AN INCOMES POLICY FOR
THE UNITED STATES

CONTRIBUTORS

Martin Bronfenbrenner, Visiting Scholar, Federal Reserve Bank of San Francisco and Duke University.

Michael P. Claudon, Associate Professor of Economics, Middlebury College.

David Colander, Visiting Fellow, Nuffield College, Oxford University.

Richard R. Cornwall, Associate Professor of Economics, Middlebury College.

Abba P. Lerner, Professor of Economics, Florida State University.

Thomas Mayer, Professor of Economics, University of California, Davis.

William D. Nordhaus, Professor of Economics, Yale University, formerly on President Carter's Council of Economic Advisors.

Mancur Olson, Professor of Economics, University of Maryland.

Samuel Rosenberg, Professor of Economics, University of California, Davis.

Isabel V. Sawhill, Director, Research on Employment and Labor Policies, The Urban Institute.

Laurence S. Seidman, Professor of Economics, University of Pennsylvania.

John Sheahan, Professor of Economics, Williams College.

Sidney Weintraub, Professor of Economics, University of Pennsylvania.

AN INCOMES POLICY FOR THE UNITED STATES:

New Approaches

Edited by
Michael P. Claudon
Richard R. Cornwall

Martinus Nijhoff Publishing
Boston/The Hague/London

Distributors for North America:
Martinus Nijhoff Publishing
Kluwer Boston, Inc.
160 Old Derby Street
Hingham, Massachusetts 02043

Distributors outside North America:
Kluwer Academic Publishers Group
Distribution Centre
P.O. Box 322
3300 AH Dordrecht, The Netherlands

Library of Congress Cataloging in Publication Data
Main entry under title:

An Incomes Policy for the United States.

   "Consists of several of the papers presented at the first annual conference on economic issues held at Middlebury College in April, 1979."
   Bibliography: p.
   1. Wage-price policy — United States — Congresses. I. Claudon, Michael P. II. Cornwall, Richard.
HC110.W24I52   339.5'0973   80-13334
ISBN 0-89838-048-0

Printed in the United States of America

CONTENTS

Introduction
  Richard R. Cornwall and *Michael P. Claudon*   **1**

I A CALL FOR A NEW APPROACH

1 TIPs against Inflation
  Sidney Weintraub   **7**

II RATIONALES FOR ANTI-INFLATION POLICIES
USING DECENTRALIZED INCENTIVES

2 ''Incentives-Based'' Stabilization Policies and the
Evolution of the Macroeconomic Problem
  Mancur Olson   **37**

3 Tax- and Market-Based Incomes Policies: The Interface
of Theory and Practice
  David Colander   **79**

III SPECIFIC PROPOSALS

4 There Is a Cure for Inflation
Abba P. Lerner and *David Colander*   **101**

5 Insurance for Labor under a Tax-Based Incomes Policy
Laurence S. Seidman   **109**

6 Tax-Based Incomes Policies: A Better Mousetrap?
William D. Nordhaus   **135**

IV EVALUATION AND CRITICISM

7 Incomes Policies in an Open Economy: Domestic and External
Interactions
John Sheahan   **155**

8 Incomes Policy: The "TIP" of the Iceberg
Samuel Rosenberg   **175**

9 Innovative Incomes Policies: A Skeptic's View
Thomas Mayer   **197**

V COMPLEMENTS TO DECENTRALIZED ANTI-INFLATION SCHEMES

10 Labor Market Policies and Inflation
Isabel V. Sawhill   **217**

11 Some Neglected Microeconomics of Inflation Control
Martin Bronfenbrenner   **233**

INTRODUCTION
Richard R. Cornwall and Michael P. Claudon

This book contains a selection of the papers presented at the first annual Middlebury College Conference on Economic Issues, held in April 1979. The conference carried the theme "New Approaches to an Incomes Policy for the United States" and focused on how to devise a decentralized institution consistent with our political framework to inhibit wage-price spirals. An assumption underlying this approach is that substantial pecuniary externalities arise from corporate and union wage and price decisions that cannot be captured by laissez-faire decision making.

This book seeks to establish the validity of the externalities assumption, to present several leading proposals for decentralized incentive-based anti-inflation policies, to present criticism of these proposals, and to present approaches that might supplement these proposals.

The book opens in Part I with an articulate call for new anti-inflation policies by Sidney Weintraub, the joint inventor (with Henry Wallich) of tax-based incomes policies. Mancur Olson and David Colander offer a general rationale for these new approaches in Part II. Today's three leading proposals are presented in Part III by their most notable proponents: William Nordhaus, real-wage insurance (RWI), as proposed by President Carter in 1978; Laurence Seidman, tax-based incomes policies

1

(TIP); and Abba Lerner and David Colander, markets for wage-price increase permits (WIP). The workability of the schemes presented in Part III is examined from the monetarist viewpoint by Tom Mayer, from a radical perspective by Sam Rosenberg, and with a view to their compatibility with international payments institutions by John Sheahan in Part IV.

The book closes in Part V with Isabel Sawhill's examination of other labor market policies that might affect a trade-off between inflation and unemployment, and Martin Bronfenbrenner's extensive list of startling proposals to reduce inflation.

Clever schemes for changing our monetary institutions to better control inflation are not solely a product of the imagination of present-day economists. Monetary cranks, politicians, and even economists have proposed many schemes in the past — from using one type of money with which to pay wages and another type with which to pay for commodities, on the one hand, to using dated money, on the other. Indeed, the diversity of schemes for curing inflation exceeds the competence of economists to properly evaluate them, for we are currently grappling with a very basic and difficult problem in economic theory: how to provide an adequate microtheoretic basis for macropolicies. The papers in this volume (especially David Colander's paper) show how important this theoretical issue is for a proper modeling of TIP. It is possible that the focus given to economic research by this policy problem will contribute to the resolution of this problem in economic theory.

Martin Bronfenbrenner suggested that we distinguish between nitty-gritty analysis and nitty-witty analysis of the alternative proposals. This suggestion met with universal applause and an even greater outpouring of acronyms: Mancur Olson suggested we distinguish TIP from HIP, hunger incomes policies, ORP, old-time-religion policies (Sidney Weintraub's characterization for relying on monetary-fiscal policy to cure inflation), and TID, tear-the-institutions-down policies; Abba Lerner suggested that subsidies to wage earners accepting below guideline wage increases be called RIP, reward incentive policies; and Martin Bronfenbrenner suggested they are all a GIP, general incentive policies. The inventive reader can continue this analysis with such promising acronyms as DIAPER.

This book will appeal to teachers of undergraduate and graduate students as well as to policymakers with some background in economics. All the papers were written so as to be accessible to good undergraduate economics majors. They present a variety of types of argument, from institutional and political to theoretical analysis. Some of the articles will be especially good pedagogically in that they present proposals that will likely surprise most readers. The book will be a useful supplement for many courses on macropolicy and monetary policy. It will also give policymakers a good overview of new approaches to an incomes policy currently being explored in the United States.

I A CALL FOR A NEW APPROACH

1 TIPs AGAINST INFLATION
Sidney Weintraub

Until he found Grant, the revered Lincoln, whose star looms brighter, lamented the "slows" of his generals.[1] Despite a big edge in equipment and manpower, they were reluctant to do battle; they preferred the comfort and sanctuary of the drill field.

The "slows" typify our policy on inflation. For eleven years our economy has suffered too much inflation and languished in too much unemployment. Counting the inglorious unwinding of the Lyndon Johnson era, the last four administrations have pledged "war" on the price binge. The policies have been conventional and unimaginative, and supremely unsuccessful. The Carter crew, after twenty-two months in office and thus at least eighteen months late, finally mapped a leisurely, meager agenda. After well-publicized presidential flourishes on October 24 and November 1 of last year, Treasury Secretary Blumenthal reported in mid-December that prospects for containing the 1979 price ascent to even 7 percent were bleak because of the OPEC price hike for oil. In exemplary histrionics his solemn public posture was one of injured surprise.

Nonetheless, despite the bewildering procrastination of the secretary and of the chairman of the Council of Economic Advisers, the irreversible

7

fact is that the president finally pointed his regime toward facing the inflation issue. Naming Alfred Kahn as chief inflation fighter was applauded, though his on-the-job cram course to repair his lack of expertise spelled more lost time. Still, the selection was a masterstroke compared to the April 1978 fiasco of assigning politico Robert Strauss to abort inflation through old-boy, power-shaker, telephone sweet talk.

Kahn's 1978 contribution was to enrich our language by replacing the word *depression* with *banana* to avoid rumbling financial markets with gloomy tidings; later musings over the efficacy of consumer boycotts of producers who violated the vague price standards were quickly disavowed by a frowning president.

Some in this audience will recall a keynote address by Governor Devers at the Democratic National Convention of 1952. Belaboring the opposition party, who always reply in kind, the speaker would throw his arms heavenward at salient points and declaim: "How long, Oh Lord, how long?"

I am still mesmerized by this entreaty. How long will we go on this way? Inflation has become a way of life. Taking 1967 as base 100, the index of consumer prices in merely a dozen years has more than doubled. Most of the movement has been reserved for a span of six years, with about 60 percent of the rise since 1973.

Where will it end? On current policies we are destined for more of the same. Inflation remains in our future unless we adopt new policies that court the prospect of alienating a powerful constituency. Educationally, the Carter administration, like its predecessors and the economics profession generally, has failed signally. This is a strong indictment that remains to be documented.

The inflation facts are stark and sad for they conceal inequities and the anguish of income redistribution. Few who contemplate a viable civilized society would condone nonviolent mugging, burglary, theft, or pilferage. Yet this is what inflation is about — a brood of Peters being ripped off, though it does not always follow that distinguishable predatory Pauls are the beneficiaries. If the redistribution were neat and clean, amends could be made by way of obvious corrections.

Grief over eroded accumulated savings and ravished fixed-money incomes is compounded by the almost simultaneous unemployment sequel over the past decade. The conventional wisdom, inscribed by monetarist reiteration, dictates that the proper remedy for the inflation malady is a firm monetary policy, interpreted to mean a retarded growth rate and transparent unemployment. In the years since 1968, then, the Federal

Reserve has usually adopted an adamant monetary stance designed to subjugate the inflation monster; monetary officials have reminded us of their eternal vigilance in this battle. On the record, they have failed ignominiously on the inflation front. Conversely, the unemployment results have been spectacular. In almost all the years since 1969, output has dipped below potential by amounts ranging from $50 billion to $150 billion per annum. The total output loss over the period has been almost equal to a full year's output, enough to build millions of houses, cars, schools, or items in any other category of consumer or capital goods.

Defeat poses a victory in monetary policy circles; doublespeak enters another dominion. When the Fed takes careful aim at the price target, it misses magnificently and splatters jobs; on top of one affliction it heaps another. When banks are compelled to reject loans for housing, not only are construction employees thrown out of work, but a ramified multiplier chain is also set off so that a score of retail industries are adversely impacted, with unemployment widening. Statistics were particularly alarming in 1974, during the Ford interregnum, after the departure of the impeachable President Nixon.

Thus we suffer the double trouble of inflation and unemployment, the ordeal that has added *stagflation* to our jargon. (In the United Kingdom the combined output and employment decline, along with zooming prices, led to the coining of the word *slumpflation*.)

Whereas we once had *either* inflation or unemployment, our economy has been prone to the double virus over the last decade. In the boom-bust business cycles of the past we had output up, prices up, and unemployment down in the recovery and prosperity phases, with prices and production tending down and unemployment up in the recession-depression stages.

Now, all the troubles seem to befall us simultaneously. Older economists would be dismayed at this strange juxtaposition of events. It is something mind-boggling that in an age when economists are awarded Nobel Prizes, when the subject has become mathematized, with econometrics combining and the computer devouring piles of data, the only discernible macroeconomic result has been to render our system a virtual counterpart of the comic opera "banana republics" where mishaps proliferate.

At bottom, our distress reflects a paucity of ideas, and the muddled application of outmoded doctrines and mechanical remedies to modern circumstances. Economists refuse to concede that the noisy bark in the old dogmas hides a toothless price bite.

ECONOMICS AND WELFARE

Thus in the longer past, economics was subject to just one of the major economic ills, one at a time; it is now vulnerable simultaneously on the two fronts of inflation and unemployment. The unemployment virulence is mainly *iatrogenic,* induced by the monetary medicine proscribed for the inflation malady.[2] For some time now, I have contended that the inflation diagnosis is faulty and the therapy mistaken. My view stemmed from the brief and miniscule — by the last decade's standards — stagflation of 1957–58, which seemed to me an extraordinary concurrence.[3] Unfortunately, it was a small experience, and it was palmed off as inherently stochastic, explicable by multifarious causes. A 100 percent plus price upheaval over the last decade was apparently necessary to confirm the plausibility of a stagflation debauch.

Doctrinal opposition to merely tolerating the heresy that monetary analyses need updating or that old nostrums of the efficacy of monetary controls are outmoded has perpetuated the double trouble of our economy, and real live people suffer hardships not endured in the inanimate models. Inflation has come to be a vast intellectual distraction, a form of professional crossword-puzzle escapism. Over my long professional lifetime it has never lacked discussion; apparently, economists have a stake in preserving it, not banishing it! I suspect that some conference remarks will advance a plea for monetary policy or cutting government expenditures, as if the two could succeed any better in the future than in the past.

Learned works still extol monetary policy. The Federal Reserve is now sixty-five years old. I surmise that if it could abort inflation, it would long ago have acted, to the plaudits of grateful people everywhere. The Bank of England will, in about a dozen years, celebrate its 300th anniversary. Monetary policy is thus not new, notwithstanding intricate fresh-dated scribblings. When the last correlation has been traced, when the quarterly series are ultimately decomposed to daily semaphores, it still remains that money supplies can be either: (1) increased per time period, or (2) decreased, or (3) held constant. Miracles from a new monetary *modus operandi* are unlikely.

The last two Federal Reserve chairmen were dedicated inflation foes, who waged relentless war on inflation. When William McChesney Martin retired in 1971, the price level was about 56 percent higher than when he assumed office seventeen years earlier. Oracular Dr. Arthur Burns, often regarded as an indispensable man by the business community, left a 50 percent higher price level legacy after seven years. Fallibility and malign results are attributed not to a lack of zeal nor devotion to monetary policy but to the inability of monetary policy to accomplish the task.

An army general who promised "light at the end of the tunnel" for sixty-five years would long ago have been sacked, with the weaponry and strategy sedulously quizzed. Not so, however, in monetary policy. The present Federal Reserve chairman, G. William Miller, seems obsessed with the illusion that he is destined to succeed where Martin and Burns have failed. His first year is inauspicious. *La plus ça change . . . .*

So the Fed chases its tail on a merry-go-round, theologically persuaded that the latest monetary rationalization will win the day. Once the thought was to alter the monetary supply by dealing only in short-term Treasury bills, as in the 1950s; then by nudging the interest rate spectrum; more recently, by emphasizing monetary aggregates, even seeking a will-o'-the-wisp revised measure of the money supply, as in the $M_1, M_2, \ldots, M_n$ sequence, maybe running the full gamut of money assets. Hope springs eternal that a formula of monetary mechanics will make a difference in an economy where the price level reflects mainly nonmonetary forces.

However we seek to delude ourselves, the Fed can increase the rate of augmentation of money supplies, decrease it, or hold it firm. In the modern economy the sequel will hardly matter for the price level, but the consequences can be redolent or ominous for output and employment. In the context of monetary policy the inflation analysis is misplaced, although a stagflation tangle or production-employment scenario is imminent.[4]

Inflation: The One in Many

Inflation is an immoderate or zinging price rise over a limited time interval, say a year. But it embraces much as it wears many disguises and touches a variety of disparate phenomena. Clothed in so many counterfeit garments, it is rightly a "one in many." It affects our individual and national life, generally adversely by deflecting and distorting outcomes from what they would be under a fairly flat price trend.

Dollar decline in foreign exchange markets has caused consternation by raising the price of imports and by blocking the amenities of travel to Americans, while making the world safe and inexpensive for the peregrinations of Germans and Japanese. Mindless politicians and self-serving groups, however, treat us to learned disquisitions on how the erosion in the dollar is somehow a boon to us, magnificently tailored to our ends. The foreign exchange dollar descent is almost entirely a study in the consequences of inflation, with further import price feedbacks rendering the dollar drop a self-fulfilling prophecy. Quicker inflation rates at home than abroad and the expectation that the trend will persist relative to the German mark, Swiss franc, and Japanese yen play a leading part in our stormy exchange rate deterioration.

Inflation and the fall in the foreign exchange value of the dollar also impart a measure of plausibility to the OPEC cartel's extortionate price rise; they have not hesitated to pronounce their oligopolistic manipulations as mainly a response to the inflation they encounter with respect to their own industrial and agricultural purchases. Undoubtedly, without our extravagant price excesses, they would have had to proffer other excuses, though events would never have deteriorated quite so far as to knock our balance of payments into the lopsided tailspin of recent years. Cumulating international wealth transfers have occurred, to what may prove over time an enormous detriment to a stable world order.

Inflation has gone a long way toward destroying the capital markets; it has surely hampered their efficient functioning. The stock market has exhibited intermittent jitters over the decade, with the common averages, after ephemeral, skitterish ups and downs, about where they were ten years ago. A whole generation of market analysts, or financial fortune tellers, has matured in the legend that the stock market generally trends mostly down or sidewise over time, notwithstanding glowing profit reports. Old-line brokerage houses have vanished, with the surviving merged firms accepting the brokerage business mainly as a diversionary sideline that may someday revive. This segment of the financial market has virtually ceased to perform its venerable function in our economic system; corporate investment issues have languished, with a tilt to the largest firms least in need of direct financial market access.

Inflation has disrupted government budgets, which are partly culpable for the nearly bankrupt state of such large cities as New York and Cleveland. With costs for existing programs reflecting the higher price trends, with welfare payments swollen by the incipient unemployment through the misguided tight-money ventures, and under constricting property-tax bases, municipalities are in dire straits. Financial planning has become futile in the inflationary era.

Nationally, perplexities abound. Whatever the ideological priorities, inflation acts as the villain, condoning temporizing: pollution control — proceed with care for it is costly and inflationary; ecologic concerns, likewise; better health care, postponed as inflationary; rebuild our transportation network, inflationary; a crash program to mitigate our energy dependence, inflationary; more arms, inflationary but. . . . So it goes.

Visible, projected, or illusory inflation confronts us at every turn, disfiguring our national and personal lives, consigning us to a bleaker fate than the resourcefulness of our people would compel or the real situation warrants. It creates economic divisions, it exacerbates political divisiveness. It has chipped away at the viability of many of our cultural and educational institutions. By disconcerting our personal planning, it narrows our horizons as longer range economic calculations are frustrated. Truly, the phenomenon is "the one in many." Banish the inflation demon, and our way would soon be clear to resolve many of our national and personal woes.

The Destroy-to-Revive Fantasy

An acute visitor to our world from outer space would express disbelief over the illogic in our national policy. The observer would learn that every time we approach full employment, with jobs for all, we tend to fear "overheating" (whatever that is exactly) in our economy and to take steps to dampen the pace of economic activity. Consciously we strive to create unemployment to fight inflation — so we are told. In sight of the Promised Land, the bugle call to retreat is sounded. Shortly thereafter, we denounce government for creating unemployment and urge expansory policies to restore jobs — until the process gets repeated.

So it is boom-and-bust. It is as if a fighter knocks an opponent to the canvas, only to pick him up to demolish him again, it being somehow unmanly to mete out punishment when he is down. Yet there are codified rules for prizefights; presumably we also have officially sanctioned recessionary behavior for the economy. At least we have acted on the latter premise.

Growing labor force, with growing productivity under technological improvements, should make each year the best on record: It is no cause for jubilation that aggregate production today vastly outruns the totals in colonial time. Last year happens only to be closer on the calendar than 1776. Productivity results each month and year should be the best on record. Too often, however, we have had to settle for second and third best as the Federal Reserve acted on the conventional wisdom to "fight inflation," and thus nibbled at the job and production house and, as soon as this was accomplished, set about to do the restorative patchwork. When it applies the hammer, the results are forced in tales of jobless misery, with finer moments marred by mild price creeps as idle labor is absorbed.

At least this was the past pattern. Over the last "decade plus one" — eleven years — the Fed fantasy has meant mainly stagflation. Absolute growth generally was sustained over this period, but too often at the snail's pace of far less than our productive potential.

This unwholesome syndrome of "destroy to revive" should be rejected, supplanted by policies that facilitate steady growth according to our productivity gains and labor force accretions under conditions of a steady price level, edging sidewise.

The Half-a Stability Phillips Curve Loaf

The notion of fighting inflation by embracing unemployment derives from the professional absorption with Phillips curves, now, I am happy to say, receding from the faddish centrist spot it once occupied in the technical literature. On other occasions I have chided this fascination as playing a hoax on Keynes when adopted by Keynesians. In his name — plastered on some common technical bagggage of his that Keynesians lugged around for identification — they prescribed unemployment as a "trade-off" for inflation. It was as if a doctor declared — with positive "scientific" glee — that we must always be content to live with either kidney trouble, or coronary disorders, or some combination thereof. Even more than connections in physiology, the inflation-unemployment nexus was heralded as immutable, not institutional.

Physicians, in similar circumstances, would at least concede some failure in insight, for medicine at peak practice strives to eradicate all ailments, to rehabilitate the full patient, and not to substitute one insidious disease for another. Yet economists seem to revel in the dilemma, positing it as a profound illumination, rather than proffering it as an explanation of what tended to happen under labor market institutions of the past and as something eminently worth erasing.

Phillips curve devotees should have been the first to devise alternative policies to banish both unemployment and inflation. Fortunately, even as they were engrossed in the intricate studies, history performed some of its ironic tricks and twists for, after about 1970, it was widely discerned in several countries that *both* inflation and higher unemployment rates proceeded apace! Rather than Phillips curve points clustering SE, they ran NE. So what was originally heralded as a predictive law became transmuted into an elegant post mortem, with wayward Phillips curves "predicting," in the fashion of historical studies, the events of yesterday.

Rarely in the history of economic analysis has so heralded a scientific breakthrough had so short-lived an existence. Indulging a penchant for complacency, the explorers in the land of *Shifting* Phillips Curves, instead of occupying themselves with methods to break the vicious circle of stagflation and slumpflation that emanates from the wayward Phillips curve aberrations that entail far too much inflation and too heavy unemployment rates, went on to carve out a new fiction, declaiming loudly that "expectations of inflation" were father to the facts. It has become a spectacle of absurdity in economic performance, where thinking makes it so, disdaining any progress in perception through support of actions to erase the incongruity.

Acceptable economic policies, compatible with the operation of a market economy and harmonious with the tenets of democratic performance, drew no sustenance from the "scientific" Phillips or "expectational" misadventures.

This is a choice episode in which a mixture of friends of the market economy and its basic freedoms joined in a misalliance with the foes of the prevailing order, who prefer to see the system collapse, the two allies comprising thereby an odd couple resisting even modest innovations in the institutional framework.

MISGUIDED THEORIES OF INFLATION

So the human comedy of inflation anguish and unemployment distress has raged on for a decade plus one. Destroy-to-revive philosophies and Phillips curve revisionism still flourish. Inaction is cultishly venerated as economists stick to their last in unfathomable complacency even as the economy writhes and our country displays its economic wounds in faltering and feeble world leadership. Though our country's productive potential and awesome military capabilities make it still the main best hope of weal in the free world, events trumpet our infirmities to implant doubts of our resolve.

Comment on some misguided theories of inflation, held staunchly by public opinion and addressed more subtly in professional literature, is incumbent, considering the extent to which they pervade contemporary debate.

Government Expenditures

Inflation, higher money incomes, and the bite of a progressive income-tax structure have undoubtedly enhanced popular consciousness of government expenditures as a prelude to taxation. Succumbing to both the fervor aroused by the Jarvis amendment in California and the homespun doctrines of fiscal conservatism espoused by the Bert Lance old-boy network, President Carter has revived the myth that our inflation virus emanates from government expenditures. Not unlike most of his predecessors and most presidential aspirants, he stands five-square against profligate expenditure.

This is perhaps the demagogic delusion of our times, a barrier to clear thought. On Calvinistic principles, and certainly on an economic perception of alternative resource use of public funds, every president should denounce spendthrift outlays and act to protect the taxpayer's interest. But to argue that lavish government expenditure has been the instrument of inflation constitutes sheer confusion and serves to mislead, rather than to educate, the American people.

As a percentage of GNP, federal government outlays have hardly been soaring; instead, a faint downward drift can be detected; the federal government thus has not been absorbing a greater portion of output or input of our productive resources. Secondly, if government is culpable, much the larger expenditure strides have been occurring at the state and local level, not in Washington. In GNP purchases, state and local outlays absorbed 13.2 percent of the GNP in 1978, while the federal government took about 8 percent. Excluding Defense Department aggregates, Washington absorbed about 3 percent in 1978, hardly greater than in Herbert Hoover's time. Proliferation of transfer payments, however, obscures the interpretation somewhat.

Too, if expenditures incubate the inflation, the president should counsel *all of us* to cut expenditure — to cut our outlay for cars, food, furniture, and all other things that individuals buy that correspond to government purchases. The purchase of, say, 100,000 vehicles by government is scarcely different in impact than that by individuals. Actually, to foster purchase restraint the president ought to recommend *higher* taxes to compel moderated outlays.

Obviously, no such recommendation has been forthcoming. And fortunately so, for over the last decade plus one, bounding real demand has not been our problem in any serious sense of the word, considering the unemployment of our times.

Talk of fighting inflation by curtailing government expenditure is thus vacuous, despite noisy yelps to the contrary. All of us should oppose squandering public funds on the basis of inefficiency, but not as an anti-inflation phenomenon. Ultimately, whatever validity the ideas contain is of a Phillips curve nature, with a curtailment of expenditure (government or private) leading to unemployment, which, pursued far and sternly enough, can slow up the money wage ascent and establish an *indirect* incomes policy by a circuitous loop.

Magnitudes underscore the current magnification of the insignificant and the miniaturization of the momentous. Federal government expenditures for Fiscal 1979 are projected at $500 billion. Employee compensation, consisting of the wage and salary aggregate, amounts to $1.4 trillion. The paybill is nearly threefold the size of government outlays. At a 10 percent annual pay increase, in merely three years the cumulative *addition* to the wage-salary bill will exceed total government outlays! Apparently what is needed are restraint on the average pay move, amounting to about $150 billion per annum, and a moratorium of sorts on valorous posturing over cutting budget outlays by a paltry (in contrast) few billions that pretends that the serious problem is being attacked.

Calmly appraised, without being fed by the popular mood and ideological meanderings, rising government expenditures are more the result of inflation than the cause, propaganda to the contrary notwithstanding. Whenever wage costs in the private sector escalate and prices respond so that government has to pay more for defense hardware, construction, or purchases of all sorts, government outlays must go up unless we retrench on programs. When civil service pay bounds up, as it must when events in private sector labor markets dictate, it becomes inevitable that government outlays rise; the rise is a consequence of the inflation swell, not the cause. Thus if prices rise at the rate of, say, 8 percent per annum for the next five years, we should not feign astonishment as federal outlays on present programs approach, say, $800 billion, regardless of who is president (unless we axe the defense budget, which will not occur). The only surprise is that we profess surprise and excoriate government as the inflation pacemaker.

While an economizing image makes good political fodder, it also betrays deceptive analysis. At 1963 prices, the Fiscal 1979 outlays of $500 billion would be $240 billion, roughly. The total grew as a *consequence* of higher prices; the higher sum was not the cause.

To guard against misattribution, I wish to make clear that this is not a plea for higher government expenditures. It is easy to stand six-square against "waste"; like others, I am appalled at huge misdirected outlays and wanton corruption. But to flag government outlay as the inflation demon is no more valid than to condemn consumers, firms, or foreign importers as devils — all sectors make purchases and absorb national output portions commensurate with their outlays.

Anarchy in Proposition 13?   Deficits and Debt

Proposition 13, the so-called Jarvis amendment limiting property taxes in California, whose message spread like wildfire with the pontifical blessings of certain economic high priests, scatters seeds of anarchy in refusing to pay the piper for community services while not rejecting the provision of services. Jarvis rebels commonly flail "wasteful" outlays — score near unanimity on that. Programs aimed at helping others, the poor or minorities especially, are lumped indiscriminately in the censure so that an ideological flavor prevails. There is a quaint philosophy afoot — to wit, that taxes are a dispensable feature of the enterprise system. There is also the winsome theory that the best tax is one on somebody else. Not precluded from enactment are sales taxes, sustainable in their regressive incidence on nonsupporters of the vociferous lobby. The Soviets undoubtedly would be most gleeful, and willing to nourish the movement, if the Jarvis mentality could develop sufficient momentum to hamstring our defense outlays or to prune social outlays severely enough to turn our society into a snarling explosive jungle of demoralized and disaffected people finding life futile and hopeless.

The Jarvis tax convulsion reversed the prevailing logic of deciding on communal programs as a first step, and then arbitrating the mode of finance, whether by tax, or loan, or the more judicious exercise in mutuality of juggling expenditure and revenue projections together, matching them up or down to some equitable reconciliation. The Proposition 13 mumbo jumbo and its political fallout have mainly confused the scene, not least in fostering bizarre ideas that taxes can be slashed without concern for expenditures and that in so doing inflation would be arrested. The revolt would be more entitled to decent respect, even in ideological disagreement, if proponents were to cite particular programs slated for oblivion. It takes little courage and less nobility of character to oppose taxes that pinch us personally.

Compounding the confusion, the anarchical tax attitude bangs against the parallel emotional theory of deficits as the inflation vehicle! The notion of deficits as an inflation maker is a simon-pure myth. Historically, the last fifty years have yielded only nine years of federal surplus, several of piddling amounts. Yet the price level over most of this period, by the last-decade-plus-one standard, behaved quite well. In 1933–34, the year of the largest percentage deficit, amounting to 55 percent of the expenditure total, or about 5 percent of GNP, the price level actually dropped 12 percent! Obviously, deficits are not automatic price tinder.[5]

Logical causation undoubtedly runs from deficits to expanding output and employment to (Phillips curve) rising wage-salary incomes to higher unit costs to price upsurges. Manifestly, the job picture takes precedence in the sequence; the deficit must be appraised in the light of total market experience. For those who see the deficit as a route for increasing the money supplies through acquisition of the debt by banks, the deficit theory loses its identity as a direct inflation ingredient and emerges instead as a theory of "too much money," a monetarist slant.

In any event, it is mainly proof by growl to allege that taxes should be slashed before expenditures and to fan the strident conviction that in so doing inflation would be instantly stopped.

Linked to the deficit dogma is the affiliated premise that government debt feeds the inflation pyre. The inconvenient facts reveal that since World War II, government debt has advanced more warily than private debt, making the assertion inconsonant with the facts.[6] In the decade-plus-one stagflation period, government debt bore a smaller ratio to GNP than it did twenty years earlier.

None of this is intended to extol deficits of debt per se, regardless of circumstances. Nonetheless, Polonius's injunction should be confined to Shakespeare: A capitalist system thrives on debt, for borrowing and lending is its very essence; banks survive only as effective middlemen. On debt, the fact is that we are where we are in time; the debt has accumulated over the past, and we cannot revise yesterday. We can, today and tomorrow, act to reduce the debt total if this is our objective. Contrary to the anarchical canons of Proposition 13, the action would generally impel higher, not lower, taxes. Circumstances, however, are hardly propitious for an extreme debt amputation.

Blaming government for all our ills appears cathartic for some. The mental purge may work psychological splendors, but to think that an inflation remedy lies on this route is a reprehensible deception, whether practiced by sputtering amateurs or prestigious economic luminaries.

Money As the Source of All Inflation

Long respectable is the dictum that money is the root of all inflation. Although some monetarists may chafe at the minor liberties taken with the pristine expression of their ideas, when stripped of the jargon, the theory boils down to too much money chasing a limited amount of goods. All would be well, this school teaches, if only the Federal Reserve didn't print so much money. (Sometimes the printing becomes the object of censure; one wonders how else paper money can be prepared — can it be grown?)

I have examined the views at more length elsewhere. What needs to be said is as follows:

(1) There is no intention to deny the potency of money supplies. Manifestly, money supplies, whether increased or decreased, affect the volume of output and employment directly.[7] Price level impacts, however, are at best only indirect.

Monetary theories of the price level are an implicit extension of Phillips curve thinking in a production economy. Slowing the pace of money emission by denying funds to business firms or making them more accessible operates to enlarge, say through tight money, the total unemployment figure. By creating enough unemployment, the wage-salary escalation *may* be slowed, and thus indirectly the price thrust may be tempered. This *may* happen; clearly in recent years, in the experience of too many countries, it has *not* occurred — so, the genesis of stagflation.

(2) The monetarists' "new quantity theory" posits a connection between money supplies and money incomes, of $MV = Y$, with the causal connection of M to Y being subject to lags of vague duration. Thus in conditions of unemployment such as have been commonplace over the decade plus one, inasmuch as money income $Y = PQ$, the "new" theory lacks a decisive identification between the amount of money and the price level as in the old equation of exchange formulation of $MV = PQ$. That is, in $MV = Y$, where $Y = PQ$, the separable effect of ΔM on ΔP is *indeterminate*. Monetarists, by their own admission in the more rigorous statements of their doctrine, are impeded from unequivocal statements of whether more M will affect P or Q in any time frame other than the "long run."

Yet it makes an enormous longitudinal difference to central bank policy, with its focus on the short-run here-and-now horizon, whether their endeavor to influence the money supply will impact P or Q. An enlargement of Q is welcomed; a jump in P, on the other hand, is to be avoided. Monetarism thus loses in policy relevance in the light of its acknowledged murkiness.

(3) Monetarism emphasizes the "quantity of money," though by eagerly fashioning various definitions of money and admitting possible "disintermediation" — the highbrow name for changes in velocity — the theory is compelled to aver that a persuasive, watertight operational definition of money is elusive. The corollary follows that changes in "money work" can be executed independently of money supply; the money *stock* may yield in any time interval an importance to money velocity, or money-use practices.

So it is often bewildering to note the emphasis on the "right" money measure, along with scanty notice of money velocity. Better accounts, however, posit high stability in the money-demand function, professing that the annual *percentage* changes in velocity are fairly constant. Stability of money demand, in the short and long period, is nonetheless more suspect now than it was in the heyday of monetarism, about a decade plus one ago.

(4) Omitted too often is the fact that purchases are generally arranged and prices agreed upon *before* payment for transaction; money thus would seem to *follow* prices rather than to lead them. We leave it to monetarists to unravel this, rationalizing somehow that the central bank "ratifies" the inflation — and leaving the subject suspended in convenient vagueness.

(5) Monetarists generally talk as if the central bank *forces* money upon people and firms, as by illustrative helicopter drops, rather than providing more money in the marketplace in exchange for government bonds in open-market operations. Generally, while the central bank attempts to "fight" inflation and curb money supply emissions through moderated open-market operations, as prices nonetheless continue to rise and unemployment develops, the central bank, sooner rather than later, is thereby compelled to mitigate the unemployment by making more monies available.

To monetarists the scenario "ratifies" inflation. To nonmonetarists the interpretation is markedly different: In *recognizing* the new higher price level drama, the central bank alleviates an unemployment debacle. The augmentation *at the higher prices* salvages jobs and output.[8] Monetarist predilections distort this simple story.

(6) Prominent monetarists commonly urge steady growth in the money supply, at about a rate equal to the long-term trend of output growth, in the conviction that this will stabilize the price level.

This is premised on the tenet that by abiding by the formula there would not be any residual money to sustain a price creep — or lift-off. On a nonmonetarist evaluation, if the wage-salary moves outpace the productivity development so that prices wend upward, the "steady-money rule" will be a sure recipe for unemployment. By ignoring the wage-price spiral, which adduces the impact of the rule on jobs and output rather than prices, the monetarist diagnosis evades the issue, overlooking the monetarists' own finding of indeterminacy in the effects of ΔM on ΔP and ΔQ.

Amid this negative evaluation of the "steady rule," it is possible to declare that the monetarist estimates are probably on course, *if* the price level was stabilized through nonmonetary means. The objection, however, is that they take the antecedent condition as established fact, as already accomplished via monetary maneuvers. Nonetheless, in lieu of a steady rule, nonmonetarist advocacy of discretionary augmentation might come to the same thing *if* the price level was stabilized by nonmonetary forces, while allowing more flexibility in liquidity cases.

My "proof" of the superiority of using intelligence rests on about the same foundations as the monetarist rule — faith in brains, as against the premise of *no* brains.

(7) While it has long been the mode for intellectuals to deride military brass hats and brass heads, in the art of policy planning no general would progress to battle without a contingency plan. Yet monetarists never harbor the thought that they *may* be wrong. What if, despite money control tight enough to appease their most cherished dreams, prices still kept rising and output collapsed in severe slumpflation? How much patience would they extol in pursuit of the steady rules?

(8) Finally, central banks have been around for a long time now and, as I remarked earlier, all the fresh learned articles on money notwithstanding, at the end of the subtleties the central bank can only increase, decrease, or keep the money-enlargement pace constant per period.

Unquestionably, sufficiently scarce and costly money can engender a job and output recession. But can prices be kept in check with outsized pay hikes?

Monetarists should — if they were not immune to any new idea — at least accept some policies to *supplement* their own thinking on money emissions, especially ideas that are unlikely to menace the market system to which they are committed ideologically. It should not take a devastating economic crisis to make them willing to adopt policies that are compatible with the functioning of a market economy and that could facilitate and hasten the effectiveness of money policy. Even on their own reasoning, what must be established is a balanced alignment of factor and product prices — a fancy euphemism for money incomes and productivity developments. Otherwise, any prospect of price level stability must be abandoned, with a yielding to varieties of stagflation or slumpflation under constricted money policies.

THE WCM THEORY

The wage-cost markup (WCM) theory of the price level holds that movements in unit labor costs govern the price level. Price level stability thus requires an alignment of *average* pay boosts with average productivity increments economywide. Misalignment would spell a price level perturbation — or upheaval, depending on the severity of divergence in the two variables.

Assault on the Laws of Arithmetic

The WCM theory suggests that we have been engaged in an egregious assault on the laws of arithmetic in the last decade plus one. Average productivity has been inching up, not even creeping by the 2 to 3 percent of our long historic past, but crawling by under 1 percent in the 1970s, while we have been grabbing off extravagant pay gains of 8 to 10 percent per annum on the premise of an open money income freeway to national well-being. Inevitably, the gap between the disparate numbers has been closed by an inflationary price climb. In the United Kingdom and Australia, the mad dash has on occasion been stronger, approaching 25 percent. Consternation ensued as prices surged to fill the productivity and pay void. Canada has had parallel experience, intermediate between our own splurge and the English-Australian splash.

In these circumstances, the efforts of the respective central banks, manifestly including our seven-member Federal Reserve Board, have resembled the wild antics of the seven maids with seven brooms futilely sweeping back the seven seas; hence, the decade-plus-one frustration. Events attest, not to the unwillingness of the Fed — so often maligned by economists — to inhibit the price disaster, but to its inability to do so in the money income and productivity circumstances; it simply lacks the tools, except by creating unemployment under exemplary Phillips curve parameters, to accomplish the task.

The Fed can, however, be properly chided for not performing a sufficient educational job to publicize the lack of tools in its armory.[9] It has exposed itself by claiming *ad nauseam* in public forums that its vigilance and tight money maneuvers (on revised manipulations of money-supply formulas) will finally squeeze inflation bugs out of the system. So we go on, with more inflation, more unemployment, and more lapsed time as our great country writhes in its traumatic experience. The time is overdue for the Fed to confess that it will be unable to stem the price tide in the face of extravagant pay hikes.

On the supposition that these criticisms are misplaced and that the Fed can do the job, as the monetarists contend, there is no reason why pay hikes should be moderated. Everyone can be made an instant billionaire. When union leaders announce that they will seek an average increase of, say, 8 percent, we could invite them to raise the ante, even berate them for their modesty: Why not 800 percent? 8,000? 8,000,000?

Once we admit that the latter numbers are outlandish, then we are intimating that there is an *optimal* rate of pay increase. The answer must be one that substantially aligns pay hikes with productivity creeps, approximating 3 percent per annum, if we are serious about aborting the inflation excrescences of our age.

The Mad Pay Scramble

Pay scales are obviously not raised uniformly and simultaneously in our economy. Some pay bargains materialize in January, others in February, and so on. Too, the "average" pay hike hides many individual discrepancies. Yet poking through all the details reveals that a general pay scramble has occurred and fairly universally reflects a variety of diverse labor market tags, here pulling upward by perennially extravagant amounts, there by frequent increments. At the end of it, despite the lack of simultaneity, pay levels have risen as if by fiat. Undoubtedly, power grabs in particular industries have yielded some rich harvests, as in the construction sector and trucking. Labor has its own internecine social structure of "princes and paupers."[10] Implicit is a form of "class struggle" not really anticipated by Marx and of interest to sociological investigation.[11]

Withal, it has been as if the full pack of all employees has somehow quickened the pace, all to run faster so that the upshot has been that relative positions have remained, if not frozen, in degree nearly so. To introduce some rationality in it all, for in a noninflationary climate it is relative wages that count, some means must be found to stem the pell-mell dash in which all stride faster to end in about the same relative place, while prices surge generally, with some relative disproportions, to end in inflation and to afflict too many by unemployment as the money screws are applied.

A More Schematic Statement

Obviously these remarks can be given a more schematic formulation.

$$Y = PQ, \tag{1}$$

where Y = money income,[12] P = price level, and Q = aggregate output.

$$P = \frac{Y}{Q}. \tag{2}$$

$$P = \frac{\left(\frac{Y}{N}\right)}{\left(\frac{Q}{N}\right)}, \tag{3}$$

where N = number employed, so that

$$P = \frac{y}{A}, \tag{3'}$$

where $y = (Y/N)$ = money income per employee and $A = (Q/N)$ = average product per employee.

Equation 1 is a simple truism of money income being equal to the multiple of prices and quantities. Equation 2 contains only the surprise that its implications have so infrequently been appraised: A stable price level implies that the total money income must grow apace with total output. It carries the profound fact that *regardless of money supplies,* money incomes can not grow faster than output. Money supplies thus constitute an *indirect* means, at best, of controlling money incomes and the price level. To control the price level *directly,* money incomes constitute the proper lever.

Equations 3 and 3' reduce equation 2 to a per capita basis: Price level stability compels an alignment of per capita money incomes and average labor productivity.

The ends of theory are better served by recognition of what I regard as the *fundamental national income identity*, namely, $Y = kwN$. In this, w denotes the average wage (and salary), so that $wN = W$, where W is the aggregate wage-salary bill. The k term is, at this stage, simply the multiple that equates Y and W. Hence:

$$PQ = kwN \qquad (4)$$

$$P = \left(\frac{kwN}{Q}\right) = \frac{kw}{A}, \qquad (4')$$

where (w/A) = unit labor costs and k = average markup of prices over (w/A).

Equation 4′ embodies the WCM theory of the price level. Of all the "great" ratios in economics, k is most nearly constant, year to year or over the long period.[13] Thus we may write $k = \bar{k}$ for all practical purposes: It will also be noted (from $k = [PQ/wN]$) that k is the reciprocal of the wage shares. Imputing right to left causality — whose origin, like the golf swing, lies in the head — any rise in unit labor costs will compel a price rise.

Only a misreading can label these ideas a "wage-push" theory. On the cost side, the wage bill constitutes more than half of business gross costs, with depreciation over 85 percent of the total. In consumer markets, in our mass production and mass consumption economy, wage-salary incomes comprise perhaps as much as 85 percent of consumer purchases, running even higher in the past before the surge in welfare incomes.[14] Thus a money wage increase impels a cost-push for producers and a demand-pull in consumer markets, and rather simultaneously.[15]

The analysis can be briefly extended at this place to note where money supplies enter under the WCM theory. Carrying the venerable equation of exchange a step further, then:

$$MV = PQ = kwN, \qquad (5)$$

$$\left(\frac{\Delta M}{M}\right) + \left(\frac{\Delta V}{V}\right) = \left(\frac{\Delta k}{k}\right) + \left(\frac{\Delta w}{w}\right) + \left(\frac{\Delta N}{N}\right), \qquad (5')$$

neglecting $(\Delta M \Delta V)$ and $(\Delta k \Delta w \Delta N)$,

$$m\left(\frac{\Delta M}{M}\right) = \left(\frac{\Delta w}{w}\right) + \left(\frac{\Delta N}{N}\right), \qquad (5'')$$

where $\Delta k = 0$ and $m = [1 + (\Delta V/V)/(\Delta M/M)]$.

Taking $m = [(\Delta Y/Y)/(\Delta M/M)] < 2$ as the money income elasticity, which monetarists assure us is fairly stable for the United States, equation 5″ reveals that if money wages jump by, say, 8 percent, unless money supplies expand by upwards of 4 percent, $(\Delta N/N)$ will turn negative. On this view, equation 5 reveals that with Δw having much of a life of its own, eluding monetary influences, the impact of money supplies falls on employment and production.

The ideas have been developed more fully elsewhere. They are introduced at this place to put the theoretical basis for incomes policy on a firmer foundation.

The Downward Drift in k

As for k, there has been a glacial descent in its magnitude; according to available data, k has fallen by about 12 percent since 1950. On the score of price margins, therefore, prices should be lower today than in 1950! Actually, they are about 150 percent higher, affirming the runaway ascent of average pay relative to average productivity. Relations are made graphic in the semilog graph in figure 1.

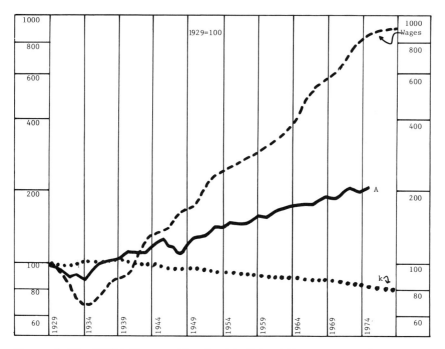

Figure 1. The WCM Theory: The Double-Edged Demand and Cost Blades (index numbers of k, w, A, 1929–1975)

INCOMES POLICY OF INCOME GEARING

To control the future price level we will have to do a better job in *gearing* money wages to productivity. This axiom pervades the modern theme of incomes policy. Inevitably, attention narrows on wages and salaries, which comprise about 75 percent of our national income. Too, knowledge of the empirical track of k gives added warrant to concentrate on the w/A ratio on the presumption that other incomes will stay in line. Meanwhile, we are always relieved to utter the typical platitudes in support of higher productivity.

The big fight concerns the kind of incomes policy. Popular opinion veers to the more obvious direct controls of wages and prices, as in World War II, the Korean War, or under the Nixon phases from August 1971 to January 1973. Professionally, it is mainly that supreme and serene iconoclast, J. K. Galbraith, who was early and astute on the inflation ordeal, who has espoused their use.

With high respect for his courage and judgment, I doubt that controls have a future for the United States economy. The Carter administration may yet come to them, considering its dilatory follies so far and the approaching presidential election. But controls are apt to be too politicized, bureaucratic, harassing, and costly in time, resources, and administration. A "no muss, no fuss" program more compatible with the market system is likely to win more enduring support.

A TIP Package

Support has materialized for a tax-based incomes policy (TIP), as originally proposed by Dr. Henry Wallich and myself, and for the variants of Drs. Okun and Seidman. Public awareness of the ideas has widened. In the United Kingdom a version of the concept is on the parliamentary docket for enactment.

On the premise that the "carrot" and the "stick" will both influence conduct, the following package reflects my current concept of a proper TIP legislative design:

1. *Amend the Davis-Bacon Act.* According to law, prevailing wages must be paid on current government or government-assisted construction. The government is thus already operating an incomes policy. Labor and business now lobby for contracts which create jobs, and shortly thereafter there are strikes for higher pay, in-

volving raids on the public purse. A new clause, however, can require that over the life of the contracts, average pay increases for all personnel are not to exceed 5 percent per annum.

A construction authorization incomes policy (CAIP) should help hold the line on construction excesses. Penalties can include disallowing overpayments on the corporate income tax form and remanding sums equal to the excess above 5 percent to the government.

2. *Amend government procurement contracts.* CAIP can be applied to government procurement generally, especially to defense contracts, where pay increases are paid for by the public.

3. *Reduce personal income taxes.* Reduce the personal income tax by a credit of 2 percent on employee compensation, with a minimum tax reduction of $200 and a maximum of $300 on all incomes rising by 5 percent or less per annum. This borrows from the original Okun proposal. Largest percentage benefits would redound to wage earners' advantage and help induce wage restraint.

4. *Implement the (modified) Wallich-Weintraub TIP.* All business firms employing 500 or more employees or having an annual wage and salary bill of five million dollars or more, would be subject to the following tax provisos:

   a. For average employee wages that increase by not less than 3 percent nor more than 5 percent per annum, the firm's tax rate would be lowered by (at least) 2 percent below the standard corporate tax rate.

   b. If the average annual pay increase exceeds 5 percent, the firm would be subject to progressive penalty tax rates.

   Essentially, (b) is the original Wallich-Weintraub TIP. Proviso (a) is inserted (from Dr. Seidman) with the 3 percent floor intended to preclude greater rewards to firms that beat down pay levels; it dispels any possible allegation that TIP is a plan to "create slave labor." It should also encourage pay moderation to foster price stability. Restriction to large firms should render the proposal administratively feasible. Others may prefer to include only even larger firms.

5. *Implement TIP-CAP: A productivity bonus.* Firms reporting average value-added per employee surpassing the economywide 2–3 percent trend of the past might be granted a pay prerogative above the 5 percent norm. Calculations would have to be made for average product corrected for price level inflation (CAP, or corrected average product). This would be a bit more complicated than TIP calculations, but would involve only simple subtractions

(of cost of materials from sales receipts) and the application of standard price level indexes as a deflator.

This would operate as a productivity bonus. Perhaps one-third of the superior productivity increase of about 6 percent might be added to the 5 percent standard increase. Not all of the productivity gain should be commanded by employees, however, for the firms should be motivated to reduce prices.

6. *Implement TIP supplements.* Various supplements can be attached to TIP-CAP to assume compliance. For example, certain firms might be in cash-flow financial straits if their 5 percent settlement offer were rejected by labor, resulting in a strike. Such firms might be cleared for a government-guaranteed loan to meet fixed charges. Clearly, loan availability would have to be monitored to prevent collusion.

    Labor, in rejecting a settlement at 5 percent (or a trifle more), might be subject to penalties ranging from mild to stringent, depending on strike duration and the (vague) national interest. Labor specialists should promote this discussion.

7. *Amend the antitrust laws.* To allay objections that prices are absolved from sanctions, the Federal Trade Commission (FTC) might be mandated to report quarterly on trends and profit margins, especially among the 2,000 largest firms, measured in terms of sales or employment.

    Firms reporting extra productivity improvement should be expected to lower prices. Where there is evidence that they are not doing so, the FTC might be empowered to report and to seek remedial policies.

    Profit margins have been declining. Until contrary evidence emerges, further action can be deferred.

8. *Limit average pay increases for government employees.* Average pay increases for federal employees would be limited to 5 percent per annum, with corrections every two or three years if the private sector trend exceeds this norm. State and local employees would be brought under the same 5 percent tent through the leverage of federal grants or other federal aid programs.[16]

Criteria for Incomes Policy

Committing myself thus to a more or less complete incomes policy package, I shall make a few remarks on criteria appropriate for a price level stabilization program.

1. *Minimize intervention.* It seems to me that the policies should make the minimum wrench with the market system that commands the widest ideological following. Our immediate objective is not utopia, but to remove the grave flaw in the market economy. Few people want to center more power in the federal government. Minimal administrative and compliance cost is an implicit point.
2. *Align incomes with production changes.* Without this objective, all is lost except perhaps by happenstance.
3. *Provide productivity incentives.* Full employment without inflation is likely to encourage more capital formation, the primary source of productivity achievements. An incomes policy that contributes to labor productivity, that curbs featherbedding practices, and that encourages labor to accept technological change has signal virtues.
4. *Be compatible with the market economy.* This is implicit in item 1. The objective is to stop inflation and not to remake the economic system or to perpetuate vacuous and impractical discussion.
5. *Facilitate bargaining over relative incomes.* Injection of equity and egalitarianism aspects leads us far off the money income beat. These are perennial and multifaceted issues. However, a policy must permit scope for bargaining and ultimate agreement over "relativities," or the money income scale. Under TIP, for example, where the concentration is on *average* increases, this remains possible.

CONCLUSIONS

Many, in some complacency, will prescribe more monetary perseverance. Yet today, after a decade plus one has elapsed, the time is overdue to explore new options. Too much of the double trouble has afflicted us after promises unlimited; events need not reach epidemic proportions to make action imperative. Intelligence should anticipate catastrophe, though democracy has a propensity to muddle and dawdle until the crisis deepens.[17]

The exigencies test our resolve to stop inflation and press on with the other vexing issues of our age. The times also constitute an opportunity to provide the free world with the economic leadership that our military might commends and our economic and political potential inspires. Universally, the inflation ordeal has provoked direct distress and concomitant unemployment and political turmoil. Other countries, bereft of leadership or world influence, are reluctant to act, holding in self-deprecation that inflation is a world phenomenon; they eye the United States and rationalize their failures by ours.

Economists have seldom been renowned for their boldness. Illustrious figures, to be sure, have carried heretical messages addressed to the issues of the times. Adam Smith's acumen perceived that self-interest and the human propensity to truck and barter could get goods produced and resources allocated, without the deliberate mercantilist statecraft. David Ricardo fretted over the corn laws: It was not high rents that meant high bread prices, but high bread prices that led to high rents. A practical phenomenon inspired the profound classical ratiocination.

John Stuart Mill, witnessing capitalism's birth pains with idealistic socialist godfathers at the celebration, envisaged distribution as an institutional innovation and prophesied improvement in the quality of life even in the stationary state that beckoned limited material affluence. Nearly forty-five years ago — it is that long — Keynes drew images of full employment. Because he lived and implanted his message, economies fare far better today in providing jobs.

Inflation now bedevils economic betterment. On conventional policies it remains obdurate. We must have the courage to adopt new ideas, compatible with the market system and consistent with our democratic ways.

Our founding fathers set forth our "unalienable" right to "life, liberty, and the pursuit of happiness." Confronted with the immorality and frustration of unemployment, Jefferson, whom John Adams depicted as having a "peculiar felicity of expression" in declining entreaties on his behalf to draft the Declaration of Independence, might today, if alive, be induced to insert a phrase on the "unalienable right to the dignity of a job." But nobody has an "unalienable" right to inflate, to wreak havoc on others through market actions. Adam Smith would never condone this in his most rapturous fealty to the market system, in awe at the efficiency of self-interest; the human trait to trade was to promote the commonweal, not to endanger it. As Mill argued, in his superb essay *On Liberty*:

> That the only purpose to which power can be rightfully exercised over any member of a civilized community, against his will, is to prevent harm to others. [Chapter 1]

Not too far from here, nearly thirty-six years ago, the Bretton Woods conference was held. Under its consensus an international monetary order evolved that was to serve the world reasonably well for most of the intervening period. Of course, that conference was held under official auspices and its deliberations were implemented thereafter.

We are not an official body. Yet ideas have a transparency and a vitality of their own, whether embossed with a government stamp or not. Keynes saw all vested interests, however powerful, as a tyranny crumbling before the play of ideas. The time for TIP, or a program akin to it, has come. It is already overdue. Constructive thoughts will be welcomed, for market economies are writhing in a despair that awaits correction by ideas. My earnest hope is that notions will emanate from here to the huge profit of mankind.

A world of stable full employment is the booty, with $50 to $150 billion as the annual GNP award. The price, on TIP techniques, is trifling. To start, we must shuck the "slows."

NOTES

1. See T. Harry Williams, *Lincoln and His Generals* (New York: Knopf, 1952), chapter 7.

2. Hyman P. Minsky, symposium entitled "The Carter Economics," *Journal of Post Keynesian Economics,* Fall 1978:42.

3. Sidney Weintraub, *A General Theory of the Price Level* (Philadelphia: Chilton Books, 1959).

4. Cf. my elaboration in *Capitalism's Inflation and Unemployment Crisis* (Reading, Mass.: Addison-Wesley, 1978), chapter 4.

5. This is *not* to advocate larger deficits. In recent years a slightly larger deficit, depending on the outlay types, might have absorbed some of the unemployment. Too, it would have had some money market influences, but here we encounter the conundrums of what the Fed monetary policy would have been compared to what it was under the actual deficits. More labor market tightness might have meant somewhat higher money wages or diminished labor productivity, and thus higher prices and costs. If employment would not expand, and deficits mounted, we would have a "profit inflation" through an upward life in k.

Dr. Arthur Burns, in some fashionable rhetoric, still denounces deficits as the inflation maker (*New York Times,* December 28, 1978). After presiding over our sordid three-year inflation record, he is in the position of the boy who killed his parents and asks for clemency on the grounds that he was an orphan. His article speaks of the "stiffening" Federal Reserve policy and a deficit-conscious administration. Burns *was* a close adviser in the Nixon-Ford years.

6. From 1945 to 1976, the interest-bearing federal debt has grown by just over 100 percent, while private debt has jumped 1,800 percent. As a ratio of GNP, the former has fallen from 1.2 to 0.3.

7. Cf. Sidney Weintraub, *Capitalism's Inflation and Unemployment Crisis* (Reading, Mass.: Addison-Wesley, 1978), chapters 4, 9.

8. Cf. Weintraub, *Capitalism's Crisis,* chapter 4, where the added *demand* for money is developed as a reflex to the higher wage level and ensuing price upswing.

9. Dr. Henry Wallich must obviously be exempted from the indictment.

10. Weintraub, *Capitalism's Crisis,* chapter 5.

11. Cf. John Goldthorpe, ". . . Towards a Sociological Account," in *The Political Economy of Inflation* (Cambridge, Mass.: Harvard University Press, 1978), edited by Fred Hirsch and John H. Goldthorpe. The volume, interesting for noneconomist views, offers a minimal policy focus.

12. Interpreted usually as Gross Business Product (GBP), the output of the market sector.

13. Cf. Lawrence R. Klein and Richard F. Kosobud, "Some Econometrics of Growth: Great Ratios of Economics," *Quarterly Journal of Economics* (May 1961); also Weintraub, *Capitalism's Crisis,* p. 47ff.

14. For some discussion, see my *Some Aspects of Wage Theory and Policy,* (Philadelphia: Chilton Books, 1963), chapter 1. On the wage bill and consumption, the significance appears in Lawrence R. Klein and Richard F. Kosobud, "Generalizing Kalecki and Simplifying Macroeconomics," *Journal of Post Keynesian Economics* (Spring 1979).

15. Cf. my article on "The Missing Theory of Money Wages," *Journal of Post Keynesian Economics* (Winter 1979).

16. Reprinted with permission and with slight changes, from *Challenge* (September/October 1978). In a memorandum of November 1977, ideas on amending Davis-Bacon were circulated to Washington officials; indications are that it has provoked support in a variety of disguises.

17. Cf. Robert Heilbroner, *New York Times,* December 22, 1978, op. ed.

II RATIONALES FOR ANTI-INFLATION POLICIES USING DECENTRALIZED INCENTIVES

2 "INCENTIVES-BASED" STABILIZATION POLICIES AND THE EVOLUTION OF THE MACROECONOMIC PROBLEM

Mancur Olson

Inflation is by definition a rise in the price level. We cannot say whether there is a case for what I prefer to call "incentives-based" stabilization policies, such as those proposed at this conference, without first confronting the question of why prices change. Obviously one reason that prices in general change is that aggregate demand frequently fluctuates, whether because of changes in monetary or fiscal policy or whatever, whereas the economy's capacity to produce usually does not change appreciably in the short run. If the demand in money terms for output increases substantially when the supply of output in real terms is unchanged, there will, of course, tend to be a rise in prices — more money will be offered for the same amount of goods and a given amount of money will buy less in the way of goods than before.

The author thanks the Environmental Protection Agency, the National Science Foundation, and Resources for the Future for support of his research. He is grateful to the organizers of the conference for agreeing in advance to publication of portions of this paper elsewhere and to Brian Cushing, Douglas Kinney, and Howell Zee for assisting him with this research. Moses Abramovitz, Dudley Dillard, Paul Meyer, Michael Parkin, and Donald Whitehead have in conversation provided suggestions that helped in writing this paper. The author is solely responsible for the paper's shortcomings.

Undoubtedly the price level often changes because of such changes in aggregate demand, and very large changes in the price level surely could not occur without changes in aggregate demand. If changes in aggregate demand are also the *only* source of general changes in prices (as opposed to changes in the relative price of particular commodities), then none of the incentives-based schemes discussed at this conference, or any other such schemes, could make any sense, for they do not address the fluctuations in aggregate demand. We may still argue about the relative roles of monetary and fiscal policy in explaining changes in aggregate demand, but only better management of aggregate demand will stabilize the economy. On the other hand, if prices in general are significantly influenced even in the short run by something beyond fluctuations (or expected fluctuations) in aggregate demand, then stabilization proposals that involve more than demand management are admissible.

Unoriginal as the foregoing paragraphs are, they are needed to take us to the inescapable starting point for the major issues debated at this meeting: the question of whether there is anything beyond actual or expected changes in aggregate demand that can influence the general price level, or even such a large and important proportion of prices that this could (in a way that will be discussed later) be important for macroeconomic policy.

Both the Keynesian and the monetarist theories in their staple or classical forms would explain inflation solely in terms of aggregate demand. A number of ingenious and stimulating models have been developed in recent years, mainly in response to stagflation, or simultaneous increases in inflation and unemployment, that would go beyond both actual and expected changes in demand in attempting to explain recent behavior. The existence and interest of this more recent work do not, however, alter the point that at least the classical or "core" Keynesian and monetarist models explain inflation solely from the demand side. It is also, I think, fair to say that neither the classical Keynesian model nor the early core work in the monetarist counterrevolution *predicted* the simultaneous inflation and unemployment before it occurred, or even alerted economists and policymakers to the fact that this was one of the important possibilities. Thus the fact that a theory can be extended, even in enlightening ways, after the fact to account for simultaneous inflation and substantial underutilization of resources does not contradict the criticism I am making of the classical Keynesian and monetarist paradigms. Neither does the fact that some recent descendants of the theories offer a richer explanation of price determination alter the fact that the core theories themselves explain inflation overwhelmingly from the demand side.

THE KEYNESIAN MODEL

Though the classical Keynesian explanation of inflation is no less demand driven than the monetarist, it is important to note that Keynes *began* his book with (and built his theory in substantial part upon) the idea that one very large and quite crucial set of prices was influenced by *something* beyond changes in demand, and indeed beyond supply and demand. This part of the Keynesian foundation should be considered rather carefully, for it is, I shall argue, related to the stagflation problem that has given rise to the incentives-based plans and other incomes policies.

Keynes began his argument by attacking the "classical" or orthodox postulate that "the utility of the wage when a given volume of labour is employed is equal to the marginal disutility of that amount of employment." Pre-Keynesian economists could argue that if groups of workers through unions agreed not to work unless they received a stipulated wage, and that wage resulted in unemployment, this unemployment was not really involuntary unemployment, but rather was due to collective choices of workers themselves. Keynes then assumed just such a situation:

> A reduction in the existing level of money wages would lead, through strikes or otherwise, to a withdrawal of labour which is now employed. Does it follow from this that the existing level of real wages accurately measures the marginal disutility of labour? Not necessarily. For, although a reduction in the existing money-wage would lead to a withdrawal of labour, it does not follow that a fall in the value of the existing money-wage in terms of wage-goods [i.e., a rise in the cost of living] would do so, if it were due to a rise in the price of the latter. In other words, it may be the case that within a certain range the demand of labour is for a minimum money-wage and not for a minimum real wage. . . . Now ordinary experience tells us, beyond doubt, that a situation where labour stipulates (within limits) for a money-wage rather than a real wage, so far from being a mere possibility, is the normal case. . . .
>
> But in the case of changes in the general level of wages, it will be found, I think, that the change in real wages associated with a change in money-wages, so far from being usually in the same direction, is almost always in the opposite direction. When money-wages are rising, that is to say, it will be found that real wages are falling; and when money-wages are falling, real wages are rising. . . .

> The struggle about money-wages primarily affects the *distribution* of the aggregate real wage between different labour-groups, and not its average amount per unit of employment . . . the effect of combinations on the part of a group of workers is to protect their *relative* real wage.[1]

The central role of sticky wages in Keynes's theory and one of the institutions that can cause this stickiness are also emphasized in Keynes's chapter 19, "Changes in Money Wages":

> Since there is, as a rule, no means of securing a simultaneous and equal reduction of money-wages in all industries, it is in the interest of all workers to resist a reduction in their own particular case. . . .
>
> If, indeed, labour were always in a position to take action (and were to do so), whenever there was less than full employment, to reduce its money demands by concerted action to whatever point was required to make money so abundant relatively to the wage-unit that the rate of interest would fall to a level compatible with full employment, we should, in effect, have monetary management by the Trade Unions, aimed at full employment, instead of by the banking system.[2]

To be sure, Keynes's explanation of underemployment equilibrium did not merely consist of the assumption of sticky wages; pre-Keynesian theory already ascribed unemployment to unrealistically high wage levels, and Keynes was anxious to differentiate his theory from the orthodoxy that preceded it. Indeed, as is well known, Keynes argued that reductions of money wages need not bring full employment and that if they did, it involved in essence "monetary management by the Trade Unions." As we know, Keynes also had new ideas about the demand for money as an asset and other matters, and these other new ideas played significant roles in his theory. Still, the fact remains that though Keynes's theory argued for changing aggregate effective demand, especially through budget deficits and surpluses, and explained inflation solely from the demand side, it nonetheless began, and in substantial part rested upon, the assumption that there were forces, such as trade unions, that influenced wages and that within limits and at least for a time did so in ways that could not be explained in terms of increases or decreases in the demand for labor or individual decisions to trade off more or less labor for leisure. This familiar point is, I think, important in ways that will be evident when we consider how the macroeconomic problem has evolved over time, as well as when we consider differences in this problem across countries.

Unfortunately, Keynes never provided a theoretical explanation of why wages were sticky or of what it was that determined why they stuck at one level rather than another or for how long. This is all the more troublesome because, at least on first examination, this stickiness is not consistent with the optimizing or at least generally purposeful behavior that economists seem to find when they study behavior at a detailed or microeconomic level. This incompleteness of the Keynesian theory — this reliance on an unexplained premise that has not been reconciled with the rest of economic theory — is not only intellectually unsatisfying, but it is, in my judgment, one of the significant sources of the macroeconomic failures of the 1970s.

THE CLASSICAL MONETARY MODEL

In the classical monetary theory, there is of course no appeal to sticky or rigid wages or prices that are themselves unexplained. Though diverse frictions and lags are admitted, the emphasis in the classical monetary argument is on full employment's being the natural or equilibrium state of the economy. Changes in the quantity of money tend to bring about proportional changes in nominal income because the price level readily adjusts, and real output is determined by resource availability, technology, and other factors outside the scope of monetary and fiscal policy.

Though the old monetary theory is not guilty of assuming arbitrary wage levels, it certainly is guilty of providing no explanation of massive and prolonged unemployment. Indeed, the theory (in at least its classical and simpler forms) goes so far as to predict that such unemployment will not occur. To be sure, in more recent years a variety of enlightening arguments that can explain *some* unemployment have been introduced by monetarists or other economists. Both search and implicit-contract models, for example, can be used to explain some involuntary unemployment and in ways that can be consistent with monetarism as well as Keynesian approaches. These models, in my opinion, surely shed light on significant truths. Then there are the accelerationist (or decelerationist) and rational-expectations arguments, which grow out of the monetarist theory itself and can be reasonably considered integral to it, which can explain some economywide, if temporary, unemployment. If there is a lower rate of inflation (or a higher rate of deflation) than expected, various decisions that were made on the basis of the false expectations could cause unemployment. Wages or prices, for example, that can change only slowly will remain for a time at higher than market-clearing levels when there is less inflation or more deflation than was expected, and these disequilibria will cause some temporary unemployment.

Both the accelerationist/declerationist and rational-expectations arguments are to my way of thinking important contributions to macroeconomic and monetary debate (ironically, they are reminiscent in some ways of Keynes's emphasis on expectations), and there is no doubt that they can explain *some* underutilization of resources. The expectations arguments are, however, far from sufficient to explain the depth and duration of unemployment in the interwar period. If the economy is always at a full employment level of output, except when, and only for as long as, the rate of inflation that was expected exceeds that which occurs, why did the depression that began in the United States in 1929 and ended only with World War II involve such an enormous and prolonged reduction in employment and real output? Consider also the case of Great Britain in the interwar period. Britain then, as now, used a system for measuring unemployment that by comparison with current U.S. practice understates the degree of unemployment; yet from shortly after World War I until World War II Great Britain never recorded less than 10 percent unemployment. This interwar experience could be explained on an expectations hypothesis only if people, in the midst of the greatest depression ever, expected an inflation so dramatic it would justify setting various wages and prices far above the levels that would clear current markets. This is, to put it mildly, doubtful, and it is even more doubtful that most people would have persisted in such wildly erroneous expectations for a dozen years, in the case of the United States, or twenty years, in that of Great Britain. Neither is it credible that, when unemployment and welfare arrangements were so much less generous than today and when most workers were the only source of support for their families, the "natural rate" of unemployment could leave a tenth to a fourth of the work force unemployed. This inability of the monetarist theory to explain the magnitude and tenacity of unemployment in the interwar period suggests that the monetarist model is, at best, incomplete.

The shorter and milder periods of unemployment since World War II are within limits that a monetarist model focusing on expectations can hope to explain. Nonetheless, the existence of unemployment in many countries in the interwar period that was of greater depth and duration than can plausibly be explained on monetarist grounds implies there is or can be some *other* cause or causes of unemployment beyond that which may be implied by a divergence between the expected and actual rates of inflation. No one has shown that this other cause was (or other causes were) not in some degree present in the postwar period also. Thus monetarist explanations of postwar recessions are, despite some attractions, not necessarily sufficient or compelling.

PHILLIPS CURVE CONSIDERATIONS

Those accounts of recent stagflationary experience that rest on Keynesian foundations are also less than compelling. Some Keynesian accounts of recent experience refer to negatively sloped Phillips curves and perhaps also to shifts in such curves. There is no need to invoke the monetarist criticisms of the Phillips curve notion to show that such accounts are inherently inadequate, for the simple reason that neither Keynesian theory nor neoclassical microeconomic theory explains why there necessarily should be a negatively sloped Phillips curve; as others have said, the Phillips curve has been a finding in search of a theory. In this respect, it is like the widespread observation that wages are sticky. An explanation of stagflation is not an explanation at all unless it includes a general explanation of why a Phillips curve should have this or that slope and why the curve shifts if it is alleged to shift. Any Phillips curve relationship must, in other words, be derived from the interests and constraints faced by individual decisionmakers. The lack of an adequate explanation in Keynes of sticky wages or of realistic behavior of Phillips curves — especially the tendency for short-run Phillips curves to move upward and become steeper over long periods of inflation — must have a lot to do with the apparent growth in skepticism about Keynesian economics in recent years. (Though he certainly exaggerated, Lord Balogh surely did not miss the direction of change when he lamented that anti-Keynesianism was the world's fastest-growing industry.)

The search and implicit-contract approaches do endeavor to relate aggregative experience to motivations and conditions of individual decision units. Because of this, as well as the fact that they can be constructed to be consistent with simultaneous inflation and increased unemployment, these approaches deserve a great deal of encouragement and attention. They were, however, generally developed after the facts they set out to explain, and it remains to be seen how wide a range of additional information models of this sort will illuminate. This consideration and the fact that no one of the search or implicit-contract models has generated a professional consensus leave one with the hunch that these approaches, just as they clarify important aspects of reality, also miss something of decisive theoretical significance.

COST-PUSH INFLATION ARGUMENTS

The fact that classical Keynesian and monetarist models did not even alert people to the possibility that inflation and unemployment would increase together helps explain the prevalence, particularly among laymen, of cost-push explanations of inflation. But as others have shown before, the usual cost-push arguments are manifestly unsatisfactory. These accounts ascribe higher prices or wages to the monopoly power of big business or big unions, but they usually offer no explanation of why there should be continuing inflation or why there should be more inflation in one period than another. The typical cost-push argument does not explain why an organization with monopoly power would not choose whatever price or wage it found most advantageous as soon as it obtained the monopoly power, after which point it would have no more reason than a pure competitor to increase prices or wages. In the absence of some adequate explanation of why organizations with monopoly power did not take advantage of that power when they first acquired it or some explanation of why monopoly power should increase over time in a way consistent with the history of inflation or stagflation, the cost-push arguments are obviously inadequate. As many others have pointed out, they must also be accompanied by some account of why monetary or fiscal authorities would provide increased demand after the alleged cost-push had increased wages and prices, so that the cost-push would culminate in inflation rather than in unemployed resources.

CROSS-COUNTRY PERFORMANCE COMPARISONS

There is further evidence of the incompleteness of the Keynesian and monetarist theories (and also a hint about how to improve them) in the association between rates of real economic growth in different developed countries and each country's success in combating inflation and unemployment, and also in the historical evolution of the macroeconomic problem. Let us look first, though only very briefly and unsystematically, at the relationship across developed countries.

Since World War II, the two developed countries whose growth has been most surprising are Japan and West Germany. Though the predictions about their economic futures just after they were defeated in World War II were bleak, these two nations have grown exceptionally rapidly, after having rebuilt their economies and recovered their prewar living standards. The major developed democracy with the slowest rate of growth since World War II, is, of course, the United Kingdom, though the United States, Canada, Australia, and New Zealand have experienced rates of growth that are about as slow.

Admittedly, we have mentioned only extreme cases, but it is nonetheless instructive to note how differently the fast-growing and slow-growing nations have fared in dealing with the only really serious disruption of macroeconomic stability in the developed democracies since World War II, the inflation-stagflation of the 1970s. Obviously, there is a problem in measuring the extent to which a nation has achieved macroeconomic stability, since both the inflation rate and the extent of unemployed resources need to be taken into account, and it is not clear how heavily each of these should be weighted, or how much the weight should be changed as nations come to have unusually bad performance by one of these measures and unusually good performance by another. In the extreme cases upon which I have chosen to focus, however, we can get around this weighting problem rather readily by noting that, broadly speaking, West Germany and Japan have done far better than the United Kingdom, and often also better than the United States and the other slowly growing countries I mentioned, in dealing with *both* inflation and unemployment. From 1972–1977 the annual average rate of inflation in the United Kingdom was 14.8 percent, whereas in West Germany it was 5.6 percent and in Japan 11.6 percent. If we look at the number of unemployed resulting from this inflation, we do not by any means get a Phillips curve type of relationship; Britain has 1.38 million unemployed, Germany .99 million, and Japan (a much more populous society) 1.24 million unemployed.[3] West Germany and Japan, moreover, have had to rely totally on imported oil.

To be sure, many factors are involved (such as the special role of guest workers who can be sent home when unemployed in West Germany), and only polar cases have been considered, so no conclusions are yet in order. There is also no lack of explanations in the prevailing orthodoxies. Some monetarists will say that together monetary expansion and inflation generate inflationary expectations that are built into wage and price levels, so that when the inflation slows down there is more unemployment than there would otherwise have been — inflation causes recession. Some Keynesians will say that the greater growth of productivity in the rapidly growing countries makes it easier for them to keep both stable prices and full employment, since for any given wage level (and wages are sticky), there can be lower prices with higher productivity; the lower labor cost per unit of labor will also induce employers to take on more labor and lower the unemployment rate. Some Marxists will say

that the social tensions or class conflicts that give rise to inflation are
easier to resolve when growth makes it possible to give more to everyone.

Clearly nothing of theoretical importance has been established, nor
could it be established even with a systematic and complete assessment
of the relative performances of all the developed countries — there are
special circumstances that may be decisive in each of them. Yet, in
combination with the temporal pattern, to which we shall turn next, there
is perhaps a hint that certain structural differences that favor rapid growth
also favor macroeconomic stability. This hint, as we shall later see,
becomes stronger when we note how very much more concern about
incomes policies, social contracts, and inflationary wage settlements
there is in Great Britain (and to some extent also in Australia, Canada,
New Zealand, and the United States) than there is in Japan and West
Germany.

LESSONS DRAWN FROM HISTORY

Historical differences in macroeconomic problems and differences in
macroeconomic problems across societies of widely different levels of
economic development have not been examined as often as one might
wish. Perhaps one reason is that both the Keynesian and monetarist
perspectives, at least as they are usually presented, do not claim to rest
on the special institutional conditions or other factors that might distinguish the advanced capitalistic countries in, say, the last half century
from the societies in earlier times or in various developing nations. It is,
of course, well known that neither monetarist nor Keynesian models are
intended to apply to barter or subsistence economies but rather to economies where goods can freely be exchanged for money. Monetarists, and
for that matter Keynesians mindful of the significant role that money
plays in Keynes's model, are obviously also interested in banking and in
other financial and credit institutions. Keynesians will mention, and monetarists will emphasize, the instability of U.S. and even world banking
systems in the twenties and early thirties and quite rightly relate these
instabilities with greater or lesser emphasis to the onset of the Great
Depression. There are still other institutional differences that are occasionally mentioned, such as the Keynesian references to the growth of
automatic stabilizers, but on the whole the typical presentations of both
Keynesian and monetarist doctrines do not say much about the institutional or other conditions in which the theory is supposed to apply and
instead emphasize the generality of the theory that is espoused. Keynes

could readily have used various assumptions of his theory, such as the assumption that savers and investors are in substantial degree different people who may have inconsistent intentions or the assumption of sticky wages, as a basis for restricting its application to certain societies and historical periods. Unfortunately Keynes did not — at any event, with any regularity — do this. Indeed, he went so far as to justify the mercantilism in Europe in the sixteenth, seventeenth, and eighteenth centuries, largely on the ground that export surpluses from mercantilistic trade restrictions and export subsidies countered unemployment. *The General Theory* of course also carried indefinitely forward in time, perhaps even until "euthanasia of the rentier." Keynes was not much more expansive than the monetarists who keep repeating that inflation is always and everywhere a monetary phenomenon.

There are certainly *some* features of macroeconomic and monetary history that are consistent with the supposedly eternal generality of both major theories. The association of hyperinflations and vast increases in the money supply certainly holds across diverse societies and historical periods; the experience of the Confederacy in the U.S. Civil War, assignats in the French Revolution, and many triple- or four-digit inflation rates in Latin American countries at diverse levels of economic development suggest that the monetarist connection between the money supply and nominal income holds at least to some degree in a wide variety of conditions. There is probably also a rough association over historical epochs between smaller changes in the quantity of money and less dramatic changes in the price level, as in the rising prices in Europe after the discovery of gold in sixteenth-century Latin America. The quantity theory of money goes back, after all, at least to David Hume.

In a similar way, there is also a broad association over different historical periods between wars, deficit spending, and investment booms and changes in at least money income. This is entirely in keeping with Keynes's model. Since money can also play a quite significant role in a Keynesian or IS-LM model, the broad connection between monetary changes and nominal income is also compatible with a Keynesian framework, unless of course the connections were so precise and regular that they implied there was never any case for anything beyond the quantity theory of money.

When we get to the monetarist assumption that the level of employment of resources, whatever the change in the price level, tends to the "natural" or full-employment rate, and the Keynesian postulate that short-term or cyclical fluctuations in both the level of real output and the price level are due in general to changes in aggregate effective demand, the situation is no longer so simple or insensitive to historical change. Let us look first merely at changes in the United States over the relatively brief period since World War II. Since monetarists have in general been more resistant than Keynesians to suggestions that structural and institutional changes were among the causal factors in postwar inflationary experience, it may be expedient to take our facts initially from a leading monetarist writer, Phillip Cagan.

Cagan examined data on the changes in prices and output for the United States since 1890. Not surprisingly, he found that the tendency for prices to fall during recessions has declined over time:

> The change in rates of change [of prices] from each expansion to the ensuing recession became less negative and, in the last two cycles, the change became positive — that is, the rate of price increase in the recession exceeded that in the expansion, perverse cyclical behavior not exhibited before. The distinctive feature of the postwar inflations has not been that prices rose faster in periods of cyclical expansion — many previous expansions had much higher rates — but that they declined hardly at all, or even rose, in recessions. . . . The startling failure of the 1970 recession to curb the inflation was not a new phenomenon. . . . but simply a further step in a *progressive* post-war development. . . . the phenomenon of rising prices in slack markets is quite common. . . .
>
> Part of the smaller amplitude of cyclical fluctuations in prices reflects the reduced severity of business recessions since World War II, for which some credit goes to the contribution of economic research to improved stabilization techniques. Nonetheless, in addition to the smaller cyclical contractions in aggregate expenditures, the response of prices to a given amplitude of contraction has declined, so that now proportionately more of the contraction in expenditure falls on output.[4]

The finding that what is loosely called stagflation has emerged recently is, of course, commonplace; however, there are two features of Cagan's observations that deserve to be emphasized. The first is his insistence that there has been a *progressive* or *gradual* emergence of this problem. This is certainly correct — the puzzling experience of the seventies was foreshadowed, for example, in the fifties, when the cost-push arguments first appeared. Yet nothing like this was evident early in the century or in previous centuries. This suggests that we should look not simply at the Vietnamese War and rising oil and food prices to analyze the current inflationary situation, but that we should be alert also for gradual and cumulative changes in American society or policy that may be implicated in some way in the current inflationary problem.

A second feature of Cagan's observations that should be underlined is the point that because of the changing behavior of prices, over time an *increasing* proportion of the effect of any reduction in aggregate demand shows up as a reduction in real output. There are, in other words, apparently some *gradual* developments that are bringing at least the more discerning monetarists and Keynesians closer together; both are noting the significant and apparently increasing extent to which the level of real output can vary with changes in the level of aggregate demand.

The gradual changes that Cagan and others have pointed out in modern experience are, as is often pointed out, also evident in many other countries. More importantly, they are also evident, and evident in a more dramatic way, when we take a really long-range historical perspective. Though the reliable data that are needed to make definitive judgments about macroeconomic and monetary history in prior centuries are lacking, the qualitative evidence and the scattered data that do exist are sufficient to have generated almost a consensus among economic historians about certain broad outlines of historical experience. These broad outlines, well known as they are, have wondrously somehow not been taken into account in either the Keynesian or the monetarist theories.

One of the most prominent, if not the most prominent, trends in aggregative economic history is the tendency for reductions in aggregate demand, whether due to monetary developments, fiscal choices, investment behavior, or whatever, to have an increased effect on the level of real output as time goes on. Though there have apparently been fluctuations in the price level about as long as there has been a money economy, and certainly for the last five centuries, substantial drops in the level of real national output for monetary or macroeconomic reasons are a relatively recent phenomenon. There were, of course, crop failures and other such sources of fluctuation in the real output of societies from the earliest times, and individual towns, communities, and industries could suffer depressions, but at the aggregative and national level a drop in aggregative demand would result mainly in a fall in the price level rather than a reduction in real output. Though things were beginning to change somewhat in the latter part of the nineteenth century, the years from the peak of inflation of the Napoleonic Wars in 1812 to the low point in 1896 will nonetheless serve to illustrate the point dramatically. Over that period in Great Britain, then the most advanced and important country in the international economy, the price level fell by more than half. Experience in the United States and other countries was not greatly different. Yet during that period the industrial revolution was completed in Britain and spread to most of Western Europe and North America. Broadly speaking, the longest and most widespread period of peaceful growth in per capita income that the world has ever seen took place in a period in which the price level was more often than not falling. As the nineteenth century wore on, the bottom years of the cycle probably brought increasing unemployment, but by comparison with twentieth-century experience the downswings in the cycle brought relatively small reductions in real output.

There were, of course, many "panics" and "crises" even in the early nineteenth century. It was naturally when the price level fell that those who had borrowed money tended to have the hardest time paying it back — they were paying a higher real interest rate than they would have paid had the price level not fallen. As the Populist movement in the nineteenth-century United States reminds us, those who had borrowed money when prices were higher certainly did not like the deflation. When prices fell and some firms could not pay their debts, there might of course be a "panic," especially in view of the unstable banking system (particularly in the United States) that often led to bank failures. These panics and crises naturally depressed expectations and led to some reductions in employment and real output, but in terms of the experience of the 1930s, or our sense of what would result from comparable falls in the price level today, the effects were relatively minor and brief.

This can best be illustrated by comparing the depression of the inter-war years with what was perhaps the greatest previous U.S. monetary contraction. Milton Friedman and Anna Swartz say that "to find anything in our history remotely comparable to the monetary collapse from 1929 to 1933, one must go back nearly a century to the contraction of 1839 to 1843."[5] Indeed, as some detailed estimates by the distinguished economic historian Peter Temin show, the contraction in the money supply was even greater in 1839–1843 than in 1929–1933. *The fall in the price level was substantially greater: −31 percent in 1929–1933 and −42 percent in 1839–1843.* But consumption in real terms, which decreased by 19 percent from 1929–1933, *increased* 21 percent in 1839–1843. More dramatically still, *the real gross national product, which decreased by no less than 30 percent from 1929–1933, increased by 16 percent from 1839–1843* (see Temin's table, table 1).

As Temin aptly points out in another book, the unemployment of resources in the United States in the depression that started in 1929 had no precedent in *any* prior contraction:

> The economic contraction that started in 1929 was the worst in history. Historians have compared it with the downturns of the 1840s and the 1890s, but the comparison serves only to show the severity of the later movement. In the nineteenth-century depressions, there were banking panics, deflation, and bankruptcy, in various proportions. But there is no parallel to the under-utilization of economic resources — to the unemployment of labor and other resources — in the 1930s.

Table 1. Comparison of 1839–1843 with 1929–1933 (percent)

	1839–1843	1929–1933
Change in money stock	−34	−27
Change in prices	−42	−31
Change in number of banks	−23	−42
Change in real gross investment	−23	−91
Change in real consumption	+21	−19
Change in real gross national product	+16	−30

SOURCE: Peter Temin, *The Jacksonian Economy* (New York: W. W. Norton, 1969), p. 157.

NOTE: The 1839–1843 data are taken from peak to trough of the respective series, and dates differ somewhat. Data on money and banks are from late 1838 to late 1842; data on prices, from calendar-year 1839 to calendar-year 1843; data on GNP, etc., from census-year 1839 (year ending May 31, 1839) to census-year 1843.

The value of goods and services in America fell by almost half in the early 1930s. Correcting for the fall in prices, the fall in the quantity of production fell by approximately one-third. Unemployment rose to include one-quarter of the labor force. And investment stopped almost completely. It was the most extensive breakdown of the economy in history.[6]

The difference between the character of the macroeconomic experience between the nineteenth and twentieth centuries is evident even in the language of daily life. Though some writers have exaggerated the newness of the term, the fact remains that *unemployment* is a term that came into common use only late in the nineteenth century. The *Oxford English Dictionary* states that the word *unemployment* has been in common use since only about 1895, but F.P. Thompson points out that the word can occasionally be found in Owenite and Radical writings as early as the 1820s and 1830s.[7] Early observers of unemployment tended to use such circumlocutions as "want of employment" or "involuntary idleness." The usual German word for unemployment, *arbeitslosigkeit,* was also rarely used before the 1890s. The usage of the French word *chomage* goes back to the Middle Ages, but this word also has connotations of leisure, as in the expression *un jour de chomé* for a day off.[8] If the falling price level in the early nineteenth century had led to widespread and continuing unemployment of labor or other resources, some word to describe such an important, if not tragic, state of affairs would surely have come quickly into common usage in the languages of all the relevant countries.

The extent to which a reduction in aggregate demand is reflected in unemployment of resources and reductions in real output must be distinguished from the magnitude of fluctuations in aggregate demand. The years since World War II, as Cagan pointed out, have by historical standards been relatively stable, in part because of what economists and governments have learned about stabilization policy. But the evidence cited shows that because of increasing inflexibility of prices, our stagflationary economy is likely to suffer more unemployment and a greater loss of output for any given reduction in aggregate demand.

Obviously something is accumulating or progressing over time, such as changing policies, structures, or institutions, which is changing the character of the macroeconomic problem. We know, both from the tendency for real output to vary more with changes in aggregate demand and from direct observation of the prices themselves, that stickier prices and wages are crucial to the change that is taking place. But we do not *explain* the change by referring to sticky prices, any more than we explain anything by referring to ad hoc assumptions like "rigid wages" or merely descriptive concepts like Phillips curves. The *cause* of the fact that most wages and prices were less flexible in the interwar years than in the nineteenth century and are still less flexible in these stagflationary times must be found. That cause, in turn, must play a leading role in our macroeconomic theory.

THE POLITICAL ECONOMY MODEL

I am of course partial to the explanation of increasing stickiness of wages, as it derives from my general model on the political economy of comparative growth rates. But that partiality should not concern the reader unless he or she knows of some *other* theory that also fits the facts at issue. If an alternative explanation is or has been found, the judgment about the relative suitability of the different theories then arises. Scientific judgments must then be made in terms of such criteria as how many correct predictions about *other* matters (e.g., growth rates) each theory makes, how parsimonious each theory is, and so on. But any such judgments are matters for other occasions and other economists. The task now is to spell out the implications of the political-economy-of-comparative-growth-rates model for wage and price stickiness. Since that model is described in detail elsewhere, I shall merely refer to its main features here.

The political economy model begins with all those organizations or collusions of firms or individuals that attempt to further the interests of their members, either through combined action in the marketplace or through lobbying government. All such organizations provide what is, analytically speaking, a public or collective good for the group whose interests they serve, even if other groups are harmed by their actions. Individual voluntary action is, for familiar reasons, unlikely to provide group-optimal amounts of a collective good. Other things being equal, the more numerous the set of individuals who benefit from a collective good, the less likely that an individual in the group will act to provide any of the collective good, since the "external economy" or benefit to others will be relatively greater. It follows that optimal group action will, at the least, usually require extensive and time-consuming bargains, and that only reasonably small groups will be able to cooperate in this way. Larger groups will require coercive power to support any organizations, just as the state requires compulsory taxation, or some privileged or lucky situation that makes it possible for them to bribe individuals to support a collective effort through some sort of tied sale. The most important large common (special) interest organizations in American society, at least, do have either coercive power or other selective incentives. Since the logic of the present argument is set out in *The Logic of Collective Action*,[9] no more will be said about it here.

This model of collective action, in combination with the straightforward microeconomic theory of markets, leads to the following four working hypotheses:

1. Since some groups, such as consumers, taxpayers, the unemployed, and the poor, will never organize because they are large and without selective incentives, the society has not and cannot reach the point where representatives of all its groups can meet together and bargain for a more efficient ("core") allocation.
2. Since selective incentives are hard to obtain, collective action is problematical and will occur only in relatively favorable conditions for those groups that have the possibility of organizing; *societies will accumulate more such organizations over time* as additional groups enjoy unusually favorable conditions.
3. At least when they are not large in relation to the whole society, such groups will on balance reduce both economic efficiency and growth; they will often do this partly through the market, by blocking entry and setting supracompetitive prices, and often through lobbying for special government policies that favor them while reducing economic efficiency.
4. If such groups encompass a large part of the labor force or the owners of a large part of the capital stock, their own members will bear a large enough share of the costs of any antisocial action to tend to countervail adverse effects on efficiency and growth.

The model leads to the prediction that countries like Germany and Japan that have had totalitarian government and occupying armies that destroy common-interest organizations or reconstitute them on a more encompassing basis will have relatively high levels of economic efficiency and growth. Those societies, such as that of Great Britain, that have had stable freedom of organization and security from invasion the longest will tend to grow more slowly. Societies with very encompassing organizations, such as that of Sweden, will sometimes do better than similar societies with less inclusive organizations. Recently settled states of the United States will have had less time to accumulate common-interest organizations, as will those states that were defeated in the Civil War, and both new states and ex-Confederate states will tend to grow more rapidly than the states in the Northeast and older Middle West, which have had a longer time to accumulate common-interest organizations.

IMPLICATIONS OF THE POLITICAL ECONOMY MODEL

Although some of the implications of the foregoing theory for macroeconomics are obvious, others are not. Before turning to the implications of the model for the change of macroeconomic problems over time and across countries, let us turn to some of the implications of the theory for an economy of relatively advanced age, which thus has a fairly high degree of "institutional rheumatism."

One immediate implication of the theory is that a great many prices or wages will be determined in part by one or more special-interest organizations. In some cases the special-interest group will be a cartelistic organization that can choose whatever price its members or leaders find most advantageous, given the demand curve and cost conditions that constrain it; in other cases, the cartel-type organization will confront other such organizations or units across the market, in which case there will have to be negotiations between the bilateral monopolists. In a great many other cases, the price will be set or greatly influenced by the governmental or quasi-governmental body or bodies, in which case the lobbying power of the special-interest organization is what matters most. Sometimes a special-interest organization will derive some of its monopoly power from government, and at other times it will have to be cautious lest the exercise of its monopoly power provoke government intervention against it. Such considerations as these and the fact that the organizational strength needed for coordinated action in the market entails that the group also have some organized political power suggest that there will be a great many situations where both market power and lobbying power are relevant.

Decision making within special-interest organizations involves *consensual bargaining,* or *constitutional procedures,* or both. Consensual bargaining means that the parties must bargain with one another until they achieve unanimous agreement on some course of action or else the action will not be taken. This is the case when oligopolists choose to collude; they must at least tacitly agree on some price or set of output limitations or at least on some procedure by which these things will be determined, and if even one firm disagrees, the purposes of the collusion may not be realized. In particular cases, there can be a firm that for some reason is incapable of producing enough even at the cartel price to lower the price by very much, but this is certainly a special case, and even then all those who are necessary to the collusion must bargain until there is unanimous consent or else there can be no gains from consolidated action. Whenever there is bargaining across a market, as when a labor union bargains with management, the bargaining must again go on until there is consensus, for both the workers and the company are legally free not to agree to any contract that is proposed.

What I call "constitutional procedures" emerge whenever a special-interest group agrees that unanimous consent bargaining is so time-consuming or so unlikely to achieve agreement that it is advantageous for individual members to give up some of their rights and to abide by whatever decision emerges from some process of voting, meetings, periodic election of leaders, and other familiar democratic procedures. Of course, there will often also be many who must abide by the collective decision that emerges from the constitutional procedure who would have preferred the right to make their individual choices; it follows from the fundamental logic of the model that coercion will often be necessary for collective action, and so the decisions resulting from the constitutional procedures may be binding on some who wanted to decide for themselves. At least within some elite or cadre of organizers, however, there will normally have been agreement to the constitutional procedures, so that they will to some degree limit or share the power of the leader or at the least require that that power be exercised only through various specified and often time-consuming procedures. Governmental intervention and appeal to the courts also ensure that constitutional procedures will at least limit the speed with which leaders can get their way. Even a union with an unusually powerful and dictatorial leader, for example, may not be able to strike unless the membership or some other representative body votes in favor of the strike or explicitly delegates its power to the leadership. This is not surprising, for a strike that does not have widespread support will not generate picket lines strong enough to keep out those who would like to cross them.

Both consensual bargaining and constitutional procedures slow down decision making. Bargaining until there is unanimous consent may take a good deal of time, not only because the bargain may be complicated and each party has something to argue about, but also because a "hold-out" is often a rational strategy. If unanimous consent is necessary and all but one have agreed to the bargain, the remaining participant can perhaps get the major share of the group gain from coordinated action in return for his or her indispensable agreement. But each of the other participants is also indispensable to the consensual agreement, so each may find it expedient to hold out for better terms. Thus it can take a very long while to agree on mutually profitable joint action, if it is agreed to at all. Tacit collusion is probably the more common kind, and it must take even longer than if explicit communication were allowed. When, because of an emergency or other reason, the stakes involved in reaching agreement become enormous, however, this provides an incentive for more intensive bargaining, and then naturally a less tardy decision is likely.

Constitutional procedures would usually not be adopted unless they promised faster action and a greater likelihood of coordinated action, and so for a group of any given size, constitutional procedures will normally be faster and more likely to produce action. The groups that have a reason to use constitutional procedures are, however, naturally larger on average, and this tends to increase the diversity of the viewpoints and factions that must at least be considered, if not taken into account. Thus those (mainly large) organizations with constitutional procedures are not necessarily able to take faster action than those (mainly small) collusions and organizations that require unanimous consent bargaining. When there is a manifest emergency or a case for change that is so compelling that it generates virtual unanimity, however, constitutional procedures may be abridged or evaded and decisions made somewhat sooner.

In both consensual bargaining and constitutional decision making, the status quo normally prevails until some alternative gets the unanimous consent or the approval under constitutional procedures. If the cartel has established price X in a previous period, and there is a proposal to raise the price to X plus 10 percent, the price will remain at X until there is unanimous agreement on a different price (or until the cartel breaks up). A similar priority for the status quo is evident in Robert's *Rules of Order* and is either explicit or implicit in the bylaws of most organizations. Thus if the College of Surgeons in some area voted the last time the matter came up that the normal fee that Blue Shield ought to pay for an operation of a certain type is $1,000, then that will be the ordained fee until the college goes through whatever procedures its bylaws specify to make a new choice.

We finally now have a plausible explanation for "sticky" wages and prices — for the unexplained rigidities in money wages with which Keynes began *The General Theory* and for many of the ubiquitous and unexplained "lags" in monetarism. There is not much dispute about the facts. Many wage rates unquestionably do remain at given or predetermined levels for significant periods of time, often refusing to fall even if the demand for labor falls off and often rising only after much delay when demand rises. As Keynes suggested, real and money wages do often move in opposite directions. Though this pattern appears to be less general for prices than for wages, there are also many prices that exhibit precisely the same behavior. The empirical evidence that this is the case is voluminous and is emphasized by observant monetarists, as well as Keynesians. Phillip Cagan has again summarized the evidence clearly and fairly:

> While manufacturing prices have at times fallen precipitously, as in the business contractions of 1920–21 and 1929–33, usually they do not. To be sure, the available data do not record the secret discounting and shading of prices in slack markets, and actual transaction prices undoubtedly undergo larger fluctuations than the reported quotations suggest. The difference between reported and actual prices [will be] discussed further. It is not important enough, however, to invalidate the observed insensitivity of most prices to shifts in demand.[10]

The stickiness in goods prices is also greater in relatively concentrated markets in which coordination among firms is easier:

> It turns out that concentrated industries (defined as industries in which the four largest firms account for a high percentage of sales) do display less amplitude of cyclical price changes . . . concentrated industries are more likely to be characterized by some discretionary price setting big firms, as distinct from the highly competitive markets for many agricultural products and raw materials, which are characterized by market determined prices. . . . The importance of price setting is that firms in industries where it is the rule appear to coordinate price changes with each other so far as possible. The various methods of coordination require these firms to disregard short-run shifts in demand and to concentrate instead on changes in cost. As a consequence, their prices exhibit smaller fluctuations over the business cycle and less sensitivity to accelerations and retardations of general inflation. They appear to

be less flexible, and they impede the propagation of inflationary pressures through the economy. Their lags of adjustment are evident in an inflationary upswing by the fact that basic commodity prices move earlier and faster. As inflationary pressures wane, they make catch-up increases that present the paradox of rising demand at a time when demand is slackening.[11]

The evidence is *exactly* as the model offered here predicts. The markets where either organization or cooperation of an informal kind is a factor have on average less flexible prices than markets where this is not the case. Strictly speaking, it does not matter whether we are talking about wages or about prices, or whether individual firms are pure monopolists or one of a vast number of competitors. Though there is on the whole a higher degree of either formal organization or informal cooperation in most labor markets than in most goods markets and on average less price flexibility, this is not a necessary connection. When firm-specific human capital, esprit de corps, and other factors making stability of employment profitable for employers and cooperation or organization easier for workers are not relevant, wage rates may fluctuate very rapidly. The typical economist's experience and direct observations tell him or her that the pay of consultants, or the wages of unorganized day laborers, or the tips received by waiters can vary dramatically in response to fluctuations in demand. Conversely, the prices charged in highly cartelized goods markets, or the rates of regulated public utilities, or goods whose prices are controlled by government can be quite as sticky as any wage levels. The single firms and individuals who find themselves enjoying a monopoly at, say, a small but growing seasonal resort are often able to change prices with the season and even the weather, whereas the thousands of farmers who vote on whether the government should impose compulsory output or acreage restrictions in the interest of higher prices can change their decisions only on infrequent dates. In general, the degree of stickiness varies, as the model predicts, with the degree of collusion or organization, not with wage-price monopoly-competition distinctions that microeconomic theory tells us should have no relevance.

Note that this explanation of "sticky" wages and prices, in addition to fitting the historical and cross-sectional evidence better than prior models, also does not rely on ad hoc abandonment of the assumption of rationality (or bounded rationality) by appealing to a "money illusion" to explain wage behavior at the same time a variety of other behaviors are assumed to be rational. Since information is costly and humans are at best imperfectly rational, there may be a significant lag before workers adjust policies to any *unprecedented* inflation. But sooner or later there is learning, and then the notion of money illusion can only be a source of mischief. Similarly, the model here does not postulate any blind and permanent refusal to accept lower money wages if that should be in the interest of the workers making the choice. The idea that money wages are quite flexible upward but utterly and permanently rigid downward is not only inconsistent with the evidence that most wages rise more slowly during an unexpected inflation than do the prices of at least those goods that are traded on uncontrolled markets; it is also controverted by documented instances in which even formally organized workers have chosen to accept reductions in wage rates or other benefits.[12] A complete historical account of certain situations might need to take account of the fact that information and learning are costly and of the fact that the gains in employment from lower wages (in the absence of employer monopsony) are probably not so obvious as the gain from higher wage rates and thereby may be understood less quickly. But any such asymmetry would not justify the conclusion that money wages are free to vary in only one direction; it would rather show up in the length of lags.

The argument offered here also predicts that the process that mainly accounts for sticky wages and prices will also tend to make these wages and prices higher than is socially optimal and also higher in most cases than will clear the market. The fact that the wages and prices are set or influenced by cartelistic or lobbying organizations whose very purpose is to generate rents for their members makes it obvious that this will often be the case. If organizations of physicians or plumbers or oil producing nations did not raise the price of what they sold above the Pareto-optimal level, they would be passing up major opportunities to increase their members' incomes. Though second-best problems, bargaining under bilateral monopoly, and other special circumstances could sometimes imply that a wage or price increase obtained by special-interest organizations would increase economic efficiency, cases of this sort would surely be exceptional.

The supracompetitive prices will often also not clear the market, but will instead lead to some kind of queue of unutilized or underutilized resources. The higher wage or price obtained by the special-interest organization means that in general a smaller quantity of whatever its members sell will be demanded. At the same time the higher wage or price makes sale of the labor or good in question more advantageous. Thus some way of rationing the valuable opportunity that has been created is required. This rationing may be done partly by the purchaser, as when employers choose any new employees they want out of the queue, provided that the union wage be paid and that workers with seniority are not laid off. In other circumstances the special interest

limits the supply directly, as when organizations of physicians make it
more difficult to gain entry into medical school. Whatever the method,
there must be nonprice rationing at some stage. Some of the resources
that would have entered the market with the supracompetitive price will
crowd into areas where there are no restrictions, so that there will be
underemployment but not unemployment. The fact that it sometimes
pays to spend time queuing or searching for a supracompetitive wage or
price, or for the credentials or licenses that provide access to it, ensures
that there will be at least some unemployment. At some stage there
cannot be a market-clearing price (unless the opportunities to take advantage of the supracompetitive price are auctioned off), and at this point
there will be some unemployment of resources in queues or searches.

AN ETERNAL PHILLIPS CURVE

The sticky wages and prices, set normally at above market-clearing and
Pareto-optimal levels, insure that there will be a negatively sloped Phillips
curve. In the case of the short-run Phillips curve, this is obvious. If there
is unexpected inflation, the real wage and the relative level of those
prices influenced by special-interest organizations will fall. This will
mean that in the rheumatic economy a huge set of wages and prices will
no longer be so much above market-clearing and competitive levels.
Employers or other purchasers of the labor or goods provided by the
members of the special-interest organizations will take larger quantities
at the lower real prices. So unemployment will decrease, and in addition
there will be some tendency toward a lesser degree of monopoly. The
unexpected inflation, as experience also tells us, will result in greater real
output.

   Though the point is not of any importance for practical policy, it is for
theoretical reasons useful to point out that this is not just a short-term
phenomenon. It would be a pity if governments used it as a basis for
policy, but the fact remains that there is an "eternal Phillips phenomenon." As a first approximation, monetary policy can be changed in days
(if not sooner). Some of the effects of monetary changes will be evident
promptly, as soon as the change in monetary policy is noticed, though
some of the effects may, it is true, appear only after a considerable lag.
By contrast, the minimum wage laws, collectively bargained wages, public utility prices, and legislation abolishing or creating monopolies can be
changed only over a period of many months or even many years. Given
that the administration can marginally change the rate at which appro-

priated monies are spent, the lags in fiscal policy are probably somewhere in between. But fiscal policy probably has rather prompt effects. (There is also a difference in the division of powers, with the executive branch of at least many countries given complete control over monetary policy, only partial control over policy on stationary prices and monopoly policy, and almost no control over collective bargaining.) Further, it is normally also true that at least in the short run the social cost of the real output lost from recession exceeds the social cost of the less than optimal size of real money balances and other subtle costs of inflation, unless the inflation has reached very high levels indeed. It follows that the quickest way, and sometimes the only way, an administration can raise the level of employment and real output and reduce the costs of monopoly power is through inflation. Monetary and fiscal policy can be changed faster than "rigid" wages and prices can be changed, so it won't be possible for the organized interests to maintain the real wages or prices in the short run. A somewhat inflationary policy in the short run is accordingly advantageous in the short run for the society.

Moreover, even in the long run, and even with rational expectations, the Phillips curve arising from the foregoing aspects of reality will *never* become vertical. Even if the public knows what the government is doing, the fact that the crucial wage cannot change as fast as monetary policy at least means that the government can always generate more real output and a lesser degree of monopoly by taking advantage of the possibility of lowering real wages during the crucial lag period. The only possibility that could make the Phillips curve vertical, even in the longest run, is institutional change great enough to do away with the fundamental features of reality described above. The priority for the status quo and the lag in adjustment would themselves have to be done away with. It is by no means certain that the coalitions that give rise to the political or monopoly power behind the whole process could ever acquire the capacity for immediate decision making or would want to. Even if indexing is used, a lag in the collection and publication of the cost-of-living index, or any stable imperfection in it known to the government, or any sticky-wage area to which the index did not apply would permit an eternally nonvertical Phillips phenomenon.

The reader may object that any policies designed to maintain higher levels of employment over a long run through inflation will result in ever higher rates of inflation and ultimately in a disastrous runaway inflation. This objection is correct, but not relevant. The point is not to recommend that government and the central bank always conspire to increase real output by inflating, but rather to point out the *permanent* structural

differences in capacity to change policy quickly and their permanent
relevance to our understanding of government behavior and macroeconomic reality. It is sometimes said that the monetary authorities can
affect the level of real output only by tricking the private sector, and this
only temporarily since the public will soon catch on. But, quite apart
from any trickery, there are the crucial matter of the different speeds at
which decisions can be taken and the fact that this difference is fundamental rather than ephemeral. Expectations matter, but it is a mistake to
suppose that *only* expectations matter. The view that the monetary authorities can influence the level, if not output, by trickery is akin to
saying that a running back in a football game can get through the defense
only by trickery. Admittedly, if the defense knew in advance just where
the back would run, they would stop him. But it doesn't follow that there
will be no more successful broken-field runners once each of the tricks
and feints that can be performed has been learned by defensive squads;
so long as there are running backs whose reflexes are sufficiently fast,
there will always be at least the possibility that they will elude even the
most muscular defense.

MARKET POWER AND THE INFLATION PROCESS

The orthodoxy, emphasized most often by monetarists but widely accepted by other economists, is that monopoly and oligopoly power,
whether exercised by firms or by unions, cannot be even a contributing
cause of inflation or of recession. Each monopoly or oligopolistic combination will bring about a once-and-for-all change in relative prices when
the market power is first acquired, and this will usually involve some loss
of social efficiency, but monopolistic firms, cartels, or unions will not
continuously raise prices that would generate inflation or (if aggregate
demand does not respond) recession. Most proponents of the cost-push
do not realize this and do not offer any reason why the prices or wages
they emphasize should rise secularly; thus they have naturally not suc-
ceeded in overthrowing or amending the orthodoxy.

If the basic model out of which this paper grows is correct, there is a
tendency for special-interest organizations and collusions to accumulate
over time in the stable societies. This involves more cartelizations and
collusion in markets and more government intervention of the lobby-
inspired and -directed type. This gradual accumulation and the great
change over time in the nature of the macroeconomic problem described
earlier in this paper suggest that the orthodoxy is a bit too simple and

indeed that it leaves out a fundamental element in the simultaneous unemployment-and-inflation problem that has emerged since World War II. The analysis of decision lags and Phillips curves we have just completed shows, if it is correct, that neither the standard Keynesian nor the classical monetarist theories are theoretically complete and deal adequately with the Phillips curve phenomena in a mature economy only if extended to include an argument of the sort offered here.

That analysis assumed a substantial but unchanging degree of institutional rheumatism. If, as suggested by the basic model from which we began, there is a *continuing* accumulation of special-interest organization and collusion in a stable society, it follows that the *short-run Phillips curve will shift upward even if no inflation whatever is expected.* Over time new organizations and collusions are created and existing ones get stronger, so that there are more cartelized or collusive markets and more lobby-influenced interventions by government. This raises the relative price or wage in additional markets to monopolistic and nonmarket clearing levels. This alone increases the time individuals and firms spend in queues or searches rather than in production and thus entails that, if there is no other change, and particularly no change in monetary and fiscal policy, there will be an increase in unemployment. The new and strengthened organizations and collusions will, for the reasons set out above, not be able to change prices and wages as quickly as the government can increase aggregate demand. The result is that there will for a time be a reduction in unemployment and a reduction in the social loss from monopoly prices if there is an unexpected inflation. The increasingly rheumatic character of the economy may therefore show up as an increasing degree of unemployment, or as a higher rate of inflation, or (more probably) as some of each — as stagflation.

The quantitative importance of the foregoing process will of course vary from case to case. Over some periods of two or three years there might be so little institutional accumulation that the short-run Phillips curves would not be affected significantly. Moreover, if this two or three year period has been unprecedentedly inflationary, expectations could have changed, and that would tend to shift short-run Phillips curves in the familiar way. Thus there can be inflationary episodes that have not much of anything to do with the further accumulation of special-interest organizations and collusions. In the mature economy there can even be stagflationary episodes, or simultaneous increases in inflation and unemployment, that are *not* due to any *increase* in special-interest organization or collusion but rather to the *combination* of a *high,* but essentially constant, degree of such organization and collusion and the emergence of inflationary expectations. There are other periods of even a decade or less in length in which there can be a substantial increase in the degree of special-interest organization or collusion, and then even the *increase* in accumulation can be a decisive factor in causing the stagflation. There is widespread, if scattered, evidence of a great increase in special-interest organization and collusion in most Western societies in the late sixties and seventies; this was, for example, a period of unprecedented growth in the share of national output spent or redistributed by governments throughout the Western democracies.[13] Thus the recent stagflation probably is due in significant part to a *further* accumulation of special-interest organization and collusion and is probably *not* due entirely to the inflationary policies that emerged during the Vietnamese War. In the absence of further empirical work, however, we cannot be sure on this latter point. The earlier point that the unemployment and underutilization of other resources during the stagflation (and the interwar depression) cannot be adequately explained without taking the high degree of institutional rheumatism into account seems irrefutable, but the quantitative importance of the further accumulation of common-interest organization in the last decade and a half has yet to be determined.

GOVERNMENTAL INFLUENCE ON THE EXERCISE OF MARKET POWER

The orthodox view that firms, unions, and other institutions with monopoly power or capacity to collude will choose whatever price or wage is most advantageous for them (and thereafter respond to changes in demand and cost conditions in essentially the same way that pure competitors do) so that they will have only a one-time effect on prices is based implicitly on a particular conception of the way these institutions make decisions. It assumes that these institutions are cavalier about the exercise of their monopoly power and do not consider the loss to others that will result from their monopoly; that they can calculate the optimum price or wage for themselves in a reasonably short run; and that they have reasonably well-defined and stable objectives, such as maximization of profits or sales subject to a minimum profit constraint. There is a good deal to be said in favor of these presuppositions; simplifications and abstractions from reality such as these are needed for parsimonious theory. Nonetheless, when the role of government in economic life is very large and particularly when cartelistic and lobbying groups are at issue, these presuppositions can occasionally miss the essence of the matter.

In an environment in which government intervention is ubiquitous and a special-interest group may even have won its monopoly position by lobbying, any organization or firm that has just acquired market power is not likely to be cavalier about the exercise of its new power. Though it is not likely to give the public interest or the interests of those with whom it deals much, if any, weight in its objective function, it is nonetheless likely to spend something on public relations and on arguments that what it is doing is really in the public interest, or required in the interests of simple justice, and so forth. As even the most casual sampling of the media of communications reveals, institutions that exercise market power or win favor from government devote more than trivial amounts of advertising money and leadership time to gaining and maintaining a favorable image. If there is this concern about public relations and alertness to the blessings that the government can both bestow and take away, a monopolist would be foolish to choose the "optimal price" the moment it acquires the capacity to charge this price — that would attract adverse attention, perhaps even from politicians looking for enemies of the people to attack. So the prudent debutante monopolists may approach the profit-maximizing price in stages over a considerable period of time. Even the established monopolists may not take full advantage right away of a substantial increase in demand. Martin Bronfenbrenner, starting from a different perspective, has made the same point with an engaging literary allusion: The monopolist, he said, will approach the profit-maximizing price "on little cat's feet" (apparently from Carl Sandburg's "the fog crept in on little cat's feet"). One of the reasons that the Organization of Petroleum Exporting Countries (OPEC) has attracted so much attention, Bronfenbrenner pointed out, was that it exercised its power with dramatic suddenness.[14] Obviously, many cartelistic and collusive groups, as well as individual firms with monopoly power, will have to approach the optimum price in a slow and stealthy way, which will give them a longer-run, if less dramatic, effect on stagflation and will further delay the adaptation of their prices to sudden changes in demand. This also means that one cannot empirically see the full effect of the creation of new special-interest organizations until some time after they have become established.

When the organizations and collusions that this paper emphasizes are the issue, the very idea that there are a unique optimum and a decision rule capable of attaining it is, at the least, questionable. In one period in this cartel or that lobby, coalition A may be in control and have chosen a given price and allocation of rights to produce; by the next period, bargaining may have revealed that a new coalition B can defeat A; and so on for perhaps several future periods. Indeed, as we know from the work of Kenneth Arrow and others, under commonplace decision procedures like majority rule, there may be no stable outcome and perhaps some bases for objection to *any* democratic decision rule that would generate a transitive preference ordering for the special-interest organization. The orthodox analysis of stagflation accordingly errs in assuming a once-and-for-all adjustment in prices as a result of any new monopoly. If, as is so often the case, the new market power (or political clout) comes from some organization or collusion of different firms or individuals, it may take quite some time for a dominant coalition to emerge and in some cases there may not even be one. Thus we cannot simply look at membership figures in special-interest organizations or the dates the organizations were created and immediately see all of their macroeconomic consequences.

In the case of labor unions, there is not even a single goal akin to profit maximation that could possibly explain their behavior. As is well known, if a union were to maximize wage rates, this would (except in special circumstances where firms have monopsony power) entail that it had no concern whatever about unemployment among its clients, so wage maximization cannot be the typical union's goal. Unions manifestly do not maximize employment either, since they often reduce employment by seeking higher wages and will sometimes control apprenticeship or hiring halls to restrict entry. There is further evidence that unions are often interested both in higher wages and in preserving members' jobs in the fact that unions often bargain for limitations on the extent to which management can reduce employment or in the fact that unions even demand overmanning or featherbedding at the same time they seek to maintain or increase wages. A similar ambivalence must characterize professional associations.

Since unions undoubtedly want to obtain higher wages and to preserve members' jobs, it follows that they must consciously or unconsciously, knowingly or unknowingly, trade off wages against jobs. How do they decide what trade-off point on the employer's demand curve for labor they want to bargain for?[15] Though the process surely varies from case to case and the differences among union leaders must be particularly important, almost every union must contain some members whose security in their present employment (or prospects of more or less equally attractive employment elsewhere) are so good that their interests are normally best served by demanding a much higher wage. Similarly, there must be some members who sense that if the employer must reduce the work force, they will probably be among those laid off (and without comparable opportunities elsewhere). Typically, unions will insist that seniority be at least the principal basis for decisions about who, if anyone, must be laid off. The correlation between seniority and influence in the work group and the union commends this principle to the union, and its unambiguous simplicity and predictability commend it to all. The employer would rather not lose the freedom to select those retained, but the correlation of seniority and relevant experience will often make this rule seem less objectionable than the available alternatives.

Thus there will almost always be some members of each union (normally the most senior) who will have an interest in bargaining for the highest wages consistent with the viability of the firm and others (normally less senior) whose interest will be severely damaged by any wage increase that will bring about an absolute reduction in the work force. (Professional associations face similar divergences of interests when professional fees are set.) Somehow, the union must reach some decision about how much weight to give the interests of senior or secure workers in a higher wage and how much weight to give to the interests of junior or insecure workers in continued employment. It would be most imprudent for a union leader to call attention to this divergence of interest in the membership; the union leader will be better advised to emphasize the common interests of the members. This fact and the fact that there are almost never organized opposition parties within special-interest groups will go a long way to obscure this fundamental conflict of interest, but it is an *inescapable* consequence of a downward slope of the demand curve for labor (which will govern even monopsonistic situations, once the union excludes dominated alternatives) and the varying degrees of confidence different members can have in their security of employment.

Though the trade-off between wages and employment is inescapable, there is no necessity whatever that a union will, as the orthodoxy supposes, choose its optimal point as soon as it obtains its power of combination and thereafter make no changes other than those dictated by changes in demand or other external conditions. On the contrary, the outcomes of the political struggles among the groupings or cliques representing different interests can change from time to time. Most importantly, the balance of power in the union and the preferred trade-off between wages and jobs may change *systematically* after the union first organizes the work place. There are, for example, some reasons to suspect that a newly organized union might seek a wage that is less likely

to bring layoffs among existing members than would a more mature
union.[16] There is, at a minimum, always the possibility that a coalition
of all but the more junior workers will seek higher wages, even at the
cost of possible unemployment for their less influential new coworkers.

Beyond this, there is one ubiquitous factor that makes unions choose
successively higher points along the employers' labor demand curves as
time goes on, thereby obtaining a progressively higher real wage at the
expense of ever larger sacrifices of employment. If the members of a
union display the same self-interested motivation that economists typically assume in the marketplace, the union will focus on the wage levels
and employment security of its members rather than on the effects the
union has on the (presumably anonymous) group of new workers the
employer might have hired had the union had a different policy. The
union will then choose the highest wage it can get that is consistent with
continued employment of every member who wants to work, or alter-
natively seek some still higher wage if it is willing to tolerate or risk
unemployment among some (usually junior) members of the union. As
time goes on, some members of the union will no longer be able or willing
to work; eventually, because of death or morbidity, some will be unable
to work, and others will retire. Then the union will seek a higher real
wage, *even if there is no change in the demand for labor or in any other
external conditions, because it can now do so without any reduction in
the probability that its members can keep their employment.* If, as is
usual, there are members who reach retirement or who become unable
to work each year, the union will demand a higher real wage *every* year,
until the marginal product of labor becomes so high that it equals the
average product of labor, at which point the wage has reached the highest
level consistent with the continued employment of any labor in this
firm.[17]

The result of all this is that even if there were no increase over some
period in the extent or strength of special-interest organizations or collusions, the relative real wage or price demanded by them can increase
substantially, thereby aggravating inflation if there are accommodative
monetary and fiscal policies, or increasing unemployment if there are
not. The orthodox assumption that any combination will choose its most
advantageous price when it first obtains its monopoly power and thereafter respond to changes in the environment much as pure competitors
would is wrong. The special-interest organization or collusion may make
decisions through processes that do not even generate a transitive ordering and certainly have no tendency to reach a stable outcome quickly.
Whatever price or wage a monopoly, whether a combination or not,

seeks as an ideal, it is likely to approach it very slowly, on cat's feet, because of the importance of perceptions in a political environment. The fact of retirement, disability, or death of unionized workers, moreover, means that quite apart from any change in aggregate demand, there are *always* at least *some* special-interest organizations that are obtaining increases in their relative real wages, even if their power is *not* increasing and, indeed, *even as their membership is decreasing*. The changing performance, as well as the increasing extent, of special-interest organization makes the macroeconomic problem change for the worse over time.

THE DEFLATIONARY IMPACT OF FLEXIBLE PRICES ON DECLINING AGGREGATE DEMAND

Some prices are not determined or even directly influenced by special-interest organizations, even in a relatively rheumatic economy. In our discussion of Phillips curves we noted that these flexible prices naturally rise more rapidly than do cartelized and lobby-controlled prices during an unexpected inflation, thereby making the latter, monopolized prices relatively lower and closer to market-clearing levels. What role do the fully flexible prices play when there is a substantial reduction in aggregate demand? Obviously these uncartelized and uncontrolled prices fall, both in nominal terms and relative to the sticky prices and wages. This alone makes it obvious that increases in the degree of special-interest organization or collusion, and even policies that brought secular increases in wages or prices in already cartelized sectors, would not be sufficient to cause inflation; at least so long as the number and importance of the markets with flexible prices are great enough to offset the effect of any rising prices without becoming negative, restrictive monetary and fiscal policy can always prevent inflation. We must now take a general equilibrium perspective and ask whether the fact that there are always some flexible prices would be sufficient to prevent unemployment as well.

Since the free fluctuation of prices in a market suggests (if the argument in this paper is correct) that the market is not cartelized or controlled, resources that cannot get employment at wages or prices that are too high to clear markets in the sectors under the thrall of special interests are free, if they choose, to move into what Sir John Hicks has aptly called the *flexprice* sector. Some economists would argue that this freedom of movement will insure full employment. The relative prices of those goods that are flexible will be driven down by the crowding of resources from the organized sector, and the economy will be less efficient than if perfect competition prevailed throughout. The critic may nonetheless insist that even in the highly cartelized and lobby-ridden economy, there need be neither inflation nor unemployment.

One problem with the argument in the foregoing paragraph is that it leaves out the time it would take for resources to shift sectors. The sticky character of the prices and wages in the organized sector implies that the flexible prices will initially absorb the whole of the deflation, thereby making the relative prices in the cartelized or controlled sector greater than before. The decrease in aggregate demand and greater relative price together imply a substantial reduction in the quantity of goods and labor demanded in the organized sector, and thus full employment could require a substantial migration to the flexprice sector. Some of the owners of unemployed resources may suppose that either because of government action or equilibrating forces, the recession will be temporary and it then may not pay to move to the flexprice sector. Such a move will, after all, sometimes involve considerable direct or psychic costs, for example, the uprooting of families in major cities in order that they may find employment in the rural areas where many of the goods with flexible prices are produced. Moreover, many of the resources used in the fixed-price sectors will not have more than a fraction of their normal value if shifted to a different sector; factories and machines are often constructed to serve only specialized needs, and workers with considerable industry-specific or firm-specific human capital may be able to do only unskilled work, at least for a time, in other industries or firms. Some people do at least describe themselves as unemployed if the only available work involves not only a change of occupation but a great change of status as well; and at the same time they may also be too old to make investments in a new skill that requires as long an education, training, or service with a single firm as that which gave them their prior skill. Some of this unwillingness to invest in a second profession may be due to a deplorable conservationism in many individuals of middle age or older, but it surely often exists, and when it does, a full employment equilibrium can arrive literally only after most of those in the class at issue are dead, or at least retired.

The foregoing emphasis on the fact that the time required for resource reallocation may exceed the duration of most "cyclical" fluctuations in the economy admittedly does not bear on the everlasting debate between Keynesians and monetarists on whether there is an "underemployment equilibrium" or only temporary departures from a normal full employment equilibrium. If the theory offered here is correct, this is a misguided debate in any case; with the continuously increasing extent of cartelized and lobby-directed markets (except during periods of social upheaval), there is, strictly speaking, *neither* an underemployment equilibrium nor a full employment equilibrium. To put it another way, the amount of unemployment that will result from a stable price level will tend to rise over time, except during catastrophes.

Even if we take a timeless view of macroeconomic fluctuations and unrealistically ignore the costs of the resource reallocation to the flexprice sector whenever aggregate demand is substantially less than expected, the fact that there are always some flexible prices need not ever insure full employment. A second problem with the general equilibrium argument adumbrated in the opening paragraph of this section is that it ignores what can best be described as the selling-apples-on-street-corners issue. Though soft-hearted journalists and demagogic politicians may love to dramatize the plight of the unemployed workers who are reduced to selling apples, the economist who knows that the economy is a general equilibrium system will, if he or she does not let emotions overcome the powers of analysis, realize that an increase in the number of those selling apples on street corners represents a helpful and equilibrating response to the situation. If there is a great increase in the number of people selling apples, we may reasonably infer that that sector is not cartelized and accordingly has flexible prices. Thus the move of unemployed resources into selling apples is a helpful shift of resources into the flexible-price sector and is symbolic of the many other such shifts that take place. This selling-apples argument is not, I must insist, a parody, but rather a correct statement of *one* aspect of the matter; that this is so can readily be seen by considering the loss of welfare that would occur for consumers as well as workers if street-corner vending were prohibited during a depression.

What needs to be added is that *if the economy is highly rheumatic and the deflation is considerable,* and if the obstacles of resource reallocation described above are overcome, the amount of resources that will have to transfer into the flexprice sector will be so great in relation to the size of the flexprice sector that prices in the flexprice sector, which already bore the brunt of the reduction of the fall in aggregate demand, will fall *much* further. The ratio of the prices in the flexprice sector to those in the fixprice sector will be most abnormal, and the returns to resources employed in the flexprice sector will become very low indeed. It is not only that street-corner vending of apples or whatever, which in normal times should provide the normal factor return for industries with free entry, will become so low that this occupation will be considered synonymous with abject unemployment; it is also that this will happen eventually in *all* the industries with free entry. In the United States in the 1930s, for example, the historic migration from farm to city was dramatically reversed. This reallocation of resources also served a purpose, but the farm prices that were associated with this shift were so abnormally low in relation to industrial prices and wages that there was widespread and effective political support for programs to "stabilize" farm prices. These prices were to some extent stabilized, and this was done by *requiring that some land and other resources by law remain unemployed* until a price ratio more nearly resembling the historic "parity" was established. It may be supposed by some that this type of action was a historical aberration. The hypothesis behind this paper is that it was not and that when a similar derangement of relative price levels occurs today, the extent of government intervention to limit this abnormal fall in prices in flexible markets is even greater (consider energy policy in the United States today).

The general point is that when the proportion of cartelized and lobby-controlled prices becomes very great, any substantial reduction in aggregate demand will lead to underutilization of resources, not only because of the difficulties of resource reallocation in the short run, but also because the shift of resources to the flexprice sector will eventually be so large in relation to the size of that sector that it will result in factor rewards so low they are not distinguished from unemployment or in additional government restriction of output or factor use to protect returns in the flexprice sector. (One result of the contribution that flexible prices make to regaining employment during a depression is that the flexprice sector diminishes further.) To this unemployment we must add the amount that occurs because the prices and wages that are held above market-clearing levels by special-interest organizations increases the incentive to wait unemployed in queues and to search.

THE KEYNESIAN MODEL RECONSIDERED

If the argument here is correct, Keynes's brilliant theory should be regarded as a special, rather than a general, theory, though for different reasons than are usually given. Keynes was writing in Great Britain in the twenties and thirties. The society in which he wrote had accumulated far more special-interest organizations and collusions than any other society at that time. The pattern of demands the British economy faced was far different than before the war, and the industries in which Britain had comparative advantage had changed somewhat too. These considerations entailed Britain's need for a new structure of relative wages and prices and a considerable reallocation of resources. In the absence of price, and especially wage, flexibility, there was a great deal of unemployment of resources. For a time this problem was exacerbated by Churchill's overvaluation of the pound. Still, as the late Harry Johnson has trenchantly argued, if the relevant wages and prices had fallen enough, British resources would have been fully employed. But the British institutional structure had been developing for a long time, and the relevant wages and prices did not fall in the short run, and some not even in the medium term. In a sufficiently long run, these wages and prices would have adjusted, but (to borrow a phrase from Keynes) in the long run we are all dead. Thus Keynes's general theory is in fact an ingenious and invaluable, but by no means general, theory. Had Britain emerged from World War I with the clean institutional slate that Germany had after World War II, he would perhaps not have had an occasion to write the book. Had the United States not experienced a modest period of stability and institutional accumulation (especially of business organizations — note the Smoot-Hawley tariff), Keynes might not have had such a profound impact upon the United States. From this perspective it is no accident that postwar German opinion has not been very susceptible to Keynes.

Though Keynes *recognized* that inflexible wages and prices could have profound macroeconomic significance, and in that respect was far ahead of many monetarists even in our own day, he did not take the trouble to *explain* the inflexibility or to show how it varies. Without any explanation of these inflexibilities, Keynes's followers in the era of stagflation have often supposed that the "rigid" wages and prices would not be affected by the increases in aggregate demand — they assumed the fixed wages and prices were simply given and would not be affected by expansionary fiscal policies, whereas they were only inflexible and would eventually change in predictable and rational ways. There is no need to dwell on the costs of this mistake, for the monetarists point it out repeatedly.

To say that Keynes's theory is crucially incomplete, and incomplete in a way that can be profoundly misleading, does not deny the colossal magnitude of his contribution to the debate on the determinants of aggregate *demand*. Keynes's emphasis on the demand for money as an asset, on the special volatility of investment as compared to consumption expenditure, and on expectations, for example, have enormously enriched our understanding of macroeconomic and monetary problems. Keynes, with the help of Hicks, also provided the intellectual framework needed to consider the supply and demand for money simultaneously with the intentions to save and invest. Having done all this and more,

Keynes can hardly be blamed for failing to provide a theory of supply-price as well. But he should have pointed out the risks and limitations inherent in this omission. It is tempting to say that Keynes's only sin was that of synecdoche.

This is a sin of which the monetarists are no less guilty. Though they never make the mistake of acting as though prices and wages would never change, they have been no more alert than the Keynesians to the organizational and collusive processes that influence these prices. If the monetarists had thought seriously about the institutional accumulation I have described (or even taken note of their own warnings about the growing role of government in wage and price determination), they would not have been so long attached to the idea that the economy is almost always at or quickly heading toward the full employment level of output — they would not have analyzed the American economy of the 1970s in a way that (at best) was appropriate to the early nineteenth century. If Milton Friedman had thought more about the gradual accumulation of common-interest organizations in stable societies, he might instead have said that if there is a natural rate of unemployment at all, it is naturally (except in catastrophes) always increasing.

CONCLUSIONS

If the theory of supply-price offered here contains any substantial degree of truth, it follows that there is definitely a need for *something* beyond demand management, such as incentives-based incomes policies. I personally have drawn a stronger conclusion than this and argued some years ago that there are a variety of incentives-based policies that, *if* properly designed and combined with the right monetary and fiscal policies, could provide crucial help in fighting stagflation in the short run.[18] I have seen nothing in the experience of the last few years that would argue against that judgment and more than a little that would argue in its favor.

NOTES

1. *The General Theory* (London: Macmillan and Co., 1954), scattered quotations from pp. 5–15.

2. *The General Theory*, pp. 262–67.

3. These data are borrowed from Patrick Minford of the University of Liverpool from his forthcoming paper "The Problem of Inflation," table 2. It is important to emphasize that the lesson that Minford draws is not the same as the one that will be offered in this paper; Minford is arguing for the superiority of the monetarist model.

4. Phillip Cagan, *The Hydra-Headed Monster: The Problem of Inflation in the United States* (Washington, D.C.: American Enterprise Institute, 1974). This quotation and the following ones are from scattered sections of Cagan's essay and leave out most of Cagan's own explanations of the facts he states. The selective quotations do, however, provide a fair summary of those facts in Cagan's account that bear most directly on the present argument. The italics are mine. I am thankful to Thomas Mayer for calling Cagan's argument to my attention.

5. *A Monetary History of the United States, 1867–1960* (Princeton, N.J.: Princeton University Press, 1963), p. 299.

6. *Did Monetary Forces Cause the Great Depression?* (New York: W. W. Norton, 1976), p. xi.

7. E.P. Thompson, *The Making of the English Working Class,* p. 776, fn. 2. I am grateful to Peter Murrell for this reference. The word *unemployed* goes much further back; it was used, for example, to describe fallow land. Note this passage from Milton's *Paradise Lost*: "Other creatures all day long rove idle unimploid, and less need rest." [4.617]

8. See John A Garraty, *Unemployment in History,* Colophon edition (New York: Harper & Row, 1979), p. 4.

9. Mancur Olson, *The Logic of Collective Action* (Cambridge, Mass.: Harvard University Press, 1965, 1971).

10. Cagan, *The Hydra-Headed Monster.*

11. Ibid.

12. See Peter Henle, "Reverse Collective Bargaining? A Look at Some Union Concessions," *Industrial and Labor Relations Review* 26 (1973).

13. Sam Peltzman, "The Growth of Government," forthcoming.

14. From Martin Bronfenbrenner's presentation to the Middlebury conference "New Approaches to an Incomes Policy," April 19–21, 1979.

15. A union may, by offering a permanent all-or-none option to an employer, obtain a wage bill or wage-quantity rectangle, part of which falls outside the employer's marginal revenue product of labor curve, as shown in the two solid line rectangles in figure 1. Any areas such as *abc* must, however, be smaller than *mno* or the employer would be better off closing down or using no labor at all. In other words, the wage bill must not exceed the average revenue product of labor. Since this is always downward sloping in the relevant range, it remains true that the higher the wage rate, the lower the quantity that can be sold. This will hold true even when the union deals with a monopsonist, after the union eliminates the dominated alternatives before it. The union can also get a wage rate that is *a* high or higher if it lets the employer specify the quantity taken; it can then choose the maximum wage rate shown by the dotted line. Only one variable factor has been assumed, but this does not affect the conclusion.

16. When the union initiates attempts to organize a workshop or craft, it needs all the support it can get among its potential clients; if any substantial group of workers, such as the less senior, should oppose the union it probably will not succeed in overcoming the opposition of the employer. There may even be a tendency for older workers to be more deferential and for those who have found it advantageous to stay with the firm for some time to be more amenable to management. The question of who is to be laid off if there is

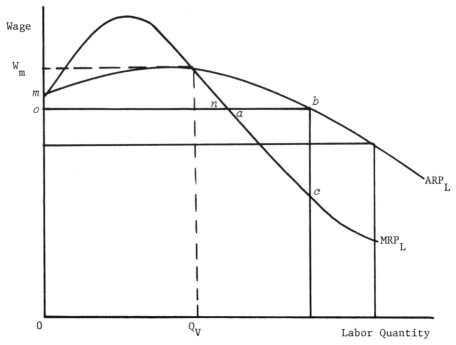

Figure 1. Union Wage Strategies

a reduction in force because of higher wages may not come up initially, and the union organizers would surely be ill-advised to raise it. Thus there probably will not initially be a seniority system or other mechanism that specifies who will be laid off if some must be. This hypothesized initial situation, in which the insecurity of the union gives it a need for the broadest possible support and in which the rules determining who must suffer from any reduction in force have yet to be negotiated, is one that systematically works against any wage increases large enough to threaten existing workers; all or almost all of the reduction in employment due to a wage increase will be borne by those who would have been hired in the absence of a union. If the risks from any wage increase are spread out over the whole membership, and the union needs only recognition and a modest victory to get itself established, then the initial tendency, I hypothesize, will be for the union to choose a relatively low unemployment point on the employer's demand curve for labor.

As the union gets stronger and rules get worked out to determine who will bear the burden of any reduction in the quantity of labor demanded, a new situation emerges. The young workers who formed the union before long have a substantial degree of seniority. It becomes clear what minority within the union will bear the main burden of uncertainty about being laid off and the increase in this burden due to a higher real wage. There is eventually, then, the basis for the formation of a coalition of senior workers that will dominate union policy and choose a different trade-off, putting relatively more emphasis on the wage increase and less on the possibility of generating layoffs. This can exacerbate stagflation even at a time when there is no increase in union membership.

17. I am grateful to Oliver Williamson for calling the influence of death and retirement among unionized workers to my attention. The influence of this demographic factor on the wages particular unions demand has apparently been familiar for a long while in the labor economics literature, but, so far as I know, its implications for macroeconomic theory and stagflation have usually been neglected.

18. "On Getting Full Employment without Inflation," in *Solutions to Inflation,* edited by David C. Colander (New York: Harcourt Brace Jovanovich, 1979).

3 TAX- AND MARKET-BASED INCOMES POLICIES:
The Interface of Theory and Practice
David Colander

Inflation is everywhere and always a full circle — prices rise because wages rise because aggregate demand increases because wages rise . . . . While questions of what is the cause and what is the effect may well serve the purpose of employing unemployed philosophers, they will always, like the chicken-and-the-egg conundrum, go unanswered. For those interested in policy questions rather than conundrums, it is useful to finesse the question of what ultimately causes inflation by concentrating, instead, on that aspect of the circular causation for which something can be done, an approach I have elsewhere called the realitic approach to economics.[1]

In realitic economics, we stop asking questions about the cause of inflation once we have found a cause we believe has a theoretical cure. The focus of the analysis then shifts to possible negative side effects and to questions of practical implementation. If the policy proves feasible,

Most of the good ideas in this paper were developed in discussion with Abba Lerner as we worked on *MAP* (forthcoming, Harcourt Brace Jovanovich). Propriety requires me to take responsibility for the bad ones.

79

we can move on to other questions; if, however, the policy proves impractical, we must return to the causation circle.

The source of inflation with which this paper is concerned is what Abba Lerner and I call a "faulty social accounting system," a problem that results from the absence of a coordinating system for nominal price and wage decisions.[2] In our view, inflation occurs because the economy has no mechanism to insure that price and wage changes are relative, not price level changes. Without such a mechanism, it is not surprising that inflation can persist. The anti-inflation proposals that theoretically solve this problem and substantiate our cause are tax- and market-based incomes policies. These policies enable us to correct the faulty individual accounting system so that it coincides with the optimal social accounting system.

The above cause may sound heretical to monetarists and monetarist fellow travelers (which I suspect includes most economists), but it is not. To attribute the cause of inflation to a fault in the social accounting system instead of to money is not to suggest that there is no role for money or aggregate policy in the cure. Indeed, the very definition of an incomes policy is a policy that coordinates aggregate policy with an incomes policy.[3] If an incomes policy is not coordinated, it degenerates into either income control or wage and price controls.[4] The problem of income policies is how to coordinate aggregate policy with the incomes policy and not destroy the market.

The Market Anti-Inflation Plan (MAP), which is described by Abba Lerner in the next paper, achieves that end by turning the market upon itself. It achieves the desired price level control in a manner fully compatible with other market forces; it simply requires anyone raising his or her nominal value-added "price" to offset the inflationary aspect of that price rise by paying someone else to lower his or her value-added "price" by the appropriate offsetting amount. All "price" changes must therefore be relative price changes. (The concept of value-added price is used throughout this paper to denote prices in their broadest sense; it includes wages, rental prices on capital, as well as all other value-added prices.)

Any market can be analogued by a tax. Therefore, theoretically, a tax-based incomes policy can achieve the same result as MAP. For this reason, the arguments I make in support of MAP also hold for a tax-based incomes policy (TIP) that analogues the MAP proposal.[5] Such a TIP would have the following characteristics:

1. It would be based on value added per unit input.
2. It would include both a subsidy and a tax so that the program is self-financing.

3. It would be implemented as a separate excise tax on above guide-line value-added increases and not as part of a corporate income tax or payroll tax.
4. It would be a permanent, not a temporary, program.
5. It would provide an equal incentive for all price changes and would not be instituted as an either-or or "hurdle" incentive.
6. It would be accompanied by a decrease in nominal aggregate spending so that there is no "excess demand."

Thus, the TIP that I see would be a type of dirty float MAP, where the tax administrator attempted to set the TIP tax in such a way that it analogued the market.[6]

Selling a new "solution" to inflation is difficult; selling a new theory of inflation is next to impossible. Therefore, instead of developing the MAP concept in our "faulty-social-accounting" framework, I shall instead sketch how MAP can be integrated with the "accepted" theories of inflation. The first section of the paper suggests the role MAP and TIP would play for three different conceptual frameworks. MAP solves the inflation problem in each, although the role it plays differs. In the first sketch of an almost competitive economy, MAP works perfectly, bringing inflation to an immediate halt. The second sketch adds some realism to the first by assuming a Phillips curve trade-off between inflation and unemployment. In this theory, MAP improves the short-run efficiency of monetary policy if there is no long-run Phillips curve trade-off or enriches the policy options if there is. In the final sociological view of inflation, inflation is a systemic problem and controls are a necessity. MAP accomplishes the control in the most efficient manner.

To accept that MAP is theoretically a cure for inflation does not mean that it should be immediately imposed; innumerable practical implementation problems must be answered before it can be considered a viable policy option. The second section of this paper addresses some of these problems. It suggests that MAP is administratively difficult, but feasible, and outlines some of the problems in translating theory into practice.

MAP AND TIP: THE ALMOST COMPETITIVE CASE

There are two requirements that any sound theory of inflation must meet. First, since inflation is a circular process, we need a theory that explains what propels the circular process. Most "simple" theories of inflation do not explain the dynamics but, instead, concentrate on what begins the process. For example, wage-push, cost-push, or administered inflation (based on monopoly) explain only once-and-for-all increases in the price level but do not account for a continually rising price level. Similarly, demand-pull theories do not adequately describe the process; once prices have risen to meet excess demand, demand has done its pulling. The second requirement is that we need a theory that determines the aggregate price level, not relative prices. Partial equilibrium analysis is of little relevance in analyzing inflation. Inflation theory must be a general theory of the price level.

While many earlier analyses of tax-based incomes policies have emphasized some important aspects of incomes policies, they have failed to consider one or both of these requirements.[7] Consequently, they have not provided an adequate theoretical base for TIP. This failure follows directly from the nature of the question posed in such analyses: What would happen to an individual firm if TIP were imposed? This question suggests that TIP will be imposed on only one firm when, in fact, all agree that to be successful an economic incomes policy would affect all or at least a large proportion of the firms in the economy. Focusing on the impact of a policy on one firm loses the important interactive effects that are central to understanding the way in which TIP works.[8] The following example reveals why these interactive effects are fundamental in TIP's operation.

Consider an economy at a 10 percent inflationary expectational equilibrium. Firms in this economy are raising their prices by 10 percent on average merely to maintain parity. (I assume the firm sets the price at the competitive level; thus it is not a perfectly competitive world, since the firm does not treat prices parametrically.) Now assume that a TIP tax on price rises is placed on a firm. The firm responds by raising its price by slightly less than what it would have before TIP was imposed. By construction, this tax will only affect the firm's actual price rise minimally; consequently, it will have little effect on inflation. Now assume that the same TIP tax is placed on all firms. The representative firm will reason that if they react to TIP by raising their price slightly less than they would have before the imposition of TIP, so, too, will other firms faced with the same TIP tax. But, if other firms are expected to respond to TIP, then the initial firm's expectation of inflation is reduced. Consequently, it can raise its price by a still smaller amount and achieve the same relative price result. But, again, if the representative firm raises its price by even less, then its expectations must be that other firms will follow in raising their prices by even less. In fact, this same reasoning applies until expectations of inflation are completely eliminated. Thus, in an almost competitive world, in the absence of excess demand, where only expectational inflation exists, the mere expectation *of imposition of TIPs* would be sufficient to douse all expectations of inflation and, by definition, inflation.

By creating a market in "price changes," MAP makes the process explicit. MAP adds an extra question to the general equilibrium system and thereby sets the price level at a specified level. Once again, consider an economy with the same 10 percent inflationary expectations equilibrium. Suddenly, MAP is imposed. Initially, all individuals and firms might want to raise their prices, but they cannot because attempts to do so will push up the price of MAP credits until it is so high that no one buys the credits. At that MAP credit price, no one will raise his or her price; however, if no one is raising his or her price, expectations of inflation will be reduced to the level of inflation — zero — and the MAP credit price will fall to zero. If some relative price changes are in order, certain firms or individuals will want to lower their prices, while others will want to raise theirs. MAP will allow such changes; in fact, it will equalize excess demands in all sectors of the economy. Thus, if one sector has a relatively greater excess demand, the marginal value of an additional MAP credit for it will exceed the marginal value in the other sectors, and it will buy MAP credits until the marginal value of an additional credit in each sector is equal.

This analysis is, of course, much too neat. The rarified expectational inflation described above exists only in competitive models. In such models, not only would TIP and MAP work perfectly, but so too would monetary policy. In fact, in this almost competitive world, any reduction in inflation that TIP or MAP achieves must be accompanied by a reduction in aggregate nominal demand; thus, an independent role for TIP or MAP cannot be deduced, and for that we must develop a richer model.

MAP AND TIP: THE PHILLIPS CURVE STORIES

Perhaps the most used framework in discussing inflation is some variant of the Phillips curve hypothesis. There are (at least) three distinct Phillips curve hypotheses.

The first might be called the Keynesian view. It posits that there is a stable long-run trade-off between inflation and unemployment. The second hypothesis might be called the monetarist Phillips curve. In this version, there is a short-run trade-off but no long-run trade-off; the Phillips curve becomes perfectly vertical in the long run. (The rational expectations hypothesis goes further and eliminates the short-run trade-

84   DAVID COLANDER

off.) The third variant is the NAIRU (nonaccelerating inflation rate of unemployment) hypothesis; it suggests that while there is no long-run trade-off at present, there would be one if there existed some method (other than the rate of unemployment) of holding the price level down.[9] In this view, the "natural rate" is not natural; it is only the "nonaccelerating" rate.

Of these three, the short-run-but-no-long-run trade-off is the most widely held. Figure 1 illustrates the case. Somehow (most advocates attribute the cause to poor money management) the economy finds itself at a high level of inflation, C, with the "natural rate" of unemployment, B.[10] To stop the inflation, the government would need to induce a certain amount of demand restraint that moves the economy to a temporarily higher level of unemployment such as point D. This lower rate of inflation would then become expected, and the economy would stabilize at a lower rate of inflation with unemployment returning to the natural rate of unemployment following the path CDE. . . . If the government once again applies demand restraint, this "wringing out inflationary expectations"

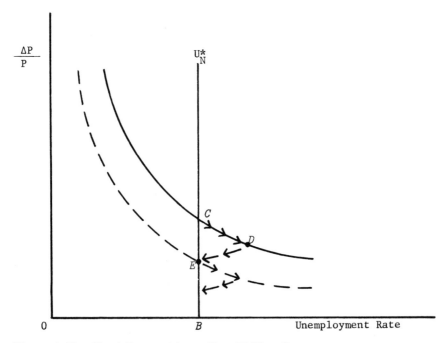

Figure 1. The Short-Run and Long-Run Phillips Curves

process will continue until the inflation is completely eliminated. Notice that because the process works through expectations, the shape of the short-run Phillips curve is essential to the argument. If the curve is horizontal, decreased demand will not eliminate inflation and, therefore, will not eliminate inflationary expectations.[11] There are varying estimates on what the unemployment cost of eliminating the inflation through this method will be, but by almost all accounts, it is high.[12]

Adding MAP to this analysis has the same effect as adding the rational expectations hypothesis. MAP makes it impossible for the government to fool people; therefore, the short-run Phillips curve is eliminated, and only a long-run Phillips curve exists. Thus, if the government wants to reduce the inflation rate, it can do so with MAP at no cost merely by reducing the allowable growth in MAP credits to the level consistent with zero inflation. Instead of reducing expectations through unemployment, the government can now reduce expectations through MAP. MAP establishes a direct connection between changes in the money supply (total spending) and changes in individual prices and the price level. It does this by internalizing the inflationary consequences within the individual's decision. Controlling the money supply controls aggregate spending but provides no way of translating that aggregate control to individual control. MAP supplies such a mechanism. Thus, MAP is the ultimate in rules; it guarantees that inflation will be stopped and allows the new equilibrium to be attained immediately.

If there is a long-run Phillips curve trade-off, MAP acquires another potential role. Instead of having a two-way trade-off between inflation and unemployment, the government has a three-way trade-off among unemployment, inflation, and MAP credit prices as shown in figure 2. If

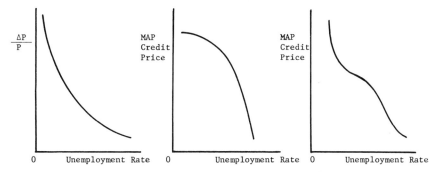

Figure 2. Government's Three-Way Trade-Off

the government chooses, it can reach a higher level of employment without inflation merely by using the MAP credits price as an offset to the inflationary pressures. The government can now choose the level of employment it desires and achieve that higher level of employment without inflation. Instead of causing inflation, the demand pressures will result in a higher level of MAP credit prices.

The NAIRU hypothesis is a combination of the first and the second. As in the first case, any deviations from the equilibrium level of unemployment is nonsustainable; hence, there is no long-run trade-off. The difference between the NAIRU hypothesis and the natural rate hypothesis is that under the NAIRU hypothesis, if some other method of holding the price level down existed, that higher level of employment would be sustainable. MAP provides such a method; thus, the short-run Phillips curve becomes the long-run Phillips curve. As is seen in figure 3, with MAP there is no longer one "natural rate of unemployment," but a large number of "equilibrium rates of unemployment," each one associated with a different price of MAP credits.[13] The government must choose the optimal rate.

Which equilibrium will be chosen depends on the shape of the Phillips curve, the social costs of unemployment, the relationships between the

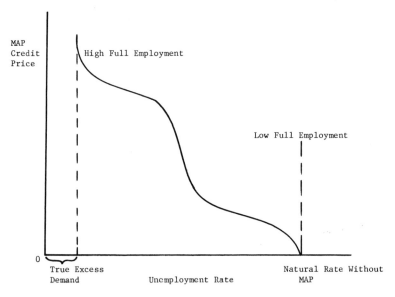

Figure 3. MAP Credits and Equilibrium Unemployment Rates

price of MAP credits and inflation, and the social costs of imposing those high credit prices. If we accept the NAIRU hypothesis, we are choosing, albeit by default, a point such as the natural rate without MAP in figure 3. This may be optimal, but it seems unlikely that it is.

Obviously, the above discussion provides only a brief sketch of how MAP will fit into the various models; the discussion is merely suggestive and glosses over many of the complications. But it should be sufficient to provide an intuitive sense of how MAP can be incorporated with different views of the inflation/unemployment trade-off. It should also provide an answer to many of the efficiency questions that have been raised about MAP and TIP. Questions of efficiency only have meaning in a given institutional setting. MAP and TIP are institutional changes and, therefore, cannot be judged on efficiency grounds in relation to the old institutional setting, as if that institutional setting were optimal. If the old setting were optimal, there would be no need for MAP. The real question is: Which state of the world is preferable, a MAP or a MAP-less world? This question is really a global question and cannot be considered in terms of local efficiency arguments. It is true that a MAP or TIP that maintains a high credit price of tax rate will have some effects on the economy, but the MAP credit price will be high only if, in MAP's absence, there would have been inflation. If the world had no inflationary pressures, the price of MAP credits would be zero and there would be no efficiency effects. Comparing MAP to an otherwise perfect world is an unfair comparison.

MAP AND TIP: STRUCTURAL THEORIES OF INFLATION

The above descriptions cover a wide range of theories. In them, once the expectations of inflation are removed, the price of MAP credits falls to zero unless a higher level of employment than would otherwise be possible is achieved. These are the optimistic theories of inflation.

The pessimistic theories see inflation as a systemic, rather than an expectational, problem. They suggest that there is a continuous upward pressure on prices that will hold the price of MAP credits positive, even in the absence of expectations of inflation and excess demand.

Such theories fall under the general heading of structural or sociological theories of inflation.[14] They suggest that given the institutional structure of the postwar economy, the excess conjectural short-run demands do not sum to zero at a constant price level. Thus, in the short run, at any level of politically acceptable unemployment, there is an upward pressure on prices. Consequently, no stable, steady state of equilibrium exists. This upward pressure does not have to be great if it is combined with expectational inflation that snowballs a slight inflationary tendency into a raging inflation.

To be tenable, such a theory must include both a political model of how governments will react to such situations and an endogenous money supply. (In almost all of these theories, money is reluctantly responsive to the inflationary pressures.) By emphasizing institutional constraints such as unemployment insurance and other built-in stabilizers, these theories, denominated in real terms, generally have such a political model, which guarantees inflationary government action whenever significant unemployment threatens. These institutional constraints limit any attempt to decrease aggregate demand and neutralize any effect unemployment might have had in holding down nominal wages or prices within the relevant period. Obviously, this situation is untenable and is consistent only with runaway inflation. Milton Friedman, commenting on a similar description, wrote:

> If this view is correct on a wide enough scale to be important, I see no other ultimate outcome than either runaway inflation or an authoritarian society ruled by force. Perhaps it is only wishful thinking that makes me reluctant to accept this vision of our fate.[15]

In these structural theories of inflation, rigidities initially save us from Friedman's alternatives; instead of causing inflation, rigidities actually postpone and retard the inflationary process. Because the normal length of contracts is one to three years, inflation occurs only as progressive leapfrogging. A second reprieve comes from economic growth. Upward inflationary pressure on factor incomes is denominated in real purchasing power; if, however, growth expands the available output by, say, 3 percent and excess demands is 3 percent, growth has provided the necessary downward pressure on the price level. But these are only temporary reprieves, and ultimately the inflation will bring down the system.

The role of MAP and TIP in these structural theories of inflation is the same as that of any other incomes policy. They install a contractual arrangement that limits the short-run powers of the sellers so that total demands are consistent with long-run equilibrium. The difference between MAP and other incomes policies is that MAP achieves this coordination in a manner compatible with the market. Administrative incomes policies duplicate market functions and create a tension that will ultimately render either the market or the policy superfluous.

IS MAP ADMINISTRATIVELY FEASIBLE?

The theories discussed above were not specified in great detail. Their purpose was merely to suggest that MAP ends inflation whatever the cause of inflation, as well as to provide the framework within which further theoretical and practical work might develop. They provide an *a priori* case for consideration of MAP as a policy option. Used in conjunction with aggregate monetary policy, MAP, theoretically, will succeed.

But even if one accepts that MAP will theoretically succeed in stopping the inflation, there is another more difficult question: Can it be implemented? I have heard countless descriptions of the administrative problems that MAP and TIP will entail, and I agree with many, if not most, of them. In fact, in a study I am doing for the government, I spend three chapters outlining and summarizing the many problems that a long-term MAP and TIP will entail. There are difficult questions of definition, coverage, enforcement, political acceptability, equity, administration, novelty, and so forth. I do not underestimate these potential problems.

I would like, however, to point out once again that the importance of these administrative problems is presupposed on the belief that MAP credits will have a high price caused by some unspecified upward pressure on prices. Without MAP these pressures would have continually increased the rate of inflation. Economists who do not believe in any systemic asymmetry or upward pressure on the price level must also believe that the MAP credit price will be zero and, hence, that there will be *no* administrative problem.

Unfortunately, I believe there is an underlying upward pressure on prices and, therefore, I believe there will be administrative problems with MAP. Still, I support MAP and believe that it is essential for economists to explore alternative methods of meeting these administrative problems. The political process wants answers, not theories. It will not allow inflation to reach a sustained 15 percent nor will it let unemployment reach 10 percent without taking some action. If economics does not have any answers, the political process will turn to others who do have answers. The other answer is comprehensive wage and price controls. Compared to this alternative, the administrative problems of MAP are minor.

In the discussion of MAP in the next paper by Abba Lerner, a very simple MAP proposal will be outlined. Naturally, many variations on the MAP theme are possible. For example:

Alternative definitions of net sales or value added could be used, such
as a consumption measure of value added.

Trend rates, rather than annual rates, could be used to determine
deviation from the guideline.

Labor inputs could be measured in a less exacting fashion.

Capital inputs could be measured by depreciation or in some other
fashion.

The administration of MAP could be placed with the Treasury, the
Council on Wage and Price Stability, or with a private concern.

MAP could be made less inclusive, and a size exemption could be
used.

Allowances for quality improvements of inputs could be built in.

MAP could be phased in gradually, and firms could be given a number
of years before they had to meet the MAP guidelines.

I will not discuss all these issues or even most of them. Instead, I will
concentrate on two issues likely to be subject to significant debate: the
use of net sales, or value added, and the question of how MAP will be
introduced.

WHY BASE MAP ON NET SALES PER UNIT INPUT OR
THE VALUE-ADDED RATE?

MAP is unique among incomes policies, not only in its use of the market,
but also because it is designed around the value-added rate and not the
wage rate. We believe that this is a significant improvement in the equity
of any anti-inflation program.

To be politically acceptable, an incomes policy must treat all forms of
income equally. In past attempts at incomes policies, wages have been
singled out for control primarily for administrative reasons. It was, and
still is, believed that product markets are relatively competitive and that
therefore nonwage income will follow wages. If this is true, even though
only wages are controlled, the program is equitable since prices are
controlled by competition. Sidney Weintraub's wage cost markup (WCM)
theory, which assumes that the share of nonwage income is constant, is
probably the clearest statement of the argument in favor of control of
wage only.

While I am in general agreement with Weintraub's WCM theory (and
certainly concur with regard to its general equilibrium approach), his

theory is subject to misinterpretation. It does not imply that wage increases, relative to the wage share, are any more inflationary than are profit increases, relative to the profit share. Both contribute equally to inflation. This point would have been clear if, instead of being specified in terms of a profit margin (a percentage amount) and a wage rate (a nominal amount), the theory were specified in terms of profit rate per worker and wage rate per worker. Then this theory would state that profit rates and wage rates increased proportionately. Wages are singled out for control only for administrative reasons, since, by assumption, controlling wages also controls other forms of income.

Controlling wages has, however, the rather significant political difficulty of being unacceptable to labor. By controlling the value-added rate, the administrative advantages of wage control are retained while the political difficulties are avoided since both profits and wages are treated equally. Thus, it is an ideal "price" to control and is, in my view, the next logical step in the design of productivity guidelines that have formed the basis of incomes policies.

The productivity guidelines were designed around the belief that a noninflationary world requires that the improvements in productivity mentioned above be passed on to the general consumer. As with the wage TIP, the productivity guidelines were applied only to wages, and competition was relied upon to hold prices down. These wage guidelines failed because competition worked too slowly and in the interim high individual-firm profits convinced workers that they had been inequitably treated. This perception of unfairness quickly led to a breakdown of the guidelines. Using the value-added rate generalizes the productivity guidelines to all factor incomes and thus provides a "normal-cost" benchmark by which to judge inflationary and noninflationary pricing behavior.

Despite this advantage in equity, the use of the value-added rate has been objected to on a number of grounds. Probably the most often heard criticism is that using the value-added rate for the base of TIP or MAP would actually make it a tax on productivity. In my view, this criticism is incorrect; using the value-added rate is no more a tax on productivity than using the wage rate is a tax on labor productivity. Both are merely taxes on increases in productivity that are not passed on to the consumer through lower prices. Moreover, since MAP gives additional adjustments in the guideline value added for investment, it actually encourages investment in productivity.

A second criticism has been that short-run profits are necessary for expansion of firms and that by limiting the profits of growing firms, we will actually reduce growth. This argument is wrong on two grounds. First, it somehow assumes that investment must come from profits and not from capital markets. There is no *necessary* reason for this. If an investment opportunity is a good investment, the firm should be able to acquire the necessary funds from capital markets. The fact that capital market funds have a higher cost to firms than retained earnings also has an overall positive effect. More reliance on outside financing would both equalize the cost of funds among all types of investment and decrease the comparative advantage existing firms have. Both these effects would promote economic efficiency by promoting competition and entry by other firms.

Second, the argument does not consider the incentive effects of firms to expand. Firms that are making high short-run profits have little incentive to expand unless they are threatened by competition. Including profits in the measure of inflation reduces the incentive that a firm has to expand slowly so as to maintain its short-run monopoly position for a longer time.

Controlling the value-added rate has one other advantage. It has been demonstrated in a number of econometric studies that profits are a significant variable in determining future wage increases.[16] By reducing profits of firms that experience good years and insuring profits of firms that experience bad years, MAP is neutral in respect to the expected profits. However, the "catch up" wage increases that often follow when a firm has high profits will be reduced. Since a value-added TIP and MAP channel the good years into lower prices rather than into higher profits, workers do not feel the need to "catch up."

The value-added rate is not a perfect concept. There are numerous measurement problems that we have not addressed in the simple MAP proposal. A few comments on these may be useful. The question of what to include in net sales or value added is relatively straightforward and parallels the arguments for and against various approaches to the value-added tax. The measurement of inputs presents, however, some new problems. The labor input is the largest and includes most of the actual input. It is subject to significant measurement problems, but these are generally felt to be manageable. Measuring capital inputs involves some new difficulties. There are two approaches one could follow: One could use either depreciation or the flow value of financial capital. Depreciation is, of course, extremely inexact; and its use introduces biases into the measure in any one year. However, since depreciation primarily presents problems of timing, for a permanent program these biases may not be significant. If a firm overdeclared its depreciation in one year, it would need to underdeclare in another. Its gain in doing so would only be in the interest in the delayed payment.[17]

We prefer not to use the physical "capital input" measure, since it is biased against nonphysical investments. By using the financial flow measure of capital input, investments and disinvestments are adjusted for in the firm independently of how the firm uses that money. We have debated a number of alternative methods by which this could be done. One would be to allow full interest cost and dividend passthrough as long as the average interest and dividend rate were below the initial rates of the firm. Since the interest rate can be expected to fall, this may be an easy solution for all bonds. New stock could be adjusted for by multiplying the income received from the stock by the average interest rate the firm pays plus an equity risk factor. Retained earnings may or may not be allowed as adjustments to capital inputs. In principle, they should be allowed; however, the present tax laws are biased toward retained earnings, and it may be desirable not to allow an adjustment as a means of offsetting that bias.

There are many other possible approaches, and the precise way capital inputs are included is not crucial to MAP. The problems do not seem insurmountable, especially when compared to those involved in correctly measuring the labor input, which forms the basis of the wage TIP.

PROBLEMS OF INTRODUCING MAP

Once in operation, the workings of MAP will not be unlike those of any other market. Unfortunately, markets do not magically come into existence, but must be administratively established.

In an "almost competitive" world, establishing a MAP market would not present difficulties; in such a world, prices would represent an equilibrium reflecting the best bargain that both seller and buyer could strike. In such a world, MAP could easily be imposed merely by formalizing the existing prices, making changes from the initial prices more difficult. In that abstract but simple world, prices are imposed by the market, and everyone accepts them. Because inflation is only an expectational problem, once it is no longer expected, inflation will cease.

In the real world, imposing MAP entails many more difficulties. Implicit or explicit forward contracts exist that limit wage and price changes to every one, two, or three years. Therefore, in the real world actual contractual prices may not at any point in time represent the best bargain that either side could have negotiated if contracts were negotiated continuously rather than at overlapping intervals. Consequently, firms and individuals will not be satisfied with the plan to impose MAP unless they are in a strong initial position relative to others. For instance, if MAP were imposed immediately after one group of workers had completed negotiations on a pay increase, they would be in a favorable position compared to those whose contracts were due to be negotiated in the near future. Additionally, if inflation were stopped suddenly, individuals with contracts that extended into the future would be subject to significant capital gains and losses. If the MAP credit price is expected to be high, these problems represent a formidable hurdle for the imposition of MAP.

Even if a set of equilibrium prices (*de facto*) exists, there is no way to ensure that the government will find it — that is, all firms and individuals will have an incentive to hide their true bargaining strength and will suggest that they could receive more. For this reason, even if we are not in the extreme case of structural inflation, the initial bargaining for starting positions in the MAP world will make it seem as if we are.

MAP does not have advantages over other forms of incomes policies in meeting these sticky issues; the conclusion that we should therefore not attempt to find this initial MAP starting position does not follow. In fact, this difficulty merely underscores the need for a long-term policy. Previous incomes policies have failed precisely because they were short-term, rather than long-term, plans. It was argued that permanent or long-run policies threatened the existence of a market economy and were consequently rejected. MAP does not undermine the market's functions; rather, it works in conjunction with it, reconciling competing and inconsistent demands. MAP's advantages only become apparent once the initial administrative barriers are overcome.

There are a number of ways that we have considered to minimize these introductory problems. Probably the most important is to insure that MAP is coordinated with macro policy to insure that there is no excess demand. Additionally, the guidelines could be phased in over a period of up to five years, with firms not being required to trade in the MAP market until the end of the introductory period. If these suggestions are followed, the MAP credit price should be low and initial allocaton of MAP credits less important.

Adjustments for future contracts could be made by an adjustment rule that sets initial guidelines on some weighted average of past value-added rates, rather than merely on the most recent year. The actual weight could be decided by the political process. Innumerable other adjustments are possible, and *any* politically acceptable rule will secure the purpose.

CONCLUSIONS

MAP and its TIP counterpart are important steps forward. They rein-corporate the problem of inflation into economies rather than relinquish-ing it as a political problem. MAP provides a technical solution to the problem, just as deficit spending provided a technical solution to unem-ployment in the 1930s.

Obviously, there is much more to be said about every issue addressed in this paper. MAP is not a finished product, only a framework. It needs much work both in establishing its underlying theory and in exploring the technical issues that make or break any new program; MAP and TIP are proposals in which theory and practice meet.

Initially, MAP will probably be shrugged off by many as too novel and too radical. My view is that MAP's novelty is a virtue, not a liability. If we have learned anything in the past thirty years, it is that the piecemeal approaches to inflation will not succeed and will likely make matters worse. Only a dramatic new initiative that promises to be a permanent and effective anti-inflation tool will be able to penetrate the tough outer shell of inflation and burst the expectational bubble. When all else has failed, novelty can no longer be a criticism.

Even if one accepts the theoretical need for MAP and believes that its novelty will not preclude its introduction, one will still, rightly, have serious concern about its administrative feasibility. In my view, these problems can be met. Any new program or new idea always involves difficult administrative decisions. Before these decisions are made, new programs always seem administratively impossible. My attitude toward these problems is one I learned from successful businessmen: Never ask whether a problem can be solved; any problem can be solved; only ask how long before you want the solution. If MAP's critics take that attitude and improve MAP's administrative design rather than merely pointing out the difficulties, each of the administrative problems of MAP can be met.

NOTES

1. The realitic/analytic distinction was first made by A.C. Pigou in his reply to R. Clapham concerning the relevance of economics. I have further developed the distinction in D.C. Colander and K. Koford, "Towards a Micro-Macro Synthesis," *Journal of Economic Issues*, 1979.

2. See A.P. Lerner and D.C. Colander, *MAP, the Market Anti-Inflation Plan* (New York: Harcourt Brace Jovanovich, forthcoming).

3. See A.P. Lerner and D.C. Colander, *Inflation* (New York: Pelican, 1972).

4. Obviously this definition does not settle the matter about what is the appropriate aggregate policy. There will likely be highly contradictory views on what is the appropriate aggregate policy. Thus, two individuals may look at the same program, and one will see it as controls, while the other will see it as an incomes policy. These differing views are about what the optimal level of unemployment is and not about the need for coordination.

5. Viewing TIP as an analogue to MAP provides an important distinction on the nature of tax-based incomes policies. TIP is not a penalty; there is a fundamental distinction between taxes as incentives and taxes as penalties. The former is simply a policy to discourage or encourage actions: If individuals do not react to the incentive, they have done nothing wrong. Penalties, on the other hand, are imposed when an individual has broken the law. This penalty-based incomes policy is merely a regulatory-based incomes policy with a specific means of enforcement.

Using taxes to deter an action that is considered wrong in a moral sense is inappropriate. For example, no one would suggest that the government should levy taxes on murder as a means of discouraging murder. Murder is wrong, and no one should be allowed to do it. After the murder has been committed, however, it makes little sense to charge the individual an infinite price; it cannot be paid. Thus, when setting penalties and fines, the government attempts to balance the after-the-fact uselessness of punishment in deterring the action with the deterrent effect of the penalty on future actions.

Such issues are relevant for fines but not for tax-based incomes policies. Raising prices or wages is not wrong per se and should not be subject to an infinite price; the incentives should merely be so arranged that price changes are relative price changes and not inflationary price changes.

6. Whether such a TIP is politically feasible is open to question; such flexible taxes have not proved feasible in the past and may not be feasible with TIP. There is also a problem of expectational stability that might make the TIP analogue to MAP difficult. Tax rates must be set prior to their payment, thus setting price and allowing quantity to fluctuate. If set too low, the expectation of raising the rate may itself contribute to inflation.

7. See P. Isard "The Effectiveness of Using the Tax System to Curb Inflationary Collective Bargains: An Analysis of the Wallich-Weintraub Plan," *Journal of Political Economy,* May–June, 1973; L. Seidman, "Tax Based Incomes Policies," *Brookings Papers on Economic Activity* 2:1978; Y. Kotowitz and R. Portes, "The Tax on Wage Increases," *Journal of Public Economics,* May 1974; and R. Latham and D. Peel, "The 'Tax on Wage Increases' When the Firm is a Monopsonist," *Journal of Public Economics,* October 1977, for examples of partial equilibrium analysis of TIP.

8. Sidney Weintraub's wage-cost markup theory of inflation and the quantity theory provide general equilibrium theories of inflation since they are concerned with price levels, not relative prices. However, their aggregate nature does not focus on the relative price/price level interaction that is central to understanding the difficulty of anti-inflation policy. Sidney Weintraub, *Capitalism's Inflation and Unemployment Crisis* (Reading, Mass.: Addison-Wesley, 1978).

9. To my knowledge, the NAIRU concept was first used by F. Modigliani, "The Monetarist Controversy, or, Should We Forsake Stabilization Policies?" *American Economic Review,* February 1977. It has since been used by Seidman, "Tax Based Incomes Policies," in his suggestion that TIP will improve the unemployment/inflation trade-off.

10. In this Phillips curve analysis, welfare is not necessarily associated with lower unemployment. Since the unemployment is serving a useful inventory function, too little unemployment can be inefficient.

11. If the short-run Phillips curve slopes upward, more unemployment will merely exacerbate the inflation problem.

12. William Fellner, a leading advocate of this view, has estimated that it should not take more than three to five years of high unemployment. William Fellner, "The Credibility Effect and Rational Expectations," *Brookings Papers on Economic Activity* 1:1979.

13. The different role for MAP in the long-run trade-off and the NAIRU hypothesis is that in the NAIRU hypothesis, inflation is a nonsustainable option.

14. These "sociological" theories do not have a good reputation in economics; they lack the formality and rigorous deductive logic of the demand-based theories. Lack of formality is not an indictment, however, and I should carefully point out that, properly interpreted, these theories are perfectly consistent with general equilibrium economic theory. They merely interpret the workings of the competitive process differently. In these theories, competition in many markets is a long-run, not a short-run, phenomenon; short-run price and quantity fluctuations can only be analyzed as implicit contingent contracts of long-run dynamic optimization enforced by social rules of conduct and standard business behavior. In these theories, rather than being exogenous, market structures are endogenous and are a method of enforcing implicit contracts.

15. Milton Friedman, "Using Escalation to Help Fight Inflation," *Fortune,* July 1974.

16. See, for instance O. Eckstein and T.A. Wilson "The Determination of Money Wages in American Industry," *Quarterly Journal of Economics,* November 1962, and Seidman, "Tax Based Incomes Policies."

17. An alternative to this approach would be to use new physical investment rather than depreciation — in a sense allowing fully accelerated depreciation. This would present a bias toward physical investment into the measure.

III SPECIFIC PROPOSALS

4 THERE IS A CURE FOR INFLATION

Abba P. Lerner and David Colander

For the orthodox theory with its dogma that inflation must "ultimately" be due to too much total spending in the economy, stagflation (inflation accompanied by economic stagnation, which implies too little spending) is a paradox. But this only tells us that the orthodox theory won't do. Stagflation is the outcome of a vicious circle of self-fulfilling expectations. We have an inflationary race in which business has to raise prices to keep up with increasing costs of production; labor has to raise wages to keep up with the increasing cost of living; and the government has to increase total spending to keep the economy functioning in spite of the rising wages and prices. But to counter charges that governmental spending is responsible for the inflation, the government restrains the increase in spending while there is still substantial unemployment. There is then too little spending for full employment and we get stagflation.

The inflation in stagflation is due not to "too much money chasing too few goods" but to the expectation of continuing inflation that fuels that vicious circle. This is not a *demand inflation* but an *expectational inflation*.

What keeps the inflationary race going is a flaw in our accounting practices. The inflationary impacts of wage and price increases are not

101

taken into account, just as environmental impacts of pollution are often not fully taken into account by industry. Appropriate antipollution incentives (usually taxes or subsidies) imposed by government can and do make individuals and firms take care not to harm the environment. Counterinflation incentives, by making inflationary price and wage increases more costly, can similarly inhibit inflationary pollution. Once this is done, the government will no longer have to keep expanding total spending in the economy to keep up with rising prices, and there will be no occasion for the "anti-inflationary" *restraint* that creates the *stag* in our stagflation.

In a free society, a cure for inflation must do two things: (1) stabilize the *average* price (the price level); and (2) leave *actual* prices and wages free to be adjusted by the market and by free bargaining to changes in tastes, techniques, and availabilities. The cure must, of course, also be *fair* and be seen to be fair, as between wages and profits, and its results must be felt reasonably soon.

PREVIOUS PLANS

A crude freeze of all wages and prices immediately stabilizes them, achieving objective 1 but not objective 2. Such measures have always been followed by attempts to adjust particular wages and prices to changing conditions, but a central administration, lacking the flexibility and the resistance to political pressures of a decentralized market mechanism, unfailingly breaks down. Wage and price regulation has repeatedly proved ineffective, but is nevertheless proposed again and again out of sheer desperation.

Recently, some ingenious and far superior anti-inflation tax-based incomes policies (TIPs) have been proposed, but these have focused the incentives only on wages and not on profits, which of course makes them unacceptable to labor. Furthermore, these incentives were to be imposed by the government in an unspecified measure.

MAP: THE MARKET ANTI-INFLATION PLAN

We believe we have avoided both of these weaknesses in our market-mechanism anti-inflation accounting credit plan, which we may abbreviate to market anti-inflation plan, or MAP. The MAP incentive is set not by the government but by the market. This insulates it from politics and adjusts it to the appropriate strength and to changing conditions. More-over, the MAP incentive is based on the (dollar) net sales of the firm. Since net sales consist of profits and wages combined, this clears MAP of any suspicion of bias against business or against labor.

FUNCTIONAL AND NONFUNCTIONAL PRICE INCREASES

Inflation tends to raise all prices and so the net sales of all firms, and this serves no useful social purpose. The counterinflation incentive must therefore be applied to all net sales if it is not to interfere with the relative changes in price and net sales that guide the efficient operation of a free economy.

If average price is not to rise, that is, if there is to be no inflation, total national net sales, the money received from the sale of the total national net output, must not rise more than the total national net output. As relative prices change, some firms will find their net sales per unit of input (of productive resources) growing more than the average national net output per unit of input (productivity). It is then essential that other firms should be offsetting this by their net sales per unit of input growing correspondingly less than average national productivity.

The counterinflationary incentive must be just strong enough to bring this about. It would then enable us to achieve both our main objectives: to stabilize the average price while leaving all actual prices and wages free to adjust to changing conditions. The crucial problem is to find an incentive of just the right strength.

ANTI-INFLATION ACCOUNTING CREDIT

MAP harnesses the market to produce an incentive of just the required strength. It does this —

1. by creating a new commodity, *anti-inflation accounting credit*;
2. by requiring each firm to buy anti-inflation accounting credit in an amount equal to its excess net sales above the increase in net sales proportional to the increase in the firm's inputs multiplied by the national increase in productivity or to sell such credit in an amount equal to the firm's deficit in net sales below that figure;
3. by letting the market set the equilibrium price of the credit.

The free market price of anti-inflation accounting credit moves to the level at which it makes supply and demand equal. Since the total demand for such credit is the sum of the excess net sales and the total supply is the sum of the deficit net sales, the two just cancel out and total net sales remains proportional to total output (which must increase exactly in proportion to the total input and the national increase in productivity). The inflation has been stopped.

The free market price of anti-inflation accounting credit is the incentive we need, is of just the strength needed, and is continually adjusted by the market as conditions change. The firms are induced by the price of the credit to set their net sales, and thereby also the wages and prices, at the appropriate noninflationary levels.

MAP RULES

MAP operates in accordance with the following rules:

1. The Federal Reserve's current responsibility for maintaining a "sound money supply" (one compatible with prosperity *and* price stability, which may not be compatible with each other) is extended by Congress to include responsibility for the maintenance of price stability through MAP.
2. A Federal Reserve anti-inflation credit (AIC) office credits each firm with a basic AIC equal to 102 percent of its last year's net sales, 2 percent being the estimated national increase in productivity. (Net sales is gross sales plus inventory increases, minus purchases from other firms. It is the firm's "value added" or its profit plus its wage bill. Profit includes interest, rents, fees, and other such income payments to individuals. The wage bill includes wages, salaries, and the cost of all fringe benefits.)
3. Hiring a new employee entitles a firm to additional free AIC equal to the employee's wage (including fringe benefits) in his or her previous employment. Conversely, the separation of an employee from a firm reduces the firm's AIC by the amount of his or her wage. New capital investment (whether financed by stocks, bonds, or reinvested profits) entitles the firm to additional free AIC equal to interest on the new investment (at the prime rate) representing the payment for the services of the new capital; conversely, the retirement of invested capital reduces the firm's AIC correspondingly.

4. Net sales in excess of the firm's AIC requires the purchase of that amount of additional AIC. A deficit in a firm's net sales below its AIC calls for the sale of its "unused" AIC.

5. The AIC office starts up a free market in AIC, buying and selling AIC freely to all comers. It neither creates nor absorbs any AIC but lets the free market price rise or fall to bring supply and demand into equality.

6. The AIC office keeps a record of each firm's AIC as it is adjusted for hirings and separations of employees, for changes in capital invested, and for its purchases and sales of AIC.

7. At the end of each year every firm's AIC is increased by 2 percent to allow for the national average increase in productivity.

8. Government agencies and private nonprofit corporations are also subject to MAP, but the place of net sales is taken by net personal income generated (i.e., the nonprofit part of net sales). Labor, capital, business, and government are thus all treated the same way.

TOTAL SPENDING POLICY

MAP cannot cure stagflation all by itself. It needs to be accompanied by a governmental spending policy that prevents too much spending or too little spending in the economy as a whole. Too much total spending causes excess demand inflation in which MAP would break down. Too little total spending results in unemployment about which MAP can do nothing.

What MAP can do is to free the government from the pressure (of rising prices and impending credit crunches) to increase total spending and the money supply; and to provide a sensitive indicator to guide the "total spending" policy. The market price on anti-inflation accounting credit will be positive when there is too much total spending in the economy and negative when there is too little. In the former case, firms will try to buy more credit (to legitimize the apparent possible increase in net sales). In the latter case, firms will try to sell their excess credit as possible net sales contracts.

EFFECT ON THE DOLLAR

Ending inflation in the United States would raise the value of the dollar as measured by the currencies of other countries. The United States would lose about as much from the fall of its export prices as it would gain from the fall in its import prices. But the stabilization of the domestic price level would make the dollar a much more desirable store of value and reserve currency for other countries than it has ever been.

HOW MAP WOULD WORK

If MAP is imposed when prices have been rising at 10 percent annually, with productivity increasing at 2 percent and the inputs of labor and capital increasing at 2 percent, total net sales will have been increasing at 14 percent. Suddenly the increase in net sales will be reduced to 4 percent, this being the total increase in AIC to which the net sales has to conform (2 percent annual increase of AIC for "productivity" plus an additional 2 percent for the annual increase in inputs of labor and capital services). This is just enough to buy the increased output at last year's prices. There will be a demand for additional AIC to legitimize an increase in net sales from any expected continuation in the increase in prices. The price of AIC will be correspondingly high. But as it becomes apparent that the actual increase in AIC and in net sales is only 4 percent, the expectation of price increases will diminish and with it also the demand for extra AIC and its price. As MAP deflates the inflation, it also deflates itself. When the inflation, and the expectation of inflation, cease, the price of AIC will fall to zero (or to whatever counterinflationary pressure is still needed to offset any remaining inflationary pressures not due to inflationary expectations).

As outlined above, MAP is directed at quickly and completely eliminating the expectational inflation. This raises serious problems of the possible necessity of abrogating contracts based on expectations of continuing or even accelerating inflation. A case can therefore be made for a slow MAP that would reduce the inflation gradually at the cost of delaying the cure.

A gradual disinflation is easily arranged by beginning with a higher but gradually decreasing basic AIC — starting with, say, 108 percent instead of 102 percent of the previous year's net sales, permitting total net sales (which will have been increasing at 14 percent) to increase not by 4 but by 12 percent the first year (8 percent in prices plus 4 percent in increased output, 2 percent from increased inputs, and 2 percent from increased productivity). The next year, with the basic AIC being reduced by two percentage points each year, net sales will increase by only 10 percent, and so on, taking five years to reach 4 percent and complete price level stability (2 percent for productivity, 2 percent for increased inputs, and zero for price increases).

As with all anti-inflation plans, there is a temptation for firms and unions to beat the gun and establish higher basic AIC claims by raising net sales before the plan starts. But once MAP is installed, average price stabilization would still be reached as soon as the rules are understood and obeyed. Such a spurt in inflation, induced by expectation of the introduction of MAP, could be prevented by making the basic free AIC equal to the net sales of the period before MAP was being seriously considered, with appropriate adjustment for the overall rate of inflation since that period.

If, as seems pretty certain, there is a lively prior discussion, the price stabilization would take very little time. MAP could be adopted only after a general expectation had been established that MAP would at least reduce the rate of inflation. Such an anticipation of smaller future price increases would create a readiness of sellers to accept lower price increases now rather than wait and a willingness of buyers to wait rather than buy now. This could stop the inflation even before MAP came into effect.

CONCLUSIONS

MAP is nothing but a new application of a device of daily experience so familiar that it is taken for granted and its very existence forgotten. Stabilizing the average quantity of some items while each actual quantity remains unregulated is no new invention. The market, an ancient and honorable device, does just this. The market sets innumerable prices at levels that make the average number of units of each item demanded per consumer just equal to the average number available, even while leaving each consumer free to choose the actual number he or she wants to buy. What makes MAP seem strange is only that the item to which the ancient device is applied is a new one. In MAP the market sets the price of AIC to make the average increase in the firm's net sales per unit of input just equal to the national average increase in net output per unit of input, even while leaving each firm free to choose its actual net sales per unit of input by buying (or selling) the corresponding quantity of AIC.

This description of the operation of a very simple form of MAP is, of course, little more than an outline. We hope to fill in the details in a forthcoming book *MAP, a Market Anti-Inflation Plan*. So far, nearly all the objections to MAP have turned out to be either misunderstandings or problems for which we have found satisfactory solutions. Problems may, of course, come to light for which there are no satisfactory solutions. Since we have so far met no fatal objections, we are led to think that MAP may indicate the way to cure our inflation-stagflation.

The plethora of current confused and contradictory policies and base-less (even if computerized) forecasts and projections that crowds the media is certainly depressing. But there is a cure for inflation and its stagflation offspring. There is no justification for despair or even for limiting our sights to moderating our inflation or perhaps only diminishing its escalation. Rather, we should address ourselves to the practical prob-lems of applying the cure — to the political and legislative procedures at the border of which our MAP ends.

5 INSURANCE FOR LABOR UNDER A TAX-BASED INCOMES POLICY
Laurence S. Seidman

Economists and policymakers have recently begun to give serious attention to a tax-based incomes policy (TIP) [4, 6–11, 14, 15]. A TIP would provide a tax incentive to employers, employees, or both to reduce wage increases. Advocates believe that TIP plus monetary and fiscal restraint can reduce inflation without increasing unemployment. In contrast to wage and price controls, a TIP would not eliminate the influence of market forces on wage and price decisions at each firm; nor would it involve direct governmental interference in wage-price decision making or collective bargaining at each firm.

Most versions of TIP provide tax incentives solely for wage increases. There are at least three reasons for the focus on wages and salaries. First, it is doubtful that a tax incentive for price increases would be administratively feasible. Most firms make products with varying quality or style, and it would be extremely difficult to distinguish a genuine price increase from a quality increase. Although this problem also exists for wage increases, it is generally agreed that it would be much more severe for price increases.

I am grateful to Eric Grossman for exceptional research assistance.

Second, both the microeconomic theory of pricing and econometric price equations support the view that price inflation is closely tied to wage inflation, so that an X percent reduction in wage inflation will automatically induce an X percent reduction (perhaps after a short lag) in price inflation [1, 8, 15]. A tax incentive to reduce wage increases should therefore be sufficient to reduce price inflation (provided it is reinforced by monetary and fiscal restraint) and should be equitable because it should not affect the average real wage.

Third, a tax incentive to reduce profit, or the profit margin, conflicts with the role of profit in promoting efficiency, from which labor ultimately benefits. "Excess profit" in a particular firm or industry rewards innovation and technological change and induces an inflow of capital where it is most productive. Moreover, if price inflation declines with wage inflation, then profit inflation must decline automatically.

Nevertheless, the equity of TIP can be improved by providing insurance for labor against two concerns: that TIP will reduce the growth rate of real wages and that TIP will shift the distribution of income from labor to "capital."

The challenge is to provide such insurance without "freezing" the income distribution or permanently altering its secular trend; without impairing incentives for efficiency; and without committing the government to a destabilizing automatic policy. The purpose of this paper is to attempt to design and analyze insurance policies that meet these constraints.

INSURANCE WITHOUT "FREEZING" THE INCOME DISTRIBUTION

The central constraint in the design of insurance for labor is to avoid permanently interfering with the evolution of returns to labor and capital, and the accompanying relative factor shares. This evolution presumably promotes economic efficiency, according to standard welfare economics. Any insurance that permanently altered this evolution would therefore risk imposing significant, permanent allocative inefficiency on the economy.

It should be recognized that insurance that tries to permanently constrain the income distribution between labor and capital would be a radical departure. Even organized labor and social reformers who favor reduction in inequality have rarely advocated such a constraint and have focused instead on the progressive income tax and personal insurance, such as social security, unemployment compensation, and medicare.

Two alternative strategies are possible in response to this constraint. Under the first, insurance can be designed to "freeze" the after-tax income distribution between labor and capital while the policy is in effect; but the insurance can be terminated after several years, even if TIP itself remains permanently in effect. Advocates of TIP might argue that such insurance allows labor to observe that TIP works to its benefit and would not shift the income distribution against it. Once this has been demonstrated, the insurance can be ended. On the other hand, if TIP would prove harmful to labor without insurance, then TIP itself can be reconsidered.

Political realism, however, makes it unlikely that insurance can be terminated while TIP remains. Indeed, it is even plausible that the insurance might remain even if TIP were terminated. It is difficult to repeal an apparent benefit to an important constituency once it has been enacted. Thus, it seems unwise to adopt the first strategy.

The second strategy would be to design insurance on the assumption that it might remain permanently in effect. The aim would be to provide one-time compensation for an adverse *change* in income shares, but not to attempt continuous, ongoing compensation. Thus, the insurance would be partial, not complete; it would protect in the short run, but not in the long run. The consequences of an adverse change in income shares would be only temporarily, not permanently, offset. The evolution of returns to labor and capital and relative shares would be temporarily, but not permanently, altered.

The value of such insurance to labor is that it would reduce its risk during the introduction of TIP, so that TIP's impact can be assessed at low potential cost. If an adverse shift in income shares occurs and appears due to TIP, then TIP can be repealed with little harm to labor having occurred. If TIP (complemented by monetary and fiscal restraint) is regarded as beneficial and the behavior of relative shares is observed to be largely unaffected, then the insurance will have allowed this experiment to take place.

A representative of labor might object to insurance that is only partial. Several points should be emphasized. First, today labor does not have even partial insurance against an adverse shift in relative shares. Second, it should be recognized that labor would benefit significantly if TIP (complemented by monetary and fiscal restraint) "works" as envisioned by advocates. The permanent reduction in inflation will especially protect senior workers approaching retirement, who must rely primarily on pensions that lose value the greater the inflation rate. Junior workers will benefit from an economy that does not require periodic recessions to control inflation. Finally, theory and evidence suggests that TIP, although focused on wage and salary increases, will not alter relative shares or affect real wages.

Thus, it can be argued that partial insurance for labor is equitable, while avoiding permanent interference in the evolution of returns to labor and capital and relative shares. This paper will focus exclusively on the design of such partial insurance.

The basic idea of partial insurance is to provide one-time compensation for an adverse change. Two kinds of insurance will be considered. The first, which focuses on an adverse change in the average real wage, will be called real-wage insurance (RWI). The second, which focuses on an adverse change in the ratio of profit to labor compensation in the whole economy, will be called profit-restraint insurance (PRI). An example will illustrate the difference between partial and complete insurance in each case.

Suppose in year 0, GNP is $2,000 billion, before-tax labor compensation is $1,500 billion, and after-tax compensation is $1,000. Consider an RWI proposal that would provide a tax cut for employees in the economy if the *growth rate* of the average real wage is less than the *growth rate* of average labor productivity. Suppose productivity growth is 2 percent, but real-wage growth only 1 percent in year 1. Then table 1 shows that a $10 billion tax cut would be required to cause after-tax compensation to grow at the same rate as productivity — 2 percent.

Suppose that beginning in year 2 and forever after, the real wage grows 2 percent and productivity grows 2 percent. Under the above RWI

Table 1.   An RWI Proposal

	Before-Tax Compensation	After-Tax Compensation	Required Tax Cut
Year 0	$1,500	$1,000	
Year 1 — hypothetical (7% growth)	$1,605	$1,070	$10
Year 1 — actual (6% growth)	$1,590	$1,060	

NOTE: This example assumes that price inflation is 5 percent in year 1 and that man-hours are constant, so that the growth rate of compensation per hour equals the growth rate of total compensation.

policy, the tax rate would return to its initial value. Yet the crucial point is that before-tax compensation, as shown in table 1, begins its 2 percent growth per year from a base level of $1,590, instead of $1,605 billion, and after-tax compensation begins from a base level of $1,060, instead of $1,070 billion. Thus, this design of RWI does not protect against this permanently lower base *level* and the loss in subsequent years, shown in figure 1.

It would, of course, be possible to provide an ongoing tax cut by using the hypothetical base $1,070, instead of the actual base $1,060 for year 1. Each year workers would receive a tax cut if the *level* of the real wage was below the level on growth path 1 in figure 1. It is this kind of complete insurance, which would guarantee an after-tax real-wage level (or path), that has been rejected in favor of partial insurance. Partial insurance provides a tax cut only in a year when the growth rate of the real wage is less than the growth rate of productivity, not in all years when the level of the after-tax real wage is below its level on path 1.

Similarly, consider a PRI proposal that would provide a tax surcharge on all firms if the growth rate of the profit-to-labor-compensation ratio for the whole economy is above "normal." For this example, assume the normal growth rate would be zero (later it will be shown that the "normal" growth rate depends on the growth rate of the ratio of actual to standard productivity). Then table 2 shows how the tax surcharge for year 1 would be calculated if the before-tax profit ratio increases from 0.15 to 0.16 (the initial income tax rate is assumed to be 46 percent). In year 1, a 3 percent surcharge (from 46 percent to 49 percent) would be imposed to keep the growth rate of the after-tax profit/compensation ratio equal to zero for that year (so that the *level* of the after-tax ratio remains at 0.081 in year 1).

Under the above PRI policy, if the before-tax ratio remains constant at 0.16 from the beginning of year 2 onward, so that the growth rate of the ratio is zero, then no surcharge would be imposed in subsequent years; the tax rate would return to 46 percent indefinitely. Thus, the new permanent level of the before-tax profit ratio would be 0.16, of the after-tax profit ratio, 0.086. The design of PRI does not protect against this permanently higher profit ratio. It does, however, provide one-time compensation in the year the ratio increases.

It would, of course, be possible to provide an ongoing tax surcharge to keep the after-tax ratio at 0.081 permanently. It is this kind of complete insurance, which would attempt to freeze the after-tax income distribution, that has been rejected in favor of partial insurance. Partial insurance

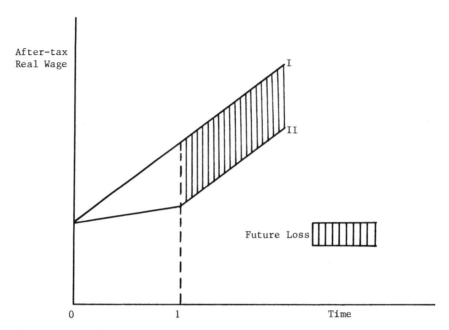

Figure 1. Real-Wage Insurance and After-Tax Real Wages

provides a tax surcharge only in a year when the growth rate of the ratio is above "normal," not in all years when the level of the after-tax ratio is above its initial level.

The remainder of this paper will explore in greater detail the design of two kinds of partial insurance: real-wage insurance and profit-restraint insurance.

REAL-WAGE INSURANCE (RWI)

RWI was originally suggested by Arthur Okun in 1974 as a complement to a policy of voluntary wage and price restraint [3]. A modified version was proposed by President Carter in his October 1978 anti-inflation speech. Under that proposal, employees at a firm that complies with a 7 percent wage guideline would be guaranteed a tax cut if price inflation exceeds 7 percent. The aim is to assure workers that money-wage restraint will not cause an actual reduction in the after-tax real wage.

Table 2. A PRI Proposal

	Before-Tax Compensation	Before-Tax Profit	Before-Tax Ratio	After-Tax Profit	After-Tax Ratio
Year 0	$1,500	$225	0.15	$122	0.081
Year 1 — hypothetical	$1,590	$239	0.15	$129	0.081
Year 1 — actual	$1,590	$254	0.16	$137	0.086

NOTE: This example assumes that the tax rate is 46 percent so that the after-tax rate is 54 percent; to obtain $129 of after-tax profit from $254 of actual before-tax profit requires an after-tax rate of 51 percent, a tax rate of 49 percent, and thus a surcharge of 3 percent.

Table 3.   Growth Rates of the Real-Wage and Labor Productivity (percent)

Year	$(w/p)_t$	a_t
1948	0.4	2.8
49	2.5	2.3
50	4.2	6.1
51	2.2	1.8
52	3.5	2.0
53	3.6	1.6
54	2.0	1.7
55	1.6	4.1
56	3.0	0.6
57	2.6	2.2
58	2.5	2.0
59	2.0	3.7
60	2.9	1.0
61	2.9	2.8
62	3.3	4.4
63	2.7	3.5
64	3.3	3.7
65	2.1	3.3
66	3.2	2.5
67	2.5	1.9
68	3.3	3.2
69	2.0	−0.2
70	1.8	0.2
71	2.1	2.9
72	2.7	3.0
73	3.7	1.7
74	−1.1	−2.9
75	−1.3	1.6
76	3.6	4.1
Mean	2.4	2.3
Deviation	0.9	1.2

SOURCE: Data are taken from table B-38, *The Economic
Report of the President,* 1978.
NOTE: Data are for the nonfarm business economy;
$(w/p)_t$ is the growth rate of the real wage (the growth rate
of compensation per man-hour minus the growth rate of
the implicit price deflator); a_t is the growth rate of output
per hour; *deviation* is the mean absolute deviation from the
mean value.

Real-wage insurance can take either an incentive or nonincentive form. If the insurance is restricted to workers who restrain their own wage increase, then RWI would provide an incentive. The incentive is weaker than that of a standard employee-TIP because under RWI workers will receive a tax cut only if price inflation exceeds a designated threshold. Under a standard employee-TIP, workers receive a tax cut if they limit their own wage increase, regardless of the rate of price inflation [8].

RWI takes a nonincentive form if the tax cut is provided across the board to all (or most) households, independent of their own wage behavior, whenever the growth rate of the average real wage in the economy is below some threshold. To protect "labor," the general tax cut (or rebate) should be "progressive," favoring low- and middle-income households. Although an automatic general tax cut would protect the average worker when TIP is introduced, thereby promoting equity, it would not provide an incentive.

The important advantage of nonincentive RWI is that it is easier to administer. It does not require measurement of the wage increase at each firm, but only an estimate of the average real-wage increase for the economy that can be provided by the standard governmental data source. A consensus has emerged that an employee-reward TIP is the most difficult version of a TIP wage incentive to administer because equity requires that it be applied almost universally [4]. Numerous small firms therefore must be included, thereby increasing the compliance cost and administrative complexity for the IRS. Opinions differ over whether an employee-reward TIP is still worthwhile, despite the additional administrative cost [4].

If minimizing the administrative task is deemed a top priority, then the original Weintraub-Wallich employer-penalty TIP should be relied upon to provide the incentive to large corporations, and nonincentive RWI (plus profit-restraint insurance, to be analyzed shortly) to assure equity for labor. Because the Weintraub-Wallich TIP is limited to large corporations, only these would have to measure their wage increases for tax purposes. Nonincentive RWI would not require measurement at each firm. The analysis that follows focuses on this kind of RWI.

One version of RWI (proposed by President Carter in his October 1978 speech) guarantees protection against a decline in the real wage, whether or not there is a simultaneous decline in labor productivity, which is generally regarded as the main determinant of the real wage. One advantage of this approach is that it enables RWI to be stated clearly and simply, without qualification.

This design, however, can be criticized. Without TIP, the average real wage normally grows at the same rate as average labor productivity — on average perhaps 2 percent per year. The norm for real-wage growth should therefore be productivity growth, rather than zero. Labor would be correct in arguing that a TIP might be reducing its normal real-wage growth, even if its real wage did not actually decline. From this perspective, the Carter administration's version does not offer sufficient protection.

On the other hand, suppose the economy sharply declines in a severe recession, so that the growth rate of productivity becomes negative. For example, from 1973 to 1974 productivity (output per man-hour) in the nonfarm private business economy declined 2.9 percent, and the real wage declined 1.1 percent, as shown in table 3. It can be argued that equity does not require that labor be protected from real wage declines due to productivity declines. From this perspective, the administration version offers too much protection.

The alternative then would be to have RWI guarantee protection against real-wage growth's being significantly less than productivity growth. This approach has several advantages. First, once it is recognized that real wages depend primarily on labor productivity, this approach will probably be viewed as a more equitable kind of protection.

Second, if TIP does not alter the real wage-productivity relationship, then the government will be able to offer more protection without increasing the average tax cut to which it is obligated. For example, under the administration version, no tax cut is provided when real-wage growth is positive, even if it is significantly less than productivity growth. If the administration version were amended to protect against any real-wage growth less than 2 percent, RWI would frequently incur a tax cut obligation. If RWI is tied to the productivity growth rate, however, only a divergence between the two will obligate the government.

Table 3 presents data on the growth rates of the real wage and output per man-hour for the nonfarm business economy from 1948 through 1976. The mean annual growth rates are nearly equal (2.3 percent for productivity, 2.4 percent for the real wage). The mean absolute deviation of real-wage growth, however, is significantly less than that of productivity growth (1.2 percent for productivity, 0.9 percent for the real wage). This suggests that real-wage growth in a given year depends partly on "normal" productivity growth and partly on actual productivity growth for that year. This exactly parallels the result of most econometric price equation research — that price depends partly on "normal" unit labor cost and partly on actual unit labor cost. Indeed, the relationship between real-wage and productivity growth can be derived from a model of pricing behavior, as shown in the appendix to this paper. It yields the following equation:

$$\left(\frac{w}{p}\right)_t = b_0 + b_1\mathbf{a}_t + b_2 a_t \tag{1}$$

where $(w/p)_t$ = the growth rate of the real wage in year t, $\mathbf{a}_t$ = the growth rate of "normal" productivity, and a_t = the growth rate of actual productivity.

The series for $\mathbf{a}_t$ is obtained by fitting a trend through data for actual productivity, as described in the appendix. If $(b_1 + b_2)$ were equal to 1 and b_0 were zero, then the growth rate of the real wage would be a weighted average of the growth rates of normal and actual productivity (equivalently, as shown in the appendix, the price inflation rate would be a weighted average of the growth rates of normal and actual unit labor cost).

Equation 1 was estimated on annual data (1953–1976) for the private nonfarm business sector.[1] It was estimated without imposing a constraint on the sum $(b_1 + b_2)$. The standard Cochrane-Orcutt technique was used to reduce serial correlation. The result was as follows:

$$\left(\frac{w}{p}\right)_t = 0.21 + 0.77\mathbf{a}_t + 0.29a_t; \tag{2}$$
$$\quad\quad (0.17) \quad (1.23) \quad\;\; (2.02)$$

$\overline{R}^2 = 0.21$, S.E. $= 1.11$, and D.W. $= 1.93$.

The numbers in parentheses are t-statistics. If $\mathbf{a}_t$ were 2 percent, it would be entered as 2.0; thus, the standard error of the regression is 1.11 percent. The sum of the coefficients of $\mathbf{a}_t$ and a_t is close to 1 (1.06). Roughly three-fourths of the weight is given to normal productivity, one-fourth to actual productivity.

An equation like equation 2 can be used to implement RWI. Given the growth rates of normal and actual productivity for any year, the equation predicts the real-wage growth rate that would have occurred without TIP. This forecast therefore provides an equitable basis for determining a norm for the real-wage growth rate under RWI. Legislation enacting RWI can specify that the norm for real-wage growth each year will be determined from the growth rates of normal and actual productivity, according to standard statistical technique. If greater specificity is required, the norm for real-wage growth can be set equal to a weighted

average of the growth rates of normal and actual productivity; according to equation 2, the weights three-fourths and one-fourth would be appropriate.

Equity does not necessarily require that a tax cut be obligated whenever the actual real-wage growth rate for the year is slightly less than
predicted. Without TIP, equation 2 of course does not forecast perfectly;
the standard error of the equation is 1.11 percent. Because employees
presumably will not incur a special tax surcharge if the actual rate exceeds
the predicted rate, the insurance need not protect them fully against a
slight shortfall below the predicted value. It seems reasonable to protect
against an "unusual" shortfall of the actual rate below the predicted rate.
The standard error of the equation provides a basis for defining an
unusual shortfall.

Suppose RWI compensates 100 percent of the shortfall in excess of 1
percent (since the standard error is 1.11 percent). It is instructive to
estimate the size of the tax cuts to which the government would have
been obligated over the sample period 1953–1976 according to equation
2.[2] In only four years (1955, 1959, 1974, and 1975) did the real-wage
growth rate predicted by equation 2 exceed the actual real-wage growth
rate by more than 1 percent. In 1974, the actual growth rate was (−1.1
percent); the predicted growth rate was +0.6 percent. Equation 2 captured an important fraction of the decline below normal real-wage growth
(approximately 2 percent), but still underestimated the decline. The dis-
crepancy in 1975 was larger; actual real wage growth was (−1.3 percent),
while predicted growth was 1.6 percent.

The largest tax cut obligation would occur under the nonincentive
RWI, in which all households receive a tax cut regardless of their own
wage behavior. The calculation for 1974 is as follows: Since the discrep-
ancy was 1.7 percent, RWI would have been obligated to compensate
for the 0.7 percent in excess of 1 percent. Before-tax compensation was
$875.8 billion.[3] After-tax compensation was approximately $643 billion.[4]
Thus, a tax cut of about $5 billion would have been required to restore
0.7 percent of after-tax compensation. In 1975, about $13 billion would
have been required because the shortfall in excess of 1 percent was 1.9
percent, instead of 0.7 percent.

The $13 billion cut would have been implemented in 1976. This cut
would not have been large enough to significantly affect the inflation rate,
even if it were not offset by a reduction in government spending or
monetary policy. If a multiplier of 2 is applied to the $13 billion tax cut,
the stimulus to GNP would be $26 billion, or 1.5 percent of 1976 GNP.
Using Okun's law as an approximation, this RWI tax cut would have

reduced the unemployment rate by 0.5 percent, from 7.7 percent to 7.2 percent. Econometric wage equations imply that this reduction in the unemployment rate would have had only a small effect on wage inflation and, therefore, price inflation [1, 5, 10, 13].

It can be argued that there are two reasons why the above calculation underestimates the RWI tax cut that might be required under TIP. First, if TIP succeeds in reducing money-wage growth, it is often suggested that there may be a lag before the decline in price growth fully matches it. In the interim, the reduction in money-wage growth may reduce real-wage growth. If this argument is correct, then TIP itself would tend to cause an RWI tax cut during the period of money-wage deceleration, which might last several years.

Second, in response to the Wallich-Weintraub employer-penalty TIP, large corporations may attempt to shift some of the burden of the TIP surcharge by raising price to cover at least part of the tax cost. It might be argued that this shifting process would raise the markup of price over unit labor cost, thereby reducing the growth rate of the real wage. Each of these two arguments — the price-wage lag and the shifting effect — will now be considered in turn.

In an attempt to assess the magnitude of the possible lag effect, a money wage growth rate was added to equation 1. The result, estimated on annual data from 1954–1976, was as follows (once again, the Cochrane-Orcutt serial correlation adjustment was used):

$$\left(\frac{w}{p}\right)_t = 0.70\mathbf{a}_t + 0.33a_t + 0.03w_t; \qquad (3)$$
$$\phantom{\left(\frac{w}{p}\right)_t = }(2.27) \quad\;\; (2.22) \quad\;\; (0.38)$$

$\overline{R}^2 = 0.19$, S.E. $= 1.13$, and D.W. $= 1.85$.

The sum of the coefficients of $\mathbf{a}_t$ and a_t is 1.03, with about two-thirds of the weight going to normal $\mathbf{a}_t$. The money-wage growth rate is insignificant, with a magnitude near zero. According to equation 3 any lag that may exist between price and wage inflation appears to be less than one year, so that the money-wage growth rate does not affect the real-wage growth rate. Alternative specifications were tested, including a polynomial distributed lag for money-wage growth. These are presented in the appendix. In no case was the coefficient of money-wage growth statistically significant with an important positive magnitude.

These empirical results provide support for the contention of TIP advocates that restraint of money-wage growth will have little effect on real-wage growth, even in a period as short as one year. Price inflation appears to respond rapidly to wage inflation. If correct, TIP would be equitable even in the short run (ignoring the possible shifting effect) and would not induce an RWI tax cut due to a price-wage lag. The previous estimates for the required RWI tax cut would therefore be unaffected by TIP.

These results should be viewed as tentative. Econometric price equations run on quarterly data usually detect a price-wage lag. Although an important fraction of the lag is usually closed within one year, the full lag effect sometimes appears to require more than a year to work itself out [1]. Further research is therefore required. Our results, however, suggest that the belief that there would be a significant price-wage lag under TIP should not be taken for granted. RWI is designed to protect labor against such a lag; but it is far from certain that such protection will prove necessary.

The second argument is the possible shifting effect. Elsewhere, I have analyzed in detail the possibility of tax shifting in response to an employer-penalty TIP [9]. Here, the implication for RWI will be briefly summarized. Under a favorable scenario, large corporations will respond to TIP by reducing wage increases close to the guideline; the average corporate tax rate will remain roughly constant, so there will be no additional tax cost to pass on (even if large, covered firms somewhat exceed the guideline, it is recommended that the base tax rate for all firms be cut when TIP is introduced so that the average tax rate for all firms will remain constant).

In the case of a very unfavorable scenario, which I regard as highly improbable for reasons given in [9], a large RWI tax cut would be induced in the first year. If large firms ignored TIP, incurred a rise in their tax rate to 87 percent, and shifted much of the higher tax cost, the shortfall of actual below predicted real-wage growth might be 4.2 percent, or 3.2 percent, in excess of 1 percent; a \$22 billion greater tax cut would have been required for 1975. Even in this case, the shifting effect would only cause an RWI tax cut initially. Once the larger markup is achieved, there would be no further effect on the growth rate of the real wage [9].

The risk of destabilization could be reduced by postponing automatically the RWI tax cut if the unemployment rate is less than some $\overline{U}$ (perhaps 6 percent) or if the capacity utilization rate is above $\overline{C}$. Once the unemployment rate has risen above $\overline{U}$ or the capacity utilization rate fallen below $\overline{C}$, the tax cut (plus interest) would be obligated. Another method would be to limit the maximum tax cut that could be obligated in one year; the remainder would be obligated in the following year (once again, including interest to compensate for postponement). Both methods could be used or perhaps better ones devised.

In conclusion, an RWI based on productivity growth can be designed that offers important, partial protection to labor, does not "freeze" the income distribution, and would not prove destabilizing (if postponement is utilized).

PROFIT-RESTRAINT INSURANCE (PRI)

An objection of labor to a TIP that provides incentives solely for wage and salary increases is that there is no guarantee that after-tax profit will not increase relative to labor compensation. In the appendix, it is shown that the same pricing model that implies that real-wage growth should be unaffected by money-wage growth (and therefore by TIP) also implies that relative income shares should be unaffected. Nevertheless, the purpose of PRI is to insure labor against an adverse shift when TIP is introduced.

It might seem natural to suggest a tax incentive aimed at the profit margin of the individual firm, just as TIP provides a tax incentive aimed at the wage increase of the firm. Such an incentive, however, would interfere with the function of profit in improving efficiency, from which labor benefits. Standard microeconomics teaches that the emergence of "excess" profit in particular firms and industries can help promote efficiency in several ways. The excess profit may be the reward for a cost-reducing or quality-enhancing innovation; without such a reward, the investment required to achieve such innovations may not be undertaken. Excess profit may result from an increase in consumer demand for the firm's product, so that the inflow of capital seeking above normal returns in this industry expands supply in response to consumer preference. Without the emergence of short-run excess profit in particular firms and industries, allocative and dynamic efficiency in the economy would be reduced.

An alternative way to address labor's concern is to focus on the ratio of aggregate after-tax profit to aggregate labor compensation for the whole economy. A uniform income tax surcharge can be imposed on all (or most) firms to prevent the aggregate ratio from shifting significantly against labor when TIP is first introduced.

This basic idea was originally proposed by Lawrence Klein and Vijaya Duggal [2]. I will call my version of their suggestion "profit-restraint insurance" (PRI). PRI would not significantly reduce the incentive of each firm to maximize its profit, in contrast to a tax incentive (such as a traditional excess profits tax) on the profit or profit margin of each indi-

vidual firm. It would, however, guarantee labor that any adverse shift in
the aggregate ratio is initially (though not permanently) offset.

The aim should be to prevent the growth rate in the after-tax profit
share from significantly exceeding what it would have been without TIP.
This suggests the same strategy adopted for RWI: Regress the growth
rate of an income distribution ratio against its major determinants. In the
appendix, it is shown that the same pricing model yields the following
equation (when the constraint that the sum $[b_1 + b_2]$ equals 1 is imposed):

$$\left(\frac{pq}{wh}\right)_t = -b_0 + b_1 \left(\frac{a}{\mathbf{a}}\right)_t \tag{4}$$

where $b_1 \geq 0$, $(pq/wh)_t$ = the growth rate of the ratio of total product to
labor compensation $(P_t Q_t / W_t H_t)$ in year t, and $(a/\mathbf{a})_t$ = the growth rate of
the ratio of actual productivity to normal productivity $(A_t/\mathbf{A}_t)$.

Equation 4 says that labor's share of total product decreases when the
ratio of actual to normal productivity increases. The intuition behind the
equation derives from the pricing model given in the appendix. b_1 is the
weight given to normal productivity, while b_2 (or $1 - b_1$) is the weight
given to actual productivity, when the firm sets its price. If b_1 were 0,
then all weight would be given to actual productivity; the firm would
respond completely and immediately to changes in actual productivity or
actual unit labor cost. Income shares would therefore be unaffected by
fluctuations in actual productivity. At the other extreme, if b_1 were 1,
then the firm would price solely according to normal productivity, ignoring actual productivity. A decline in actual productivity below normal
will therefore reduce the nonlabor share, while an increase in actual
productivity above normal will increase the nonlabor share. If b_1 is
between 0 and 1, then the product/compensation ratio will vary with the
productivity ratio, but not as much as if b_1 were equal to 1.

Equation 4 was estimated on annual data (1959–1976) for the nonfinancial corporate sector.[5] This is the broadest sector for which profit
data are reported in that data source. Data for output per hour and
compensation per hour are presented only since 1958. The result was as
follows (using the Cochrane-Orcutt adjustment):

$$\left(\frac{pq}{wh}\right)_t = -0.17 + 0.61 \left(\frac{a}{\mathbf{a}}\right)_t ; \tag{5}$$
$$(-0.64) \quad (4.41)$$

$\overline{R}^2 = 0.53$, S.E. $= 1.06$, and D.W. $= 1.89$.

Although equation 5 is run on a shorter time series and narrower
sector of the economy than equation 2, the estimate of b_1, 0.61, is not far
from the estimate of 0.77 in equation 2 (also, as the appendix shows,

equations 4 and 5 constrain the sum $[b_1 + b_2]$ to equal 1, while equation 2 is estimated without this constraint being imposed).

When the economy moves into a rapid recovery, so that the growth rate of actual productivity to normal productivity is positive, the product/compensation ratio and therefore the profit/compensation ratio will increase. Such an increase should not be attributed to TIP; nor should labor be protected with a tax surcharge against this normal increase in the profit share over the cycle. If PRI uses an equation like equation 5 to determine the "normal" increase in the income distribution ratio, then a tax surcharge will only be obligated if the increase in the ratio is significantly above normal. Even in the short run, there would be no interference in the normal fluctuation of shares over the cycle.

Equation 5 yields a prediction for the growth rate of the product/compensation ratio. This can be used to predict the growth rate of the profit to compensation ratio, as shown in the appendix. Under PRI, if the actual growth rate is significantly above the predicted growth rate, then an income tax surcharge on firms would be automatically imposed. As in the case of RWI, it seems natural to define an "unusual" excess of the actual over the predicted rate according to the standard error of equation 5, which is approximately 1 percent. PRI might impose a surcharge sufficient to reduce the growth rate of the ratio of after-tax profit to compensation to what it would have been if the actual growth rate of the product/compensation ratio had exceeded the predicted rate in the equation by only 1 percent (the standard error).

It is instructive to calculate the surcharge that would have been imposed for 1975, a year in which the predicted growth rate in equation 5 was significantly less than the actual growth rate; the excess in 1975 was the largest of any year in the sample period. In the appendix it is shown that a uniform income tax surcharge of approximately 2 percent would have been required, raising about $3 billion from the nonfinancial corporate sector. Such a surcharge (the nominal corporate tax rate was 48 percent for most firms) would have only a minor effect on the economy.

As in the case of RWI, it might be thought that if TIP reduces money-wage growth, a price-wage lag would cause an increase in the product/compensation ratio (and therefore the profit/compensation ratio), so that equation 5 underestimates the surcharge that would be required. In the appendix, empirical evidence is presented that suggests that the income distribution ratio would be unaffected by money-wage growth. Thus, it is likely that the above estimate would apply under TIP.

Finally, one design option for PRI should be considered. Thus far, it has been implied that the only condition required to impose the PRI surcharge is an excess of the actual growth rate over the predicted growth rate (by an amount in excess of the standard error). This would mean, however, that a surcharge could be imposed even if the ratio of product to compensation (and therefore of profit to compensation) declined, provided the actual decline was significantly less than the predicted decline. For example, in 1974 the actual product ratio declined 2.0 percent, but the predicted decline (according to equation 5) was 3.0 percent. Because the standard error was 1 percent, no surcharge would have been imposed, but an actual decline less than 2.0 percent would have required a surcharge.

Imposing a surcharge when the actual ratio declines may be regarded as inequitable. It generally will not promote stabilization because declines in the ratio are correlated with declines in the economy. It might therefore be desirable to add the second condition that the surcharge can only be imposed if the growth rate of the ratio is positive. Another alternative would be to postpone the imposition of the surcharge until the growth rate of the ratio became positive.

It should be emphasized that PRI is based on the growth rate, not the level, of the ratio. Only partial insurance is therefore offered to labor. There is no risk that the income distribution will be more than temporarily constrained.

CONCLUSIONS

It appears feasible to provide partial insurance to labor under a tax-based incomes policy (TIP). Such insurance would protect labor against an initial adverse change in real-wage growth or in the ratio of profit to labor compensation in the economy. It would therefore enable labor to assess the impact of TIP (complemented by proper monetary and fiscal policy) while avoiding significant risk. At the same time, the insurance would be partial, not complete; it would not protect against an eventual change in the level of the real wage or the level of the income distribution ratio. It would therefore not interfere with the evolution of returns to labor and capital; it would not "freeze" the income distribution.

Two kinds of insurance were considered: real-wage insurance (RWI) and profit-restraint insurance (PRI). RWI would give households an automatic tax cut if real-wage growth in the economy were "below normal." PRI would impose an automatic tax surcharge on firms if the growth rate of the ratio of profit to labor compensation for the whole economy were "above normal." In each case, an econometric equation was used to define "normal." For RWI, the real-wage growth rate was predicted by the growth rates of actual and normal labor productivity. For PRI, the growth rate of the product/compensation ratio (and therefore the profit/compensation ratio) was predicted by the growth rate of the ratio of actual to normal productivity.

For both RWI and PRI, the magnitude of tax cut or surcharge to which the government would be obligated would not be destabilizing. It is sometimes asserted that if TIP reduces wage inflation, price inflation will decline only after a significant lag, thereby raising the RWI tax cut and PRI surcharge. Econometric investigation, however, failed to detect evidence of a lag beyond one year. It is therefore unlikely that a price-wage lag will cause an equity problem for TIP or significantly raise the RWI tax cut or PRI tax surcharge. It has also sometimes been asserted that an employer-penalty TIP would induce large firms to shift the higher tax cost by raising prices, thereby reducing real-wage growth and causing an RWI tax cut. It is unlikely, though possible, that tax shifting would cause an RWI tax cut of significant magnitude. Even if a price-wage lag or tax shifting should cause the government to be ultimately liable for a large RWI tax cut, postponement (with interest) can reduce the risk of destabilization to near zero.

Thus, TIP need not be a policy that requires labor to bear the risk, even though it provides an incentive to reduce wage and salary increases. It should be feasible to provide insurance for labor that reduces this risk, but at the same time does not "freeze" the income distribution, impair incentives for efficiency, or commit the government to destabilizing automatic policy.

APPENDIX

The pricing model is as follows:

$$P_t = Ke^{-b_0 T} \left[\frac{W_t}{(A_t^{b_1})(A_t^{b_2})} \right].$$ (A1)

Capital letters denote levels; small letters used below denote growth rates. Variables are as follows:

P_t = price.
K = a constant.
W_t = wage.
$\mathbf{A}_t$ = normal productivity (normal output per man-hour).
A_t = actual productivity.

If $b_1 = 1$ and $b_2 = 0$, then price would be set according to normal unit labor cost, W_t/A_t; if $b_1 = 0$ and $b_2 = 1$, then price would be set according to actual unit labor cost, W_t/A_t. If $(b_1 + b_2) = 1$, but both b's are fractions, then price depends partly on normal unit labor cost and partly on actual unit labor cost. The markup, (Ke^{-b_0T}), grows at the rate $(-b_0)$; T is time.

Dividing equation A1 by W_t, inverting, taking logs, and differentiating yields equation 1 in the text.

Dividing equation A1 by W_t, multiplying by A_t ($A_t = Q_t/H_t$), imposing the constraint that $b_2 = 1 - b_1$, taking logs, and differentiating yields equation 4 in the text.

The series for a_t in equation 2 is constructed by running a_t against a constant and Time (T is 0 in the first year, 1953, and increases by 1 in each subsequent year), using the Cochrane-Orcutt adjustment. The result was obtained using equation 2 data:

$$a_t = 2.90 - 0.06T; \qquad (A2)$$
$$(3.86)(-1.24)$$

$\bar{R}^2 = 0.02$, S.E. $= 1.69$, and D.W. $= 1.89$.

"Normal" a_t in equation 2 is then defined as the value of a_t predicted by equation A2 in year T. Because equation 3 was run on data from 1954 through 1976, a_t in equation 3 was constructed from the same sample (using Cochrane-Orcutt):

$$a_t = 3.15 - 0.07T; \qquad (A2')$$
$$(3.93)(-1.47)$$

$\bar{R}^2 = 0.04$, S.E. $= 1.70$, and D.W. $= 1.90$.

The series for $(a/a)_t$ in equation 5 is constructed as follows:

$$A_t = A_0e^{(r_0+r_1T)T}. \qquad (A3)$$

Equation 3 allows the growth rate itself to vary with time. Taking logs and running the regression on equation 5 data, that is, 1958–1976 (without using Cochrane-Orcutt):

$$\ln A_t = 1.58 + 0.04T - 0.00T^2; \qquad (A4)$$
$$(132.82)(16.21)\ (-7.64)$$

$\bar{R}^2 = 0.99$, S.E. $= 0.02$, and D.W. $= 1.53$.

Equation A4 yields a predicted value for $\ln A_t$ in each year; taking the antilog yields a predicted value for A_t, which we define as $\mathbf{A}_t$. Then $(a/a)_t$ is defined as the growth rate of $(A_t/\mathbf{A}_t)$.

To test for the impact of w_t on $(w/p)_t$, several alternative specifications to equation 3 were run. First, equation 3 was run with a constant term with data from 1953 through 1976 (no Cochrane-Orcutt adjustment was required):

$$\left(\frac{w}{p}\right)_t = 1.17 + 0.46\mathbf{a}_t + 0.29a_t - 0.06w_t; \qquad (A5)$$
$$\quad (0.52) \quad (0.74) \quad (1.83) \quad (-0.34)$$

$\overline{R}^2 = 0.18$, S.E. $= 1.14$, and D.W. $= 1.96$.

The addition of the constant term reduces the t value and magnitude of the coefficient of $\mathbf{a}_t$; w_t remains insignificant, near zero in magnitude.

The remaining specifications required Cochrane-Orcutt adjustments. Polynomial distributed lags (PDL) were run on a_t and w_t. A PDL on a_t serves as a substitute for $\mathbf{a}_t$ because it captures lagged and thus "normal" productivity. To isolate the impact of w_t, an equation with a PDL on a_t that excludes w_t is presented for comparison (1956–1976):

$$\left(\frac{w}{p}\right)_t = 0.56a_t + 0.48a_{t-1}; \qquad (A6)$$
$$\quad (5.29) \quad (4.50)$$

$\overline{R}^2 = 0.34$, S.E. $= 1.06$, and D.W. $= 1.72$.

The coefficients of a_t and a_{t-1} were estimated as a second degree PDL, constrained to zero in year $t - 2$. When a second degree PDL for w_t was added (also constrained to zero in $t - 2$), the result (1956–1976) was:

$$\left(\frac{w}{p}\right)_t = 0.46\, a_t + 0.40a_{t-1} + 0.21w_t - 0.10w_{t-1}; \qquad (A7)$$
$$\quad (3.99) \quad (3.55) \quad (1.20) \quad (-0.58)$$

$\overline{R}^2 = 0.40$, S.E. $= 1.01$, and D.W. $= 1.81$.

The coefficients of w_t and w_{t-1} are not "significant," since the t-statistics are well below 2. Nevertheless, the coefficient of w_t is positive, providing weak evidence for a price-wage lag (a 2 percent reduction in w_t would reduce real-wage growth by 0.4 percent in the first year, although it would increase real-wage growth by 0.2 percent in the following year). Two alternative specifications, however, failed to provide even weak support for the price-wage lag. The same equation was run with second degree PDLs for both a_t and w_t, but with the lags extended to three years, constrained to zero in $t - 3$. The result (1957–1976) was:

$$\left(\frac{w}{p}\right)_t = 0.40a_t + 0.29a_{t-1} + 0.16a_{t-2} - 0.13w_t + 0.10w_{t-1} + 0.15w_{t-2};$$
$$\quad (2.88) \quad (4.22) \quad (1.79) \quad (-0.62) \quad (1.22) \quad (0.96) \quad (A8)$$

$\overline{R}^2 = 0.42$, S.E. $= 1.02$, and D.W. $= 1.98$.

The coefficients of the a's are similar to the estimates in equation A7 and the t's are well above 2. Once again, the t's of the w's are all well below 2. In contrast to equation A7 the coefficient of w_t is negative; taken literally, a 2 percent reduction in w_t would raise real-wage growth by 0.3 percent in the first year, though this would be offset in the following two years. Because this lag structure seemed implausible, a third degree PDL was tried for w_t (constrained to zero in $t - 3$). The result (1956–1976) was:

$$\left(\frac{w}{p}\right)_t = \underset{(2.41)}{0.34a_t} + \underset{(4.68)}{0.30a_{t-1}} + \underset{(2.16)}{0.19a_{t-2}} + \underset{(0.07)}{0.01w_t} - \underset{(-0.97)}{0.22w_{t-1}} + \underset{(1.52)}{0.35w_{t-2}}; \quad \text{(A9)}$$

$\bar{R}^2 = 0.42$, S.E. $= 1.00$, and D.W. $= 1.74$.

Once again, the result for the a's is similar, the w's are still insignificant, and this time the coefficient of w_t is very close to zero.

The conclusion from equations A5 through A9 is that a price-wage lag is *not* clearly detected in annual data for the private nonfarm business sector. It should not be taken for granted that TIP, by restraining money-wage growth, will in the short run reduce real-wage growth ("short run" is one year), thereby causing an inequity. Nor should it be assumed that TIP will induce an RWI tax cut. Even if a price-wage lag does exist, it is unlikely that its magnitude will be important. Thus, the estimate given in the text for the likely magnitude of the RWI tax cut should be reasonably accurate when TIP is in effect (ignoring any shifting).

The same method was used to test for the impact of w_t on the product/compensation ratio. Because equation 5 was run on a shorter time series and a narrower sector of the economy than equation 2, the results provide a useful check on the estimates of equations A5 through A9. First, w_t was added to equation 5 (1960–1976):

$$\left(\frac{pq}{wh}\right)_t = \underset{(-0.00)}{-0.00} + \underset{(4.26)}{0.62} \left(\frac{a}{\mathbf{a}}\right)_t - \underset{(-0.22)}{0.03w_t}; \quad \text{(A10)}$$

$\bar{R}^2 = 0.50$, S.E. $= 1.10$, and D.W. $= 1.90$.

The coefficient of $(a/\mathbf{a})_t$ is virtually the same as in equation 5. The coefficient of w_t is very small, and its t value is near zero. A second degree PDL (constrained to zero in $t - 2$) was tried (1962–1976):

$$\left(\frac{pq}{wh}\right)_t = \underset{(-0.36)}{-0.36} + \underset{(3.64)}{0.61} \left(\frac{a}{\mathbf{a}}\right)_t - \underset{(-0.34)}{0.09w_t} + \underset{(0.45)}{0.12w_{t-1}}; \quad \text{(A11)}$$

$\bar{R}^2 = 0.46$, S.E. $= 1.20$, and D.W. $= 1.88$.

Finally, the lag was extended (constrained to zero in $t - 3$) for data from 1963–1976:

$$\left(\frac{pq}{wh}\right)_t = \underset{(-0.50)}{-0.55} + \underset{(3.18)}{0.65} \left(\frac{a}{\mathbf{a}}\right)_t + \underset{(0.37)}{0.11w_t} - \underset{(-0.15)}{0.02w_{t-1}} - \underset{(-0.26)}{0.06w_{t-2}}; \quad \text{(A12)}$$

$\bar{R}^2 = 0.44$, S.E. $= 1.24$, and D.W. $= 1.98$.

These results confirm the conclusion reached using equation 5 data. There is little support for the view that a reduction in money-wage growth affects the income distribution ratio, even in the short run (a one-year period).

Calculation of the Surcharge under PRI

The calculation of the 2 percent surcharge under PRI in 1975 is as follows: In 1975 the actual product/compensation ratio increased 3.76 percent (in the nonfinancial corporate sector), but the growth rate predicted by equation 5 was only 1.42 percent. The excess gap over 1 percent was 1.34 percent. The actual value of P_tQ_t/W_tH_t was $\$875.2/\$576.6 = 1.52$. If the ratio had increased (1.42 percent + 1 percent), it would have been 102.42 percent $\times$ (1974 ratio) = 102.42 percent $\times$ ($\$808.8/\$552.9$) = 1.50. A 1.50 ratio in 1975 would require $P_tQ_t = 1.50\ W_tH_t = 1.50\ (\$576.6) = \$864.9$. Nonlabor income, N_t ($N_t = P_tQ_t - W_tH_t$) would have been ($\$864.9 - \$576.6$) = $\$288.3$ (instead of $\$875.2 - \$576.6 = \$298.6$). In 1975 the ratio $II_t/N_t = \$102.3/\$298.6 = .343$ (II_t is before-tax profit). Thus, if N_t would have been $\$288.3$, II_t would have been $\$98.9$ instead of $\$102.3$. In 1975 the effective income tax rate was $\$40.8/\$102.3 = 40$ percent. Thus, after-tax profit would have been 60 percent of $\$98.9$, or $\$59.3$, instead of $\$61.6$. With actual $II_t = \$102.3$, this would require a tax of $\$102.3 - \$59.3 = \$43$, or a tax rate of $\$43/\$102.3 = 42$ percent. Thus, an effective 2 percent surcharge would have been required, raising tax revenue by approximately $\$3$ billion in the nonfinancial corporate sector in 1976.

NOTES

1. The data are taken from *The Economic Report of the President*, 1978, table B-38.

2. If RWI were enacted, equation 2 would only be applied to postsample years. This exercise should therefore not be regarded as an actual simulation of RWI, but rather as a

means of estimating the likely magnitude of tax cut to which RWI would obligate the government.

3. *The Economic Report of the President,* 1978, table B-19.

4. From ibid., table B-74, federal taxes for social insurance were $89.9 billion; from ibid., B-75, state and local taxes for social insurance were $13.9; total social insurance taxes were $103.8. From ibid., B-74, federal personal tax and nontax receipts were $131.1; from ibid., B-75, state and local personal tax and nontax receipts were $39.2; total personal tax and nontax receipts were $170.3 (confirmed in ibid., B-21). Not all personal tax and nontax receipts should be attributed to compensation. In 1974, the ratio of compensation to personal income was $875.8/$1,154.9 = 76 percent (ibid., tables B-18 and B-19); 76 percent of $170.3 = $129.4. Thus, total tax due to compensation was about $233.2 ($103.8 + $129.4 = $233.2). Thus, after-tax compensation was about $643 billion; 0.7 percent × $643 = $5 billion.

5. Ibid., tables B-11 and B-12.

REFERENCES

[1] Eckstein, Otto, ed. *The Econometrics of Price Determination.* Washington, D.C.: Board of Governors, Federal Reserve System, 1972.

[2] Klein, Lawrence, and Duggal, Vijaya. "Guidelines in Economic Stabilization: A New Consideration." *Wharton Quarterly* 6 (Summer 1971): 20–24.

[3] Okun, Arthur. "Incomes Inflation and the Policy Alternatives." In *"The Economists' Conference on Inflation: Report,"* vol. 1. Processed, 1974, pp. 365–75.

[4] ———, and Perry, George, eds. "Innovative Policies to Slow Inflation." *Brookings Papers on Economic Activity,* 1978:2.

[5] Perry, George, "Determinants of Wage Inflation around the World," *Brookings Papers on Economic Activity,* 1975:2, pp. 403–35.

[6] Seidman, Laurence. "A New Approach to the Control of Inflation." *Challenge* 19 (July/August 1976): 39–43.

[7] ———. "A Payroll Tax Credit to Restrain Inflation." *National Tax Journal* 29 (December 1976):398–412.

[8] ———. "Tax-Based Incomes Policies." *Brookings Papers on Economic Activity,* 1978:2, pp. 301–48.

[9] ———. "Would Tax Shifting Undermine the Tax-Based Incomes Policy?" *Journal of Economic Issues* 12 (September 1978):647–76.

[10] ———. "The Return of the Profit Rate to the Wage Equation." *Review of Economics and Statistics,* February 1979.

[11] ———. "The Role of a Tax-Based Incomes Policy." *American Economic Review Papers and Proceedings,* May 1979.

[12] U.S. President, *The Economic Report of the President.* Washington, D.C.: U.S. Gov't. Printing Office, 1978.

[13] Wachter, Michael. "The Changing Cyclical Responsiveness of Wage Inflation." *Brookings Papers on Economic Activity,* 1976:1, pp. 115–59.
[14] Wallich, Henry, and Weintraub, Sidney. "A Tax-Based Incomes Policy." *Journal of Economic Issues* 5 (June 1971):1–19.
[15] Weintraub, Sidney. *Capitalism's Inflation and Unemployment Crisis.* Reading, Mass.: Addison-Wesley, 1978.

6 TAX-BASED INCOMES POLICIES:
A Better Mousetrap?
William D. Nordhaus

There is widespread agreement that inflation is Economic Enemy Number One. It has become the top priority because of a decade of benign neglect — a period in which inflation was outranked by other priorities (Vietnam, Watergate, unemployment) or in which efforts to combat inflation were short lived (as in the Nixon wage-price controls) or a joke (Ford's Whip Inflation Now).

This decade was also one in which the unexpected shocks and underlying forces were predominantly inflationary. The rise of OPEC, the depreciation of the dollar, increasingly costly regulation, and a dramatic decline in productivity combined to produce a series of upward ratchets in the underlying inflation rate (the increase in the nonfarm business deflator) from 1.0 percent in 1961–1964, to 2.9 percent in 1965–1969, to 6.1 percent in 1970–1971, to 8 percent in 1978. The only good news was that it could have been worse.

This combination of events has led to the consensus that reducing inflation should be the number-one priority. Households thinking that inflation is more serious than unemployment outnumber those with the opposite persuasion by almost 3 to 1. With an economy essentially at full employment, no relief from inflation in sight, and a clear signal from voters that they want action, now is a propitious time to wage war on inflation.

Although virtual unanimity on the existence of an inflationary disease exists, there is no agreement on a remedy. Many conservatives call for fiscal or monetary austerity or both; the people seem to lean toward balanced budgets; J.K. Galbraith has trotted out the perennial nonstarter of wage and price controls; Milton Friedman argues that reduced monetary growth will suffice; and many businessmen claim that reduction of regulation will go far.

Partially as a result of the babel of theories and remedies, there is in fact no political consensus about how to proceed. And there is no national inflation program.

The problem of inflation is akin to a crowd watching a football game. There are two stable equilibria at a game — everyone standing up and everyone sitting down. These might correspond to a high-inflation and a low-inflation equilibrium.

The problem arises because an individual or group gets excited, or "overheated," and stands up to see the field better. Others follow suit until everyone is standing. On average, the view is not better standing up — some see better, some worse. Generally everyone is a little uncomfortable; yet there is no easy way to sit them down. No single person has the incentive to sit down first because he cannot see over those standing in front of him. Yet if everyone were to sit at once, the entire crowd might be more comfortable.

How to persuade people to sit down? The following analogies with inflation are imperfect but entertaining:

1. *Old-time religion*: The proven way to get the crowd off its feet is to slow down the football game and "cool" the crowd.
2. *Jawboning*: Announce that standing up is bad and ask if everyone would please sit down.
3. *Controls*: Order everyone to sit down or be ejected from the stadium.

When these fail, one might be tempted to try "TBCC," tax-based crowd controls — reward everyone with a tuition-tax credit if they sit down.

A SIMPLE INFLATION MODEL

Before discussing alternative approaches to inflation, I must admit my personal prejudices about the inflation process. They can be summarized in three behavioral equations. First, it is assumed that wages follow an expectational (or natural rate–style) Phillips curve:

$$w_t = w_{t-1} + f(u^*/u_t) + k(y^*_{t-1} - y_{t-1}), \tag{1}$$

where

p = rate of price inflation;
w = rate of change of wages;
u = unemployment rate;
u^* = natural (or nonaccelerating inflation) employment rate;
$y = w - p$ = growth of real wages;
y^* = expected growth in real wages.

Equation 1 states that wage inflation follows an inertial process unless shocked by excess supply or demand for labor or by disappointments in real-wage growth (or in alternative versions by exogenous inflation). Each of the three terms in equation 1 can become a bottomless pit of controversy, and no attempt to justify each will be given here.

Prices are assumed to follow a cost-determined structure:

$$P_t = w_t + c_t - a_t, \tag{2}$$

where c = rate of increase in the share of nonlabor costs (e.g., indirect taxes, imported materials, and perhaps the markup of price over costs) and a = rate of growth of labor productivity.

Equation 2 states that inflation is determined by the rise in costs per unit output. It is clearly a view of price formation consistent with the predominance of "administered," rather than "auction," markets. It could be made more realistic by specifically accounting for nonlabor costs and by adding an effect of demand on the markup of price over costs, but little is gained by these further complications.

Finally, we assume that expected real-wage growth is adaptively determined as a function of past growth in real wages:

$$y_t^* = g(y_{t-1}, \ldots). \tag{3}$$

For simplicity, assume this period's expected real-wage growth simply equals last period's actual growth:

$$y_t^* = y_{t-1}. \tag{3'}$$

To solve this system for its wage and price behavior, we take u_t, c_t, and a_t as determined outside the wage-price system. The unemployment rate is determined by monetary and fiscal policy in light of competing national goals. Productivity growth and the share of nonlabor costs are determined partly exogenously by underlying trends or exchange market developments, partly by policies regarding taxation and microeconomic policies.

Solving our simple system of equations in 1, 2, and 3', we have:

$$\Delta w_t = f\left(\frac{u^*}{u_t}\right) + k(\Delta c_{t-1} - \Delta a_{t-1}) \tag{4}$$

$$\Delta p_t = f\left(\frac{u^*}{u_t}\right) + \Delta c_t + k\Delta c_{t-1} - \Delta a_t - k\Delta a_{t-1}. \tag{5}$$

Thus, in this simple view, wages and prices accelerate under two general sets of conditions. Four points are worth making. First, there is a permanent acceleration either when there is a period of excess demand and the unemployment rate falls below the natural rate or when there is a permanent shift in productivity or cost growth. Second, there is a temporary burst of inflation when there is a temporary drop in productivity growth or increase in cost growth; however, after the temporary change and after all lags play out, the inflation rate returns to the original level. Third, the effect of cost or productivity changes on the level of prices is greater than that on prices by the amount of the change, while demand affects the two variables by equal properties.

Finally, note that the wage-price system is explosive if demand is held away from the natural rate, but that it is not explosive even if workers attempt to make up their entire real income (i.e., if $k = 1$). This latter feature appears because of the adaptive nature of the income expectation.

ALTERNATIVE STRATEGIES TO REDUCE INFLATION

We noted above that there are an enormous number of competing theories concerning the remedy for reducing inflation. A brief review of the troops, using the simplified model outlined above, may help sort out confusion. In what follows, I will discuss three sets of alternatives: genuine strategies, false strategies, and new strategies.

Genuine Strategies

There are three strategies for reducing inflation that have been tried and examined in a wide variety of circumstances: macroeconomic policy, microeconomic policies, and incomes policies.

Macroeconomic Policy.   The level of overall economic slack in labor and product markets is the central factor determining inflationary pressures year after year. It is well documented that by holding a high level of slack ("old-time religion"), inflation can be reduced, and the administration's current fiscal policy opens up a bit of slack for this purpose. In the simplified model above, slack occurs when the unemployment rate exceeds a natural rate, leading to deceleration of wages that is passed into acceleration of prices.

The costs of using economic slack to reduce inflation are very high — 2.5 million person-years of employment and $100 billion of output are lost for each point that inflation is reduced. The high cost of reducing inflation through recession, combined with the political sensitivity to recessions, has up to now meant that conversions to the old-time religion have been unacceptable or followed by atheistic splurges.

Microeconomic Policies.   A second real strategy is the use of supply-side (or microeconomic) policies to reduce costs and thereby inflation. There are two general ways in which supply-side policies can affect inflation. Increases in cost-raising taxes (such as sales or social security taxes) increase prices and enter into the wage-price spiral. Policies that raise private costs or lower productivity (such as deregulating oil prices, limiting emissions into air or water, or imposing trade restrictions) raise unit costs and have a similar effect. In the simple model discussed above, supply-side policies reduce nonlabor costs (c) or increase productivity growth (a). Note, however, that most measures (trade restrictions or liberalization, oil price decontrol, regulation) represent one-time changes in productivity or costs and therefore have only a one-time effect on inflation. A policy that effected a permanent slowdown in productivity growth would lead to a permanent acceleration in inflation.

Incomes Policies.   A final genuine alternative is the use of incomes policies or price and wage controls. These policies customarily use a series of guidelines or percentage increases for wages and a markup standard for prices. At one extreme, where pure jawboning ("whip inflation now") penalties exist for breaching the guidelines, it is hard to see why any parties would change their behavior. At the other extreme, controls, the price-wage system degenerates largely into a political process. The Carter guidelines fall somewhere in between. They were designed to have significant penalties for noncompliance, but were very limited in their scope, were full of flexibility, and had modest objectives.

It has not proven easy to model incomes policies, but a little illumination can be obtained in the simple model above. The wage half of incomes policies is an attempt to break the inertial process by slowing down wages. As can be seen, in an inertial system, such as the one outlined above, if wages are successfully slowed, this will permanently slow the overall rate of wage and price inflation. Thus, if 1 percent is subtracted from the right-hand side of equation 1, this will translate into 1 percent lower w and p for all time thereafter. Again, however, it is hard to see the economic mechanism of a wage incomes policy without statutory wage controls. As in our stadium crowd, since no one wants to sit down first, no one sits down at all.

It should be noted that because prices are *not* inertial, the effect of "prices policy" is much less powerful. In effect, prices policy reduces or restrains the markup of prices over costs. Thus, in our little model, prices policy lowers the nonlabor share, reducing c_t. The problem is that this compression of the margins cannot go on for long; indeed, it seems likely that the cost level will bounce back. Over the entire price-policy period, then, c_t will rise slower at the beginning and faster at the end, for no net gain. As can be easily seen from equations 4 and 5, there can therefore be no lasting effect of prices policy on inflation unless it helps wages policy.

How well have these programs worked? Evidence from the United States is that there are at best very modest effects of incomes policies. The verdict on the Kennedy-Johnson guideposts is that they hold down inflation by 0.1 percent or so. The Nixon statutory wage and price controls over the 1971–1973 period appear to have had *no* net effect. Evidence from abroad is rather mixed, with a few successes and many failures.

Given the dismal record of incomes policies, it might seem to be a puzzle why governments come back to them time and again. For all her admiration of the free markets, Prime Minister Thatcher has not vowed to remove the Labour government's restraints in Britain. The reason we seem to come back to the rather dry well so often is simple: Incomes policies are (or appear) relatively inexpensive and, given the enormous costs of the alternatives, they are probably worth trying even if they have only a small chance of success. Even if Fred Kahn is only worth one-half point on the inflation rate, compared to macroeconomic policies he is worth $50 billion.

False Strategies

The three strategies discussed above are genuine in the sense that there are sound theoretical and empirical reasons to believe they work. In addition, there are many "snake oil" remedies that cannot be certified as efficacious and ought to be taken off the shelf of anti-inflation medicines.

Monetary Policy.   The first of these is a mechanical monetary rule of simplistic monetary linkages. Both theory and history indicate that a given monetary policy is neither necessary nor sufficient for reducing inflation. Money enters along with fiscal policy, oil prices, animal spirits, and other factors into the determination of aggregation demand. Except for some second-order effects, it is only through the levels of aggregate demand (or unemployment rate, u, in our simple model above) that money affects inflation. Other things being equal, tighter money will improve inflation. But other things being unequal, as they tend to be with pesky frequency, money has no intrinsic magical powers over prices.

If the tomes of history and journal articles are not sufficiently convincing, the most recent behavior of money should help dispel the myth about money's supremacy. Over the last six months, M_1 decelerated dramatically from about 8 percent over the first nine months of 1978 to -3 percent over the next six months. There has been no deceleration in inflation as of the latest data.

Fiscal Policy.   A second set of persuasive false remedies concerns the role of fiscal policy. There is currently a public movement, unique since Prohibition, for a return to fiscal austerity in the form of balanced federal budgets. At least part of this ground swell is in reaction to the acceleration of inflation and is seen as a way of reducing inflation.

Mechanically balanced budgets are no more a panacea than are mechanical monetary rules. The appropriate level of the budget deficit will differ depending on many things, such as monetary policy and the external sector, as well as the public sentiment about the relative unattractiveness of inflation, unemployment, and lost output. Although many would be delighted with budget surpluses, few would have applauded the 10, 11, or 12 percent unemployment rates this would have induced in 1975. As for monetary policy, lower deficits would affect inflation through the effect on aggregate demand — no more, no less.

Expenditure-Limitation Approach.   A more sophisticated version of the balanced-budget approach is the "expenditure-limitation" version in which growth in government expenditures is limited to (or in some cases below) the growth in nominal GNP. While there may be some second-order effects of such an approach on inflation (e.g., lower expenditures imply lower taxes, which in turn imply at least some one-time moderating effect on costs and prices), there is even less reason to think the expenditure-limitation approach will lower inflation more than the balanced-budget approach. In this approach there are no constraints on either tax or monetary policy, and a government can be fiscally irresponsible with either a growing or shrinking public sector.

New Strategies

The genuine and false strategies are not encouraging — they are costly at best and inefficacious at worst. Given the importance of inflation and the paucity of conventional tools, there has been considerable search for new strategies.

So far only one important new class of ideas has turned up. This is the so-called tax-based inflation policies, or TIP. The rest of this paper will be devoted to a discussion of the functioning, design, and effectiveness of TIPs.

TAX-BASED INCOMES POLICIES (TIP)

The basic rationale of TIP is simple. Inflation is somewhat like pollution. In making their own private price and wage decisions, private agents generate "macroeconomic externalities." Decisions to raise wages and prices have a macroeconomic externality because they raise wage and price indices rather than simply leading to *relative* price changes. The higher price indices lead to restrictive macroeconomic policies and real income and output losses. Thus, in a fashion that is not obvious, there are externalities here just as much as at Three Mile Island.

In response to pollution, it is customary to propose regulations (like incomes policies or price and wage controls) or effluent taxes (hence TIP). We may choose to have no inflation policy. However, if governments choose to enter into the price and wage arena, a policy should attempt to give firms, unions, and workers *decentralized incentive* to moderate their price-and-wage-raising behavior; hence, TIP.

Would TIP Work?

There are basically two reasons why a TIP might work. One is of a social contract view and the other is the buyout theory.

The *social contract* view has its roots in the European tradition of tripartite bargaining of unions, firms, and the government. For example, in Britain in 1974 and 1975, the trade unions accepted wage restraint in return for certain personal tax reductions. There is no doubt that the dramatic deceleration of wage inflation in Britain from 1974 to 1977 was in some part due to the success of this social contract.

My view is that the social contract can play virtually no role in the success of TIP (or incomes policies more generally) in the United States. The labor movement in the United States is too decentralized and the AFL-CIO leadership too weak to exercise any significant effect on the labor settlements as a whole. Given antitrust laws, there is even less room for a contract with business. Nor is there any forum for such bargaining to take place. Thus the idea that a TIP can somehow galvanize major groups into significantly changing behavior, without providing incentives for individual unions or firms, seems implausible.

A second view of the effectiveness of TIP is that it is a *buyout* of firms and workers — that is, TIP changes behavior basically because it is in the self-interest of the workers and firms whose behavior is changed. This view of TIP is based on a deep economic tradition that ascribes profit or utility-maximizing behavior to firms and workers.

It may be useful to show how a TIP will work in our simple model outlined above. We have up to now assumed that wages are a simple aggregate. TIP functions critically by working on the distribution of wages.

For simplicity, we will analyze what will later be called a one-year wage-buyout-carrot TIP, one quite similar in many respects to the Carter administration's real-wage insurance (RWI) proposal. In this example, a reward is offered to any individual (or group) whose wage rate increase (w_j) is less than a standard ($\overline{w}$). Assume that the reward takes the form of a one-time taxable earned-income credit of R percent.

What is rational individual behavior? Consider two cases:

Case 1 — a one-year contract, with any real-wage loss made up the second year. If the wage gain would otherwise have been $w_j{}^*$, then TIP is *accepted* under the condition:

$$w^* \leqq \overline{w} + R.$$

Case 2 — a long-term three-year contract in which the real-wage loss is half made up in the next contract and the rest in the third contract; then (ignoring discounting), TIP is accepted if:

$$w^* \leqq \overline{w} + \frac{R}{4.5}.$$

The important point is that the *budget cost* of the TIP will depend on where $\bar{w}$ is relative to the distribution of desired wage increases, while the effect will depend on the number between $\bar{w}$ and $\bar{w} + R$ (or $\bar{w} + \alpha R$, where α is a discount factor for loss in future years as in case 2).

An illustration is shown in figure 1 of the effect of wage-carrot-buyout on behavior. In the figure those whose desired gains (w^*) are less than the standard get a free ride with no rational effect on their behavior. Those in range from $\bar{w}$ to $\bar{w} + \alpha R$ will reduce their wage gains to $\bar{w}$. Those above $\bar{w} + \alpha R$ will not find it worth their while to meet the standard and will be unaffected. We can apply this simple apparatus to ask what the effect of a 2 percent wage-carrot TIP might be for the United States for 1979, this being a fair guess today as to the payout of real-wage insurance. A discount factor of $\alpha = 0.67$ probably is reasonable. If the average worker's private compensation increase were to average 8.5 percent, in an average year there would generally be 15 percent of workers between 7.0 and 8.0 percent (i.e., where $w^* - \bar{w} \leq \alpha R = 0.67 \times 1.5 = 1.0$ percent). This would imply that on a purely rational basis this 15 percent of workers would reduce their wage increases by

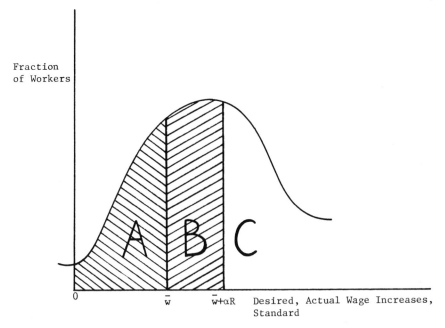

Figure 1. Illustration of Effect of Wage-Carrot-Buyout on Behavior

0.5 percent and *the aggregate wage increase would be 0.075 percent lower.* The total cost would be 2 percent of earned income for those receiving earnings increases up to 8 percent — about 40 million workers — for a total outlay of around $10 billion. Note that this cost ($1.3 billion cost per basis point on inflation) is around that for recession policy ($1 billion per basis point), but that these are budget costs rather than real resources.

There is yet a careful study to be done analyzing TIP on a "rational" basis. In preliminary work, some bizarre features turn up, such as significant economies of scale in the size of the program. Work along these lines, combined with comparisons of alternative costs of alternative anti-inflation approaches, should be high on the list of research priorities.

Critical Design Questions in TIP

Up to now, TIP has gotten no further than the proposal stage. The most carefully designed example is that of real-wage insurance (RWI), proposed by President Carter in January 1979.

The basic design of RWI is straightforward. In this proposal, employee groups that have wage increases of no more than 7 percent would receive a tax credit if consumer prices rise more than 7 percent over 1979. The rate of tax credit would be equal to the difference between the actual inflation rate and 7 percent, up to a limit of 3 percent (i.e., coverage extends only to 10 percent inflation). This rate would apply to each employee's wages up to a limit of $20,000 per job.

In constructing RWI, several important and interesting design issues arose. The following discussion looks at six of these to illustrate some of the key problems that will probably arise under any TIP plan.

Prices v. Wages. An absolutely fundamental question that is raised by TIP is whether it should apply to wages or prices or both. Some of the proposals for TIP were relatively comprehensive — they suggested taxes on excess wage or price increases. On careful examination, however, the problems involved in describing a price TIP look overwhelming. The difficulty is due to two factors. First, a TIP probably will not stand on its own, but will be part of a more general and comprehensive anti-inflation policy. Design of the administration's proposal took place *after* the wage and price standards had been formulated. This meant that many design features would have to be common between RWI and the more general program. Second, the price part of the general guidelines program was much more complicated and difficult to formulate than the wage part. Indeed, such is the nature of a complex modern economy. Whereas wages were limited to a 7 percent increase, prices had a dual standard with multiple exceptions and exemptions. As a result, it was clearly impossible to design a price program in a short time, and it was quickly dropped in favor of a wage-only standard.

Is the design of a price TIP hopeless? I admit that the problems look insurmountable. The major problem is that it would not only involve a full set of decisions on all possible industries and contingencies, but also the codification of these into law and regulations. In a sense it would require a whole new business tax code for TIP. Just for fun, here are a few random problems. How would costs be defined? Would inventories be valued with LIFO or FIFO? What base period would be used? For multiproduct firms, would the TIP apply to each product or to price indices? If the latter, with what detail would they be constructed and would they be fixed or of variable weight? How would product quality be treated? If new products are linked to old, what is to prevent uneconomic and unjustified claims of quality change? Would firms that are regulated be exempt or would they be subject to dual regulation? Would there be a small business exemption? A self-employed exemption? How would multinationals be treated? How would intercorporate transfer prices be treated among wholly owned subsidiaries? Partially owned subsidiaries? Foreign affiliates? Would auction markets be exempted? How would interest rates be treated? And so forth.

The list could be indefinitely extended. It is not that there are no answers to these questions; rather, there are no good answers. Yet to be effective, answers must be given, or firms will choose the answer that makes their case. (Indeed, the present guidelines seem to suffer from just this problem.) To close loopholes, any price TIP will struggle under the incredible complexity and bureaucratic structure necessary to answer relevant questions. Along the way, I suspect that the American political system would throw up its hands and say that the red tape was not worth the costs.

Carrot v. Stick.   Most of the early proposals for TIPS proposed taxes rather than subsidies as the mechanism for providing decentralized incentives (hence, TIP rather than SIP). The reason, I suppose, was simply that if sin is bad, the remedy is to tax sin, not to subsidize virtue. Or to change the metaphor, if the rationale for TIP is that it provides a better mousetrap, we may be better off putting out a little cheese to lure in our rationally expected working mouse.

There are several fine points to be made in the decision about whether taxes or subsidies are preferable. These include the presence of taxed and untaxed sectors, the shadow price on government revenues, and the distributional differences between the two approaches.

Although this question has the raw materials for a fine and extended theoretical debate, they are not germane today. First, Congress and the country were, and are, in an antitax mood. After Social Security tax increases, Proposition 13, and wellhead taxes, any tax on excess wages or prices would be a nonstarter. A second reason pertains to peculiar notions of equity. For reasons discussed above, the TIP was to be limited to wages; yet, if a "stick" TIP was to be used, it would only be "fair" to workers if it applied also to firms. This leaves only carrots as a possibility. Third, in this particular case, it was thought that rapid en-actment was critical to the success of the program. If the proposal languished through 1979, it would have little effect. Conventional wisdom is that subsidy schemes are more popular than tax schemes and therefore more likely to pass quickly. Again, this suggests using the carrot approach.

It might be asked how eternal these verities appear with hindsight. I continue to think that the case for the carrot is compelling *at this time*. In other circumstances, things might change. The main drawback, in retrospect, is that the program becomes very expensive with adverse inflationary shocks (see the subsection on budget cost below). This seems to me to be the major reason why a pure carrot approach has some serious drawbacks.

Insurance v. Buyout. In considering the various options, there were two competing schemes for the wage TIP. The first (and the one finally chosen) was the insurance TIP. The insurance TIP would guarantee the "real wage" of the participant by making up the difference between the actual inflation rate and the wage standard 7 percent. A different version was the straight "bribe TIP." Under the second version, participants were given an extra tax credit (say, 1 or 2 percent of earned income) if they would "join" the TIPlers club by adhering to the standard.

The insurance approach was chosen because it was (then) thought that it would be cheaper than the bribe. Moreover, the insurance feature could arguably have had added attraction to risk-adverse workers. Fi-nally, it might be easier to terminate than a straight handout. The cost was that the insurance approach looked gimmicky in a scheme that was already extremely novel. Moreover, the insurance feature meant that the costs of the program were a lottery, and random fiscal policy has few admirers.

The design feature is a much closer call than some of the others. The insurance approach may be too clever, and the government may itself get caught in the trap. A simpler and more predictable approach might be preferable for the next design.

Who Should Be Exempted?   The problem of inclusions and exclusions from the real-wage insurance is a very difficult problem. The conventional wisdom before the administration proposal was that it would be impossible to have a strict definition of eligible groups with a carrot TIP and that a good deal of money would be wasted. As it turned out, because of the influence of the hardheaded Treasury people, the scheme was very tightly drawn.

An example of the kind of problem that is raised in a carrot TIP is, What do you do with the self-employed or the farmers? The fear might be that to win the farm vote, you would have to include farmers. The administration proposal made the sensible suggestion of including only those who are employees and excluding those who are major shareholders and who might therefore simply defer wages. A similar problem arose with low-wage workers. They were exempted from the wage standard, and there might have been strong pressures, on grounds of hardship, to give them real-wage insurance automatically. Again, the decision was instead in favor of making them subject to the rules as any other workers would be.

Union v. Nonunion Workers.   Treatment of union and nonunion workers (or more generally contractual and noncontractual wages) is a very sticky question. The tension in the design arises because it is unclear whether TIP should follow the same principle as the guidelines or whether it should be an internally consistent piece of tax legislation. Should there be horizontal equity across workers or across programs?

The reason for the difficulty was that under the guidelines, collective bargaining agreements received approval as of the contract date (*ex ante*), while other wages were judged to comply after the end of the program year (*ex post*). In part, this distinction arises because contracts can be costed out in advance, while informal arrangements cannot. In part, *ex ante* treatment arises because of the key importance of slowing the key union settlements for reducing inflation.

From the point of view of tax policy, the principle of neutrality would have been preferable — that is, all workers would be treated equally no matter what their institutional wage format. This, then, would have required that *all* wages for the purpose of TIP would be measured *ex post*, at the end of each program year. Unfortunately such an outcome would have been a setback for the overall inflation program; here, as in the subsection on prices v. wages above, the fact that the TIP must be an integral part of a unified program was very important. The problems with the tax-policy approach were twofold. First, it would have provided little incentive for big unions to comply because big union contracts are usually front loaded. Second, it would actually have led to a dual standard for large union contracts — the standard for three-year contracts was 7 percent over the life of the contract and 8 percent in the first year, while the TIP had a 7 percent first-year limit. Finally, it probably would have sown so much confusion that both programs would have been subject to ridicule. Thus, the fact that the guidelines program was in place and that there was need for coherence led to the outcome that tax policy was bent to the needs of the anti-inflation program.

Budget Cost.   One of the most difficult problems that arises in TIP design involves its budgetary and fiscal consequences. For RWI, as a result of two choices — the carrot and insurance approaches — the budget costs were both highly uncertain and potentially very large. The major issues arising here were how to limit budget exposure and whether the anti-inflation gains were, in some general political sense, worth the budget costs in a year of budget stringency.

The issue of how to limit the budget is extremely difficult. Under RWI, total "costs" would be determined by the fraction of workers who qualify and by the inflation rate. Assuming 50 percent of workers qualify, with average covered earnings of $12,000, every point of inflation over 7 percent would lead to $6 billion of gross costs (or about $5 billion after tax). More refined estimates gave a cost estimate of $4.5 billion per point of inflation. In the (then perceived) very unlikely case that a repetition of 1973–1974 would occur, with inflation at 12 percent, the cost of the program would be over $20 billion.

It is clear that a very high estimated possible cost (such as $20 billion or $30 billion) would doom the RWI proposal. Moreover, there is some question about the wisdom of having a policy that leads to fiscal stimulus in a period when inflation accelerates. Three options were available to keep the costs down: (1) having a balancing *tax* (like a wellhead oil tax) that would be triggered when costs get too high (this was too cumbersome and would have doomed the whole program); (2) putting on an *aggregate* budget limit (such as $10 billion) that would lead to a scaling down of the payoff if the inflaton or participation rates rose too much; (3) using program *design* characteristics that would limit the cost — making RWI taxable, limiting qualification and, most important, giving insurance an inflation rate of only up to 10 percent. The latter approach was selected.

As it turned out, the budget *risk* problem attracted less attention than the budget *cost* problem. When RWI was proposed, it looked as if it might be cheap — for inflation was forecasted to be under 7 percent. By the time of the January 1979 budget, the forecast was 7.4 percent. A good guess now (end of March 1979) would be an inflation rate for the program year of 9.5 percent, with a consequent budget outlay of around $11 billion.

The problem arises because — Milton Friedman and popular opinion notwithstanding — the budgets of the president and the Congress must find room for the $2.5 billion or $11 billion (or whatever amount it estimates). If the budget deficit is to be limited to $30 billion, then $2.5 billion or $11 billion (or whatever) of other concrete expenditures or tax cuts must be shelved. Instead, the Budget Committees of the Congress shelved RWI.

''Finding the room'' for RWI is not a major design problem, since that is somebody else's job. However, two serious and enduring budgetary problems will probably face any future attempts to use TIP. First, any effective TIP will have to have stiff financial penalties. There are no free anti-inflation lunches; big sticks or carrots are needed for big horses. I cannot see how a serious TIP program could operate with gross taxes or subsidies of less than $10 billion or $20 billion a year. This will imply that any taxes will be fought bitterly by those they hit, while subsidies will be fought by interest groups who want the money for their own programs. Even if TIP is a ''good buy'' for the economy as a whole, the problems of selling it when large transfers are involved seem immense.

A more interesting economic problem is whether the fiscal impact of a TIP should be pro- or anticyclical. (By procyclical I mean a positive inflation shock leads to greater subsidies or smaller taxes.) Carrots need *not* share the RWI feature of being procyclical — it is the *insurance* feature that leads to the higher payout with higher inflation. For most TIP dangers we would expect the opposite — that higher inflation would lead to lower compliance and higher taxes or lower revenues, that is, they would be anticyclical.

It is not at all clear whether it is desirable that TIPs be pro- or anticyclical in the sense defined above. It is generally thought that when real output declines, an automatic stabilizer should reduce taxes, and a progressive tax system does this quite well. What is the appropriate response to an exogenous increase in inflation? This depends on the source of the inflation (temporary v. permanent) and on our attitude toward inflation (whether we should or should not accommodate inflation). Since an exogenous increase in inflation seldom leads to an offsetting decline in real growth, we would only want a TIP to be procyclical if we were more averse to real output declines than to inflation increases. Moreover, some inflationary shocks are contractionary (food-price shock), while others lead to tighter labor markets (a productivity slowdown).

TIPs are already complicated enough without their getting swamped in the debate about fiscal policy or whether we should accommodate inflation. Perhaps the best answer is that they be self-balancing (i.e., raise no net revenue). This would be useful if for no other reason than simply because we could avoid endless debates about where the TIP payout that unbalanced the budget and increased the money supply would actually be inflationary.

RWI: RIP

In early April 1979 the real-wage insurance proposal died a graceful death in the congressional Budget Committees. What went wrong?

A postmortem reveals three things. First, RWI was too new and gimmicky for many legislators to accept — its time had clearly not come. Second, there was great skepticism in Congress about whether it would work. Third, and most important, any realistic budget estimate would yield a cost of $10 billion for RWI. Congress could not accept either squeezing this out of other programs or adding this to the federal deficit with a constitutional convention looking like an iceberg on a foggy night. Better to sink the ship than to hit the iceberg.

IV EVALUATION AND CRITICISM

7 INCOMES POLICIES IN AN OPEN ECONOMY:
Domestic and External Interactions
John Sheahan

Is it possible to have an independent national incomes policy in an open economy? The question is closely linked to a more general issue of analysis and evidence: Are prices determined primarily by current changes in demand and supply in individual markets, as economists have from time to time suggested, or are they based primarily on wage costs? If the former, an incomes policy in an open economy is an extremely doubtful proposition. If the latter, it is at least conceivable to make important headway in restraining national inflation through incomes policy.

At one extreme, it is possible to argue that world forces of supply and demand determine international prices of traded goods and no national producer is able to charge any higher price or likely to charge any lower — prices of traded goods are determined by world markets and not separately within each country.[1] At another extreme, it may be argued

Special thanks are due to Anne Romanis Braun of the International Monetary Fund and Carl Van Duyne of Williams College for their detailed criticisms of earlier drafts of this study. They would not agree with much of the present version, but it has been improved considerably by their suggestions.

155

that the use of variable exchange rates can insulate national from world
price trends so that a separate national rate of inflation is perfectly
feasible.[2] Yet another interpretation, applied by Sidney Weintraub to the
United States as a very special case, is that trade is of such marginal
importance to the economy that the question of external inflation is not
significant: "The United States is obviously a very closed economy."[3]

With such a rich variety of interpretations, the temptation is to resist
all of them and offer another one. It seems undeniable that external price
changes do affect domestic inflation and most unlikely that the use of
variable exchange rates can make the interactions disappear. But there
may still be scope for gain from incomes policies depending on management of the exchange rate, on the behavior of firms in response to
external price or exchange rate changes, on the specific structural pattern
of external price movements, and on the response of domestic monetary
and fiscal policy to external impacts. The following discussion is no more
than a selective attempt to sort out some of these issues for consideration,
in the belief that the external side of inflation is far too important to
ignore in any formulation of incomes policy.

The first part of this paper sets out a simple framework of analysis in
terms of three sets of markets, based on Scandinavian models of inflation
in terms of open and closed sectors but splitting up the open sector to
take account of different kinds of price behavior for different groups of
traded goods. The second part considers the insulating properties of a
variable exchange rate. The third part is concerned with a small sample
of policy questions that might usefully be considered if the economy is
regarded as open to influence from external changes in demand and
supply. The fourth part explains two arguments in favor of domestic
incomes policy, arguments deriving from a belief that domestic and external rates of inflation do interact with each other, but (1) that there is
room for domestic gain from successful incomes policy and (2) that this
could in turn have positive effects on the outside world.

THE FRAMEWORK

It is always possible to alter the course of particular prices by direct
intervention in the markets concerned if such intervention blocks recourse to external markets. Perhaps the most important assumption about
incomes policy in this discussion is that the pursuit of methods to limit
inflation will not involve any widespread recourse to trade restrictions,
any general movement toward insulation of the economy from the outside

world. This need not mean that prices of traded goods are tightly linked to world prices at all times, but it does mean that measures to hold domestic prices distinctly below external levels will be counteracted by pressures from market forces acting to pull prices together.

A second presumption about policy is that we will not return to a regime of fixed exchange rates in the Bretton Woods sense. This is not meant to be a vote in favor of completely variable rates. Inflation might well be brought under better control through active intervention to hold the exchange rate stable. But it is also true that variable rates provide greater possibilities for independent national price trends, for better or for worse, and that in periods of sustained current account deficits the economy could be badly damaged by efforts to hold on grimly to a fixed price of foreign exchange.

A third presumption concerns the nature of the incomes policy used. If it were to consist of no more than a few isolated instances of selective restraint, most of the problems discussed here would be irrelevant. If it were to consist of a tight system of thoroughly worked-out plans to reconcile income flows, final demand, and product availabilities, it could be wrecked by external shocks. A viable policy has to be somewhere in between: It would need not only to balance demand and supply, taking into systematic account the cost and the income sides of wages and nonwage incomes, but also to provide for frequent readjustments in real incomes. To make the background assumption somewhat more concrete, the concept used here is that incomes policy is oriented toward maintaining a ceiling rate of increase in money wages of x_1, a distinct but consistent rate of increase for product price increases of x_2, and a total of real income flows to labor, to firms, and to primary producers that adds up to the level of national income possible when the economy is close to full employment. It is assumed that incomes policy will be used to help keep the economy closer to full employment than it would otherwise have been, but that aggregate demand will not be allowed to exceed productive capacity.

Different Kinds of Markets and Price Behavior

To get out of the trap of analysis in terms of a single price trend and behavioral pattern, the discussion here postulates three kinds of markets and pricing behavior. Following in part the Scandinavian models of inflation, it may be assumed that the closed sectors of the economy — construction and nontraded goods and services in general — can follow an independent path of price inflation depending primarily on wage rates and material costs;[4] that is, prices will be affected by changes in the costs of inputs, both domestic and imported, but final prices of goods and services from this side of the economy do not need to match external prices. For the closed sectors, an incomes policy based on restraint of wages could then have an effective role because wage costs will directly affect sector prices.

A totally different kind of pricing is more likely for primary commodities traded on world markets. While these markets differ enormously among themselves, it may be acceptable as a first approximation to treat them as subject to price unification through commodity arbitrage, with prices determined by world demand and supply. That is certainly not true in any complete sense because many of these markets are ridden with private and public controls and many of them feature prolonged differences between official producer prices and spot markets.[5] But it is still likely that (1) changes in domestic wages have very little effect on prices of these products, except in the indirect sense that they can in the long run change the quantities produced and traded by particular countries, and (2) domestic prices will in general be a direct translation of external prices at prevailing exchange rates. This is, of course, true for exports, such as wheat and soybeans from the United States, as well as for imports: The home market price cannot be kept indefinitely below the external price unless trade is blocked. These commodities would seem to be out of reach of any incomes policy based on wage costs.

One of the earliest and best of the Scandinavian models, that of Odd Aukrust for Norway, puts agriculture in the closed sector of the economy, rather than the open. The reason is that Norwegian agriculture is thoroughly protected from world markets, with extensive domestic subsidy arrangements.[6] Some components of American agriculture could reasonably be treated the same way, though not those agricultural products that are involved in export markets. But even those commodities that are nonexported and protected are much more likely to be market determined in the competitive sense rather than closely tied to wage costs. An incomes policy based on wage restraint would not have much effect on them. On the other hand, a more comprehensive incomes policy including explicit decisions about agricultural pricing, limited to the effectively nontraded commodities, could in principle alter their price trend.

The third kind of market behavior considered here is that of manufactures. Aukrust puts all manufacturing in the traded-goods category: Prices of manufactured goods are considered to be determined by external markets and not by domestic costs. In his model, rising external prices

increase profitability in manufacturing, and this increase in profits generates wage increases as a response. Rising wage claims in the export
sector then lead to a unifying wage reaction in the closed sectors, raising
prices there (subject to offset from productivity increases) as an indirect
consequence of rising prices for traded goods. By this path, external
price movements dominate domestic wage and price changes. "The only
ultimate prices found that explained the movement of prices and wages
in Norway . . . have been world market prices and the exchange rate."[7]

In direct contrast to Aukrust's model, William Nordhaus and John
Shoven have used the Scandinavian approach to analyze inflation in the
United States, but with manufacturing assigned to the sheltered sector,
immune to external prices except through the cost side for traded inputs.[8]
One might react by regarding this difference in treatment as perfectly
natural. After all, why expect the Norwegians to be able to set world
prices for industrial products? But then why expect American firms to
be able to set world prices either? The answer may be that American
firms do not think of themselves as setting, or even meeting, external
prices. They just set domestic prices and export if they can do so at
those prices, or seek protective restraints on imports if foreign firms
undersell them in the home market.

Which version is more nearly right, or what combination of the two
versions best fits the real situation? Do traded manufactures obey the
"law of one price" and match external prices, or are they set on the
basis of domestic costs and then traded, if at all, at such domestically
determined prices?

The most convincing empirical investigations of this question give
more support to the second view than to the first. Research by Irving
Kravis and Robert Lipsey and by Peter Isard, using entirely different
tests, lead them to conclude that prices of manufactured goods of similar
kinds can remain far apart in international trade for prolonged periods.[9]
Assar Lindbeck, drawing on this same evidence, concludes that the
Aukrust model should be modified to drop the idea of strict external
determination of domestic prices for manufactures: The heterogeneous
character of tradable manufactures permits semi-independent trends for
domestic and for imported and exported manufactured goods.[10] For reasons explained below, it seems possible that these studies may have
overstated the degree of independence, but there can be little doubt that
the evidence dispels any idea of close and consistent price unification.

Rudiger Dornbusch and Paul Krugman interpret a recent empirical
study of theirs as showing that in many industrialized countries the prices
of foreign competitors do affect prices charged by domestic producers,

but that this is not the case in the United States.[11] A different kind of test by Mordechai Kreinen, comparing U.S. export and import prices for manufactured goods in 1970 and 1972, before and after the Smithsonian Agreements, suggests much the same picture. U.S. exporters apparently passed on the effects of devaluation fully, selling at reduced export prices in terms of those foreign currencies that had risen relative to the dollar. But foreign sellers in the United States absorbed more than half of the revaluation effect, increasing their dollar prices by less than half of the change in exchange rates.[12] The U.S. firms still acted as if pricing could be independent. They could do so easily in this context because their prices went *down* relative to foreign alternatives. And they may have been constrained to do so because of the price-wage controls in effect at the time. Pressures toward price unification were neither absent nor complete, but the existence of controls may have made them move more in a downward direction than they would have otherwise.

Complete pricing independence is hard to take seriously. It is not readily consistent with profit-seeking behavior. If one assumed that firms were profit maximizing in the first place, then any change in exchange rates would alter external marginal revenue curves (if considered in terms of domestic currency) or marginal cost curves (if considered in terms of foreign exchange). In either version, the readjustment after devaluation would call for reduced prices in terms of foreign currency; in the case of upward-sloping marginal cost curves, it would call for increases in terms of domestic currency. The demonstrations of independent pricing cited above might perhaps be considered as evidence of delayed reactions, rather than as proof of anything resembling complete independence. The question may be one of adjustment speed rather than any ultimate lack of connection between prices of competing producers. The point comes out particularly well if Peter Isard's statistical tests of price behavior are examined for questions of lags.

One of the most informative measures used by Isard is a comparison of changes in German export prices expressed in dollars, at actual exchange rates, to U.S. wholesale prices for nine comparable categories of industrial products. He tracked German and American price changes for a series of subperiods from January 1968 to December 1975 and concluded that they diverge "in a manner that is strongly correlated with exchange rate movements."[13] This conclusion points to definite independence of national pricing, but if the series are considered in more detail the picture is more complex.

For the whole period of the test, four of the nine series show increases in the ratio of German to U.S. prices that are well under half of the increase in the dollar price of the German mark. These are the measures for industrial chemicals, agricultural chemicals, plastic materials, and paper products. A fifth series, that for glass products, shows a movement almost exactly one-half as strong as the exchange rate. Only four groups show anything like complete pricing independence: apparel, home electronics, electric industrial equipment, and metal-working machinery. These are categories in which product differentiation is highly marked. The others are not, and their prices could not stay apart indefinitely. As Isard expressed it, these latter groups "parallel exchange rates fairly closely for the first half of the sample period and then fall sharply during the second half."[14] This suggests an understandable picture of pricing originally formulated in terms of domestic costs, then gradually forced toward recognition of external prices. It is consistent with an underlying interpretation somewhat different from that presented by Isard: that the United States, and perhaps Germany to a lesser degree, have long had relatively independent national patterns of price formation for industrial products, but are being pulled out of this insular tendency by the force of variable exchange rates and increasing interaction in world markets.

A similar interpretation in terms of long-delayed, but still operative, pressures toward price unification may fit some of the early postwar efforts to achieve price stabilization by independent national wage and price policies. Anne Romanis Braun concludes that the relatively successful case of wage and price restraint in the Netherlands from 1947 to 1953, under conditions of fixed exchange rates, worked well because manufacturers did not match foreign prices but stayed under them with prices based on local costs.[15] But, again, forces of market unification won in the end: The very success of the export sector undercut continuing acceptance of wage restraint, and the system broke down as wages moved up to occupy the room opened by prior restraint. Aukrust's vision of wage determination by external prices was, after very considerable delay, finally vindicated.

Braun suggests that something like the same process of long-term underpricing and export expansion applies to postwar Germany, because of an initially undervalued currency held down for many years, and to Japan. In both these cases, strong export performance that might have spilled over into rising domestic prices was counteracted by deflationary monetary and fiscal policy, which permitted the export sector to continue growing at the cost of severe restraint on the closed sectors of the economy.[16] Prices of exports were not unified in world markets, and the consequence was that the open sectors of these economies grew rapidly, while the economies with the higher priced manufacturing exports were

changed by a shift of resources from the open to the closed sectors. On
both sides of the long-sustained disequilibrium, pressures grew progressively stronger to seek a new balance through changing exchange rates.
The imbalances destroyed the Bretton Woods system.

Suggested Interpretation with Respect to Independence of Prices

The preceding arguments and evidence cast doubt on both the idea of
highly unified world markets, which could make incomes policy pointless,
and the opposite idea of such a high degree of national price independence
as to make external impacts of little significance. It should be noted that
the question as considered so far does not refer to insulation through
variable exchange rates; it is directed instead to the possibility of differing
domestic and external prices at given exchange rates and thus includes
the possibility of separate national incomes policies even under fixed
rates.

Of the two polar interpretations, the idea of highly unified world
markets is probably the more unrealistic because major sectors of the
economy, including construction and most services, are hardly involved
at all in international markets and because most industrial pricing seems
to be primarily determined by domestic costs and market conditions, at
least for any short- or medium-run period. Both of these considerations
make it likely that increased restraint on money-wage increases could
hold the domestic rate of inflation significantly lower than it would otherwise have been.

The opposite polar interpretation is the less unrealistic, but it heads
for trouble if it ignores the facts that (1) many primary products and
especially industrial raw material prices are determined on world markets
and not by domestic wage costs; (2) some industrial product prices,
especially the more standardized commodities, are pulled strongly toward
prices of external competition in fairly short periods, even though many
or most industrial products are not; (3) for the goods from all sectors that
are pulled toward world prices, the impact on domestic inflation does not
come merely from the side of input costs, but also from the fact that
prices of exports will move up to external levels, regardless of domestic
wage costs; and (4) the whole structure of industrial prices, though based
primarily on costs in a proximate sense, will be driven toward world
prices over time, either by changing the exchange rate (and thereby

shielding the domestic price level) or by upward bursts of domestic costs as export success undermines wage restraint.

THE INSULATING PROPERTIES OF A VARIABLE EXCHANGE RATE

An alternative way to explain the possibility of an independent national incomes policy is the argument that for a country able to keep domestic costs from rising as rapidly as external inflation, it is always possible to offset the effects of external price increases by a corresponding appreciation of the currency. If domestic costs were stable and external prices were uniformly rising at any given rate, appreciation of the currency at exactly this rate would in principle remove any domestic impact from the external inflation. So why worry about pricing behavior of firms or anything other than wage restraint?

Two questions that cast serious doubt on the insulating properties of a variable exchange rate are (1) the likelihood of nonuniform changes in external prices and the especially troublesome problem of adverse changes in the terms of trade, and (2) the fact that variable exchange rates do not in any systematic way operate to wipe out price differentials for traded commodities or to keep the current account in balance, because their movements are at all times affected and sometimes dominated by capital flows, expectations of future changes in currency values, and, in general, all the considerations that bear on decisions of asset holders to acquire or sell foreign exchange.

Considering the first question separately, that of nonuniform changes in world market prices, it may be a helpful simplification to assume temporarily that variable exchange rates will function to keep the current account in balance. It may also help to assume that initially the domestic economy is able to ensure a workable incomes policy combining overall monetary balance with stable wage costs. In such conditions, what happens if the terms of trade change adversely, as by an increase in the price of imported oil?

If prices of particular imports rise significantly while export prices are constant in world markets, the first question to be considered is the elasticity of demand for the imports. If demand elasticity is high, total spending on the imports will fall and the currency will begin to appreciate: A variable rate will counteract the effect of the rising import prices. If, on the contrary, demand elasticity is low, as it clearly is at present for oil, total expenditures on imports will rise, and (under present assumptions) the currency will begin to depreciate. Any initial depreciation would then bring into question the combined demand elasticities at home for all imports and abroad for the country's exports, as well as all supply elasticities involved. A shortcut to minimize difficulties might be to fall back on the Marshall-Lerner condition: If the sum of demand elasticities for imports and exports exceeds unity, then the initial depreciation will be reversed. But this formulation runs into some serious conceptual problems.

If incomes policy had in the first place worked well and if the initial monetary balance permitted reasonably full employment prior to the import shock, high elasticity coefficients would generate excess demand and stimulate inflation. The adverse change in the terms of trade would require aggregate monetary deflation to reduce demand to fit the lower level of real income available as a result of the price increase for imports. The Marshall-Lerner clue does not point to the necessary solution. But if demand elasticities were favorable and monetary deflation were used to reduce domestic absorption in order to release the additional exports needed to pay for the increased import bill, would those conditions provide a sufficient solution? Probably not. Reduction of real income per capita in the process would require either increased unemployment or decreased real wages. If an incomes policy were predicated on target levels of increase in real wages, then the target would have to be reduced. If that could be done and everything else in terms of elasticities and aggregate demand management worked properly, then, and only then, could the import shock be handled without inflationary impact.

From a somewhat different angle, the whole concept of applying the Marshall-Lerner condition tends to unravel if prices of traded goods are based partly on world market competition and partly on domestic costs. Going back to the initial step of depreciation as import prices increase, the concept of demand elasticity for exports presumes that export prices are domestically determined. If they are, then export prices expressed in foreign currency decrease as the currency depreciates, and the question of foreign demand elasticity is fully applicable. If, instead, some export prices are set in competitive world markets, then the initial effect of depreciation is not to change the export price, but to change the exporter's income. It should make exporting more profitable and thus stimulate export sales, but the immediate question then is the elasticity of supply response and not the foreign demand elasticity. If the condition for getting the added exports to pay for added imports is that the price of foreign exchange stay higher than it was initially, then traded goods, both exports and imports, will end up with higher domestic prices. To retreat to the starting point, if domestic demand for the imports with higher foreign prices is not elastic, if total expenditures on imports rise, then there would seem to be no escape from the conclusion that the whole domestic price level will be shifted upward by a combination of directly higher input prices and some degree of currency depreciation.

A possible rejoinder to this conclusion is that the initial assumption about exchange rate determination should be corrected: It is not necessary that exchange rate movements be determined by the current account balance. In particular, considering higher prices for oil imports in the United States and a higher import bill for oil, it is possible both that the sellers of the imports will leave their dollar earnings in the country and that other asset holders will expect still worse import problems for other countries and will therefore purchase dollars because they expect appreciation. Higher expenditures on imports may not lead to any depreciation of the currency at all or to any increase in exports.

If capital flows do work out to compensate a current account deficit, as they in fact have for at least some of the periods since oil prices began to rise steeply, one might conclude that insulation has been accomplished, *not* by a variable exchange rate, but instead by the absence of variation in the exchange rate. This could be considered to be a lucky break for the deserving, or it could be considered to be a source of trouble.

A current account deficit offset by increasing foreign claims on the country is not in all respects an ideal solution. It is exactly the kind of trap that has undermined the autonomy of many developing countries unable to restrain borrowing as an alternative to promoting exports. But to devalue deliberately for something as specific as an increase in costs of a specific import, and in this case for an import from countries that cannot be expected to raise their own import spending in response to any lower prices for exports of their customers, does not make a great deal of sense.[17] If the only problem were that of inflationary consequences, it might be preferable to keep on with the stable exchange rate and accept growing external debt. But if increasing external debt and reliance on continued capital inflows are regarded as serious problems in themselves, then the better solution might be to tax the imports and drive up effective domestic demand elasticity for the imports.

To recognize the reality of exchange rate movements in response to factors other than current trade positions and product prices leads to more, rather than fewer, doubts about the insulating properties of variable rates. In the first place, the United States is, as a result of past deficits, in a situation of considerable dollar overhang in the sense that foreign holdings of dollars are so large, and subject in some cases to so much dependence on extramarket political pressure to restrain selling by their holders, that variable rates in the near future may have, for some time to come, a downward bias for the dollar whatever else is going on. In the second place, even if portfolio preferences do not change adversely, changes in the value of the dollar cannot be expected to offset price trends in any systematic way. Exchange rates do not move just because relative price trends begin to differ; they move when dealers in currencies change their convictions about relative values. Unless they are sure that changes in price trends will continue or that intervention may not operate to limit changes in rates, they may not take the decisions that will implement appreciation of the currency. Similarly, firms that use imported inputs that are rising in price, in terms of external currency, may not expect the domestic currency to appreciate and may raise domestic prices on the (temporarily correct) assumption that their costs have effectively risen. If they do, the rate of inflation will rise and the eventual appreciation of the currency will be less. Brian Scarfe, considering particularly Canadian experience with fluctuating rates, concludes that cost-based price increases are very likely to move ahead of currency corrections, with the consequence that "the initial response of the economy to a foreign inflationary shock may well be a phase of inflationary recession." [18] He suggests that an insulation policy would have a better chance to work if the exchange rate were not simply left to float, but rather moved up quickly by monetary intervention based on a firm and announced policy to make the exchange rate move as an insulating technique.

The conclusion is not that variable rates are incapable of providing some insulation, but that they cannot be counted on to do so in all circumstances, and specifically not in the kind of situation that has dominated U.S. problems with imported components of inflation in recent years. They do not ensure the possibility of wholly independent national determination of the rate of domestic inflation. They may easily make it *more* difficult to restrain inflationary spread of import price increases than would be the case under fixed exchange rates.

INCOMES POLICIES IN AN UNTIDY WORLD

This in-between vision of a world of limited independence, in which both the course of domestic wage costs and external impacts can affect the course of inflation, points toward the likelihood of conflicts in many areas of policy. Three such areas selected for consideration here are exchange rate management, reactions to adverse movements of the terms of trade, and the recurrent appeal of export controls as an insulating technique.

Exchange Rate Management

Conflicts in this area are inescapable because of the multiplicity of national objectives. These include, besides concern for inflation, consideration of the use of exchange rates for balance of payments purposes and for employment and also concern, at times, for the very principle of *not* managing the currency but instead leaving the exchange rate up to private market decisions with respect to asset preferences. Three particular possibilities are considered here: a generalized acceleration of external inflation, the emergence of a current account deficit in the balance of payments, and a change in preferences by asset holders leading to a depreciation of the currency not related to the current account balance.

If a combination of monetary, fiscal, and incomes policies were otherwise functioning well and external prices began to rise more rapidly than domestic prices without altering the terms of trade, the normal expectation would be that the currency would appreciate and help insulate the domestic price trend. As suggested above, the process of appreciation might well be too slow to provide the necessary insulation, if dealers in foreign exchange or producers using imported inputs have inelastic expectations about the rate. That situation would call for active management of the rate to supersede current market decisions, not in the sense of contradicting the evolution of relative prices, but in the sense of using monetary policy to lead the system to a new equilibrium with a lower rate of inflation than would otherwise occur.

If an incomes policy were functioning well, but changes in external demand or supply moved the current account of the balance of payments into deficit, then the currency would presumably head downward if not prevented by intervention. In such a situation, it would be surprising if the agencies concerned with restraint of inflation did not exert pressure to stabilize the exchange rate. This is a classic conflict of policy: To depreciate for balance of payments reasons would accelerate inflation, but to keep the currency from depreciating would raise external debt and dependence on foreign lending, add to inflationary pressures in the outside world, and maintain a structure of relative prices favoring more reliance on imports than consistent with ability to pay for them. A sustained external deficit on current account is a terribly high price to pay to protect the domestic price level.

If an otherwise stable situation were upset by depreciation due to changed preferences by asset holders, with the current account in balance, then the question of desirable policy with respect to the exchange rate is much more uncertain. If the problem is essentially one of a shift out of dollar balances into foreign assets, not related to current prices of commodities or changes in interest rate differentials, then stabilization by borrowing to offset this pressure does not have any clear adverse effect on world resource allocation. In this situation the goals of incomes policy would require intervention in exchange markets because the capital movements would otherwise increase the rate of inflation. Too many issues of efficiency in capital markets are involved to warrant any one-sided conclusion that intervention to stabilize the rate is desirable, but at least the case for such stabilization is a good deal stronger than it would be in the presence of a deficit on current account.

Adverse Changes in the Terms of Trade

It is possible that the future will be gentle, but it might be well for any incomes policy to include some way of dealing with the rough kind of experience associated with oil imports in recent years, in which the outside world simultaneously provides a specific direct price rise, an adverse change in the terms of trade, and a strong current account deficit promoting depreciation of the currency. The key element is perhaps less the direct price effect than the reduction of real income per capita.

If an incomes policy has been predicated on restraint of wages, with an accompanying understanding about the implications of this wage restraint for prices, then an upward shock to the price index could easily destroy the system of restraint. Conflicts over distribution of the burden of reduced real income could not possibly be avoided, but they might be easier to deal with if they are foreseen and if real wages are stated in contingent terms. It should not be impossible for all concerned to see the need for adjusting to real-income changes, if they can see the desirability of an incomes policy in the first place.

A conceivable approach would be to specify that such external events would be partially, but not wholly, excluded from any price index used to guide rates of increase for money wages. Any upward adjustment of money wages should be held below the initial cost increase. But that would hardly be acceptable unless there were a basic understanding that external impacts that reduce income per capita would require reduction of all forms of real income, not just wages. The problem is that any measures to block price increases for the firms that incur higher costs because of increased import prices would encourage continued demand for the import-intensive final products. A possible answer to that would be to allow full passthrough of costs and consequent higher prices relative to wages, but to impose higher taxes on nonwage incomes in order to share the necessary adjustment in terms of real income.

Export Controls

Both the period of use of wage-price guideposts in the 1960s and that of direct wage and price controls in the early 1970s led to measures restricting exports. In the earlier period, exports of hides for leather and exports of copper were placed under restrictions. In both cases, the prices of the commodities were reduced in the domestic market and held below world prices.[19] In 1973 and 1974, "export controls on industrial raw materials and agricultural products were widely used as an anti-inflationary tool."[20] The most dramatic case was the temporary restriction placed on exports of soybeans, directly threatening food shortages in other countries. No more powerful way could be devised to tell countries importing from the United States that they cannot rely on supplies in periods of stress.

To agencies concerned with a program to limit inflation, a rise in external demand or a fall in world supplies for a primary commodity produced in the United States is a menace. To respond by limiting exports appears reasonable both in terms of protecting domestic consumers and in terms of avoiding an inflationary shock. Beyond such direct implications, rising world prices for commodity exports may upset the whole framework of an incomes policy by stimulating wage claims. Even if the external price increase turns out to be temporary, the wage-price repercussions inside the United States could create an ongoing higher rate of inflation.

To analyze all the consequences of export controls is a tricky business. On one side, direct price increases and secondary wage repercussions may be forestalled. On the other side, higher export earnings in the absence of the restraints could raise the value of the dollar and thereby reduce the domestic prices of all tradable goods.[21] A period of unusually high prices for one's exports would not seem to be an ideal time to shut off the exports. Though the consequences for inflation might (or might not) be helpful, the other consequences are unambiguously harmful. Such controls weaken incentives for long-run increases in domestic supply, aggravate external inflation, and inflict lower living standards on the rest of the world.

TWO EXTERNAL ASPECTS OF THE CASE FOR INCOMES POLICIES

Staying on the Right Side of World Prices

Variable exchange rates clearly have permitted an increase in the dispersion of national rates of inflation. This does not mean simply that each country is free, with a floating rate, to establish its own pace of inflation unaffected by the others. Instead of leaving national rates of inflation unchanged, the effect of floating is to magnify departures from the average, on both sides.

Countries that are able to constrain the domestic rate of inflation below the world rate are likely to generate a current account surplus if the exchange rate is fixed and to attract accumulation of holdings of their currencies whether the rates are fixed or variable. With variable rates, appreciation is likely to moderate impacts from external price increases. Countries that begin to run rates of inflation above the external average are equally likely to experience continuing depreciation and thus aggravated impact from external price increases. In this sense, variable rates magnify the gains of any independent domestic restraint and magnify the penalties of failure to achieve it. The success of Germany and Switzerland at holding down their rates of inflation is in the first instance a tribute to domestic efforts to do so; however, a degree of success that is only slightly better than average becomes the basis for reinforcing changes in currency values.

The change to variable rates in the 1970s helped get U.S. industry off the hook of its competitive disadvantages of the preceding decade, but the process of moving to a lower value of the dollar surely contributed to the inflationary strains of the 1970s. The chances of restraining inflation in the 1980s are not necessarily better or worse than they would be with fixed rates. If the pace of wage increases stays close to the rate of productivity improvement, flexible rates will be a help. But if the rate of increase of money wages greatly exceeds that of productivity improvements, to a degree leading to a faster increase in domestic prices than the average of world market prices, a variable exchange rate will swing over from a help to a handicap. To those who hold their domestic inflation just slightly below the external rate, many blessings are given. An incomes policy for the United States might well focus on exactly that target. To keep the existing rate of inflation from rising may in itself be a major accomplishment, but to make real headway, the domestic inflation rate has to be keyed to staying close to or below the world rate.

Positive Effects on the Outside World of Incomes Policy in the United States

A successful incomes policy should in the first place limit pressures originating in the United States that raise the world rate of inflation. It should also reduce the need to rely on general macroeconomic deflation and unemployment as restraints on price increases and thereby favor a higher long-term rate of growth in demand for imports. That should help maintain export prices for primary products and foster long-term supply growth for primary products by providing greater market stability for them. To pay for higher rates of growth of imports, the United States would need to raise the long-run rate of growth of its own exports. If this is accomplished, it would exert competitive restraint on prices of goods competing with U.S. exports. The two movements together suggest the likelihood of greater growth in world income, but deteriorating barter terms of trade for the United States. Insofar as increasing productivity within the country outpaced such a deterioration of the terms of trade, real incomes could still keep rising within the country, and at the same time the distribution of income among countries should become less unequal. It is implausible that all this would work out so neatly in practice, but the general picture of external consequences is so favorable that it strongly reinforces the case for making great efforts to develop an incomes policy.

CONCLUSIONS

The answer suggested in this discussion to the question that opens and dominates it is two-sided: It is possible to have an independent incomes policy in the sense of a program that can reduce the domestic component of inflation, but it is not possible to eliminate external impacts and actually control the rate of inflation. Domestic price movements are bound to be affected by world markets. We are all in it together.

The key reference base for an incomes policy should probably be to hold the rate of increase of money-wage costs equal to or below the rate of increase of prices of the main competing industrial nations. If this is done, the current account of the balance of payments should tend to surplus, the currency should appreciate in the long run, and external inflationary shocks should be moderated. If this is not accomplished, the reverse should be expected.

Workers could not honestly be promised that any given degree of wage restraint would imply any given behavior of product prices. Independent national policy cannot ensure any specified trend in real wages. It should certainly allow for the possibility, and current fact, of increasing relative prices for imported commodities for which demand is inelastic. When that combination hits the economy, the terms of trade worsen, the current account is driven toward or into deficit, the currency may depreciate with consequent increases in costs for all industries using both imported and exported inputs, and real income is reduced. That context raises a particularly rough set of policy requirements. Any socially acceptable adjustment process would require that wage and nonwage income share the burden. As always, it is easier to prescribe a reduction of the rate of increase of money wages than to see what can be done about nonwage incomes. Since the correction process should surely allow for increased prices of those goods that use more expensive imported inputs, the solution would seem to need something like selective taxes on nonwage incomes.

The dangers of an incomes policy might be summarized under two counts. One is the pressure it creates to interfere with efficient resource allocation, and the other is the pressure it creates toward insulation of the economy. Past periods of attempted restraint through guideposts and controls have shown that the temptation to restrict exports of primary products can become severe. It is also possible that depreciation of the currency in response to a sustained current account deficit may be blocked by giving priority to protection of the price level.

The United States has no ultimate responsibility for the world as a whole, but reduction of real incomes in other countries to lessen our own rate of inflation would seem to be a violation of the sense of any meaningful incomes policy. The point of such a policy is to lessen the human strains and the economic losses associated with inflation. A more fundamental purpose, not necessarily intended but certainly implied in the approach, is an effort to create a better method of reconciling social conflicts. To step on other countries in the process would violate any such principle.

An open economy implies complex requirements for a workable incomes policy. It also means that the stakes are higher, the effort more worthwhile. It is unrealistic to view the domestic rate of inflation as a purely domestic product, and being unrealistic about things can lead to unnecessary trouble; however, it is possible to take the interactions of domestic and external markets into account without giving up the ball game.

NOTES

1. Michael Parkin, "A 'Monetarist' Analysis of the Generation and Transmission of World Inflation: 1958–71," *American Economic Review*, February 1977: 164–71; Alexander Swoboda, "Monetary Approaches to Worldwide Inflation," in *World-Wide Inflation*, edited by Lawrence Krause and Walter Salant (Washington, D.C.: Brookings, 1977), pp. 9–51.

2. Harold T. Shapiro, "Inflation in the United States," in ibid., pp. 267–94. The point was emphasized by William Nordhaus as a general criticism of the present article, at the Middlebury College conference "New Approaches to an Incomes Policy for the United States," April 1979.

3. Sidney Weintraub, *Capitalism's Inflation and Unemployment Crisis* (Reading, Mass.: Addison-Wesley, 1977), pp. 59–62, quotation from p. 59.

4. Odd Aukrust, "Inflation in the Open Economy: A Norwegian Model," and Lars Calmfors, "Inflation in Sweden," both in Krause and Salant, *World-Wide Inflation*, pp. 107–68 and 493–544; Assar Lindbeck, "Imported and Structural Inflation and Aggregate Demand: The Scandinavian Model Reconstructed," in *Inflation and Employment in Open Economies*, edited by Lindbeck (Amsterdam: North-Holland, 1979), pp. 13–40.

5. Ferdinand E. Banks, *The International Economy: A Modern Approach* (Lexington, Mass.: Heath-Lexington, 1979), pp. 47–81; Gerald Helleiner, "Freedom and Management in Primary Commodity Markets: U.S. Imports from Developing Countries," *World Development*, 1978: 23–30; E. C. Hwa, "Price Determination in Several International Primary Commodity Markets: A Structural Analysis," *Staff Papers*, International Monetary Fund, March 1979, pp. 157–88.

6. Aukrust, "Inflation in the Open Economy," pp. 109–12.

7. Ibid., p. 166.

8. William Nordhaus and John Shoven, "Inflation 1973: The Year of Infamy," *Challenge*, May–June 1974: 14–22.

9. Irving Kravis and Robert Lipsey, "Export Prices and the Transmission of Inflation," *American Economic Review*, February 1977: 155–63; Peter Isard, "How Far Can We Push the Law of One Price?" *American Economic Review*, December 1977: 942–48, and "Exchange-Rate Determination: A Survey of Popular Views and Recent Models," *Princeton Studies in International Finance*, no. 42, 1978.

10. Lindbeck, "Imported and Structural Inflation and Aggregate Demand," pp. 23–25.

11. Rudiger Dornbusch and Paul Krugman, "Flexible Exchange Rates in the Short Run," *Brookings Papers on Economic Activity*, 1976:3, pp. 537–75, especially pp. 566–68.

12. Mordechai Kreinin, "The Effect of Exchange Rate Changes on the Prices and Volumes of Foreign Trade," *Staff Papers*, International Monetary Fund, July 1977, pp. 297–329.

13. Isard, "How Far Can We Push the Law of One Price?" p. 942.

14. Ibid., p. 945.

15. Anne Romanis Braun, "Some Reflections on Incomes Policy and the International Payments System," International Monetary Fund Research Paper, August 1979; John Sheahan, *The Wage Price Guideposts* (Washington, D.C.: Brookings, 1967), pp. 96–103.

16. Braun, "Some Reflections on Incomes Policy," section 3.

17. W.M. Corden, *Inflation, Exchange Rates and Economy* (Chicago: University of Chicago Press, 1977), chapters 7–9.

18. Brian L. Scarfe, *Cycles, Growth and Inflation* (New York: McGraw-Hill, 1977), p. 257. See discussion pp. 247–55 and 272–74, and his "A Model of the Inflation Cycle in a Small Open Economy," *Oxford Economic Papers* 25 (July 1973): 192–203.

19. Sheahan, *The Wage Price Guideposts,* pp. 67–72.

20. Carl Van Duyne, "Are Export Controls Anti-Inflationary?" abstract of article in preparation for the annual meetings of the American Economic Association, Atlanta, December 1979. See also Edward Fried and Philip Tezise, "The United States in the World Economy," in *Setting National Priorities: The Next Ten Years,* edited by Henry Owen and Charles Schultze (Washington, D.C.: Brookings, 1976), pp. 167–226.

21. Van Duyne, "The Macroeconomic Effects of Commodity Market Disruptions in Open Economies," *Journal of International Economics,* forthcoming, 1979.

8 INCOMES POLICY:
The "TIP" of the Iceberg
Samuel Rosenberg

In 1944 John Maynard Keynes, while editor of the *Economic Journal,* wrote the following to an economist who had submitted an overformalistic analysis of the problem of inflation:

> I do not doubt that a serious problem will arise as to how wages are to be restrained when we have a combination of collective bargaining and full employment. But I am not sure how much light the kind of analytical method you apply can throw on this essentially political problem.[1]

While agreeing with Keynes that wage restraint at full employment is essentially a political problem (and with his criticism concerning the overformalization of economics), I would add that wage restraint at less than full employment is also a political problem. It is a more serious political problem, for the benefits of full employment can no longer be presented as an offsetting factor to those who are having their wages restrained. This is one of the policy issues being faced by the Carter administration.

In this context, some have suggested using a tax system as a tool for fostering wage restraint and fighting inflation. Behavior in the "public interest" — that is, wage restraint — would be rewarded, or behavior

175

not in the "public interest" — that is, excessive wage increases — would be penalized, or both. These new proposals are being discussed at a time when previously feasible policy options have failed to solve the problem of simultaneous inflation and unemployment. Fiscal and monetary policy are limited by the relative unresponsiveness of inflation to decreases in aggregate demand. Wage and price controls are foresworn by members of the Carter administration, at least for now, on the basis that they limit allocative efficiency and economic freedom.

Any incomes policy, be it tax-based or otherwise, must be discussed in light of the basic characteristics of the American political economy. This paper focuses on the economic problems that a tax-based incomes policy (TIP) is designed to remedy, as well as the political context in which it is likely to be implemented, if implemented at all. A conflict-based theory of inflation is developed. Certain institutional mechanisms for generating inflation are described. With this analysis of inflation as the base, a TIP is treated with emphasis on certain political elements involved in its advocacy at the current time, as well as its likely impact on factor shares and production and distribution at the level of the firm.

CONFLICT AND INFLATION

Understanding and explaining inflation requires that technical economic factors be combined with broad economic, social, and political factors. Inflation is a symptom of a more important underlying dynamic, that being the conflict between various groups in the society over the production and distribution of economic output. The most important actors in American society are workers and capitalists. While this two-class grouping does not capture all participants in the economy — for example, independent artisans are omitted — it can be used to highlight many of the issues surrounding inflation.

The conflict between workers and capitalists over the distribution of income manifests itself in workers' attempting to maintain and increase their wages while capitalists attempt to maintain and increase their returns from profits. However, behind the realm of distribution is the realm of production. Here, too, conflict between workers and capitalists exists. Capitalists hire workers for their ability to labor, but the output to be produced by a given number of workers, with similar technical skills working with similar units of capital, is variable depending on their "diligence." The "diligence" of the work effort is to a large degree based on the relative ability of capitalists and workers to influence the work process. For example, workers' output will depend somewhat on their ability to resist speedups, to punish "rate busters," and so forth. Capitalists will be able to increase output to the degree to which they can gain the loyalty of the workers, or create proper structures of organization, techniques of supervision, incentives, and so forth; or both.[2]

With their growth in size and importance, the various levels of government — federal, state, and local — have also become important arenas for social conflict. Those with limited, if any, access to the private sector, who require government transfer payments, and those unhappy with market outcomes turn to or force governments to intervene in the economy on their behalf.

Conflict in the realm of production between capitalists and workers and conflict over the distribution of income between capitalists, workers, and other social groups are the underlying causes of inflation. Inflation is commonly referred to as "too much money chasing too few goods." Inflation, rather than being characterized as merely a monetary phenomenon, might be better characterized as a situation where too many demands, made with "dollar votes" or political power, are placed on the output of the society.

When demands exceed output, several possible strategies are available to the various levels of government with the actions of the federal government being of prime importance. The particular policies chosen will depend on the relative balance of political power with political power being based on a combination of economic power, votes, and nonelectoral political initiatives. First, an atmosphere of "lowered expectations" can be fostered by those holding political power — for example, President Carter's rhetoric of scarcity — or by influential elements in the media.[3] Second, attempts can be made to delegitimize the demands of some members of the society — for example, welfare recipients. Third, strategies to increase the social product can be tried. Programs designed to increase worker productivity — for example, the "productivity campaigns" of the early 1970s — can be developed to attempt to increase output while having a positive impact on profitability. With less than "full employment," serious "full-employment" policies aimed at the production of socially needed goods and services can be implemented. These have rarely been attempted in our society because of the objections of capitalists and their allies that employment, by strengthening the power of labor, threatens corporate profitability.

If these strategies are not implemented, or if implemented, do not succeed in equating demands and the means to satisfy them, policymakers may choose a policy of inflation. In this case, monetary authorities lubricate the system by providing an increased money supply so that people's demands are met, to some degree at least, in nominal terms — for example, wages received — but not in real terms owing to the resulting inflation. If the inflation required to mediate the situation is relatively low, it serves the purpose of resolving group rivalries and social conflict relatively painlessly. The appearance is given of an impersonal, nonpolitical solution to a problem with both economic and political content. While in certain instances inflation may be functional for social stability, at other times it may lead to serious economic and political problems if high rates persist for extended periods of time.[4]

In this argument, the money supply is considered to be endogenous and not the cause of inflation. Of course, mistakes can be made in monetary or fiscal policy that manifest themselves in inflation. However, in many instances, policies resulting in inflation are said to be "policy errors," when, in reality, they are consciously chosen responses to the underlying conflicts among the populace.

For an understanding of the current inflationary period in our society, this model suggests looking at the extent to which more demands are being made upon the social product relative to the ability to satisfy them. When one is analyzing the demands being made, it is important to determine whether groups previously ignored are making demands or whether previously listened-to groups are making greater demands. When one is analyzing the ability to satisfy demands, it is important to focus on economic growth and various impediments to growth.

Many commentators of varying political tendencies have focused on recent assertions of groups relatively silent in the past. Samuel Huntington, in thinking about the political system, makes the following argument:

> The effective operation of a democratic political system usually requires some measure of apathy and noninvolvement on the part of some individuals and groups. . . . Marginal social groups, as in the case of the blacks, are now becoming full participants in the political system. . . . Less marginality on the part of some groups thus needs to be replaced by more self-restraint on the part of all groups.[5]

Whether blacks are truly becoming full participants in the political process is open to question, and whether his policy prescriptions are desirable is also open to question. However, this passage, from the writings of an eminent political scientist, by focusing on the need for self-restraint, implicitly supports the theory of inflation being developed here.

Similarly, others who have been listened to to some degree in the past have amplified, at least until recently, the nature of their demands. At a conference designed to evaluate wage-price policies from 1945 through 1971, the participants (described by Kermit Gordon as "the most star-studded cast of movers and shakers in economic policymaking ever to be assembled around the same table") discussed changes that had occurred that had made economic stabilization more difficult. They described some of these changes in terms such as "a revolution of rising expectations, an assumption of affluence and a breakdown of the caste system which weakened restraints on the assertiveness of minorities and other depressed social groups."[6]

Another example of the weakening of the inhibitions formerly imposed by the old status order, but not necessarily affecting depressed social groups, concerns public employees. Whereas twenty years ago public employees would have seen themselves as servants of the public and averse to striking, strikes by public employees are now a common occurrence.

In addition, capitalists have been interested in rebuilding rates of return to what they consider to be more satisfactory levels. The expansion induced by the Vietnamese War, coupled with the economic slowdown of 1970–71, resulted in a serious decline in profit rates. For example, the rates of return on nondepreciable assets for nonfinancial corporations fell from 16.3 percent in 1965 to 10.3 percent in 1971.[7]

For expectations to be acted upon and to be responded to somewhat affirmatively, they must be supported by bargaining power of one form or another. While more are making demands, the various conflicting groups have become somewhat more equally matched, at least until recently. Now, the power and influence of the capitalists and other wealthy individuals is on the rise, while that of organized labor and various minority groups and poorer individuals is on the decline.

Economic growth by improving absolute living standards can minimize, to a degree, social tensions arising from questions of distribution. A high level of economic activity may be desirable not only for its own sake, but also because it is a minimal requirement for the maintenance of order. Yet, while needing to grow, the economy has been suffering from stagflation.

A full account of the causes of the current stagflation is beyond the realm of this paper. However, one characteristic of the current period is poor productivity performance. Over the past decade, the rate of growth of productivity has slackened, with the slowdown becoming quite serious beginning in 1974. A study by Denison allocates the bulk of the change in rates of growth of productivity from 1948–1969 to 1973–1976 to an unexplained residual.[8] This change in productivity performance may have its roots in the antagonistic relation between workers and employers inside the firm, an area not analyzed by Denison.[9]

Poor productivity performance makes it more difficult to temporarily remedy problems of distribution and increases the likelihood of inflation. Wage increases lead to unit cost increases that tend to manifest themselves in higher product prices. Thus, conflicts in the sphere of production can exacerbate tensions arising in the sphere of distribution.

Events in the foreign sector can have the same impact, especially given the decline in the ability of the United States to control happenings overseas. For example, in recent years there has been a transfer of real resources from the advanced capitalist world, including the United States, to the oil-producing nations or to elites in those countries. The rise in the cost of oil must be paid for by some subset of individuals in the United States, given that there is no explicit mechanism to allocate the costs equitably throughout the society. If neither workers nor capitalists volunteer to pay the cost, the initial increase in the relative price of an essential resource causes people to attempt to protect their real incomes. This results in some combination of inflation and unemployment, with the unemployment designed to lessen the inflation.

It is impossible to predict the relative increases in inflation and unemployment that develop. The willingness of the public to tolerate unemployment, including the situation when the costs of unemployment fall mainly on politically powerless groups, influences the extent to which inflation, rather than unemployment, occurs. The ability of groups to protect themselves from shifts in the relative prices of essentials also influences the extent to which the rising prices of a specific good gets translated into general inflation. If most (few) workers are able to gain increased wages to compensate for the rise in the price of oil-based products, a severe (weak) price-wage spiral evolves taking a long (short) time to work itself out as firms increase prices in response to increased labor, as well as material, costs.

THE STRUCTURE OF THE ECONOMY

For a better understanding of how inflation can be generated throughout the society, an analysis is needed of the structure of the economy including areas of concentrated power.[10] The industrial structure and the labor market can be pictured as consisting of two sectors each, one being less competitive and the other more competitive.

The industrial structure is composed of an "oligopolistic core" and a "competitive periphery." Firms in the core are generally large, use more capital-intensive technologies, are more likely to be unionized, and earn relatively high profits. Firms in the periphery are generally small, use more labor-intensive production processes, are less likely to be unionized, and earn relatively low profits. Prices in core firms, set by markups over normal costs, are more fixed in the short run than prices in the periphery, set by the usual competitive mechanisms.

The labor market is composed of a *primary* sector and a *secondary* sector. Primary market jobs offer relatively high wages, relatively good working conditions, chances for advancement and equity, and due process in the administration of work rules. Jobs in the secondary market are characterized by low wages, poor working conditions, little chance of advancement, and often arbitrary and capricious supervision. Many jobs in core firms are primary, while secondary jobs predominate in peripheral firms.

Internal labor markets, which are administrative units within which the pricing and allocation of labor are governed by a set of rules and procedures somewhat impervious to market forces, are more likely to characterize firms with primary jobs than are those with mainly secondary jobs. Jobs in the primary market are hierarchically arrayed within a series of internal labor markets. These labor markets have developed both in response to the advantages they yield employers and on the basis of union pressure.[11]

Wages in the secondary labor market are based largely on supply and demand conditions, influenced to a degree by minimum wage legislation and governmental transfer payments. On the other hand, primary market wages, though influenced by market forces, are strongly affected by the relative bargaining strength of workers versus that of employers in cases where unions exist, and by union settlements elsewhere in cases where the work force is unorganized. Market factors, though being distinguished from more institutional ones, such as unions, can influence institutional ones. For example, with extensive unemployment, the bargaining strength of unions declines somewhat because of the ability of employers to recruit strikebreakers, the lesser availability of alternative jobs for strikers, and the greater difficulty of other family members to find employment.

Within firms with primary jobs, wage rates between different jobs along a job ladder cannot be explained by differential skill content, for skill content frequently differs little between successive steps along the ladder.[12] These wage differentials, insulated from the market, are determined, in noncollective bargaining contexts, by employers interested in maintaining discipline among, and long-run work incentives for, their work forces. In this case, issues of "equity" and "fairness" are important, with these being defined by the participants. With collective bargaining, unions influence the particular wage structures that develop.

While wage relations exist within firms, they exist across firms as well. Several possible factors explain this phenomenon. First, in many instances unions will engage in "pattern bargaining" whereby they negotiate with a major firm in an industry and, after settling with that firm, attempt to settle with other firms on similar terms. Second, historical patterns may develop whereby unions try to follow patterns set by each other. For example, from the early 1940s to the late 1960s, wage parity virtually existed between workers in the rubber tire industry and workers in the automobile industry. Third, nonunion employers may attempt to emulate settlements in similar unionized firms in an attempt to forestall the development of a union or to retain the best members of the work force.

Wage contours may also exist between workers in the public sector and workers in private industry. The wages of similar workers in the private sector are important elements of public sector negotiations.[13]

Within the primary labor market, two issues of importance in regard to inflation are wage contours and labor hoarding. While wage contours and pattern bargaining exist, there is no guarantee that historical patterns will continue to be maintained or that the same degree of spillover between the union and nonunion sectors will continue to exist. However, groups of workers successful in protecting their real wage from elements beyond their control — for example, oil price increases — may influence the demands of workers in the same industry, as well as in other industries. While employers in other firms or industries are not obligated to settle on similar terms, the settlements elsewhere can generate added tensions in a given bargaining situation. Wage contours then can serve as mechanisms for transmitting inflation, even if the initial "shock" is unrelated to them.[14]

Labor hoarding is more likely to occur in the primary labor market for secondary sector firms with low profitability, and low-skill jobs have less of an ability and less of a need to hoard labor. This behavior impacts on inflation through its effect on productivity.

Given the inability of specialists to explain recent productivity behavior, an admittedly speculative argument seems both necessary and appropriate. A falloff in the rate of productivity growth can result from many factors, two of which are a failure to reduce the work force by the requisite number (labor hoarding) and a failure of workers to work as "diligently" as workers in the past. These two factors become quite serious when combined with a sharp recession.

For a variety of reasons, in primary market jobs in core firms, labor costs have become less like variable costs and more like quasi-fixed costs. While hiring and training costs may be a partial explanation for labor hoarding and the resultant quasi-fixed nature of labor costs, a more compelling explanation is the desire of employers to have a loyal, stable work force. Many firms have implicit commitments of long-term employment to many of their employees, generally not including lower-level production workers.[15] A loyal, stable work force is beneficial to the employer because of the greater diligence, labor peace, and willingness to accept managerial authority that come along with it. The best way to counter the development of such a work force is to lay off people quickly the moment an economic downturn occurs. In such instances, layoffs occur less frequently than they would otherwise, and the firm incurs substantial losses before resorting to such drastic action.[16]

A second factor of importance concerns workers' attitudes toward work. People have commented that many workers see work less as a means to an end than as an end in itself. This has occurred at a time when the nature of the available jobs has not changed in line with the increased educational attainment of the labor force.[17] Such an attitude leads to questions such as, Is work worth it? Negative answers can lead to such phenomena as the growth of voluntary absenteeism, the taking of sick days when not really sick, the development of "efficiency resistance" (sabotaging the plans of efficiency planners), and "working to rule" when such action significantly slows down the production process. This has generally been an individualistic response to the conflict between workers and employers in the work process. While it seems quite difficult to quantify the importance of these factors in explaining recent productivity behavior, journalistic accounts of the work place suggest that they should not be ignored.[18]

WHY TIP?

The previous section has cursorily described various factors affecting the wage-price-productivity nexus, the central focus of any incomes policy, be it tax-based or otherwise. Given an understanding of certain elements of the environment that a TIP is designed to influence, several questions arise. First, why are TIPs being advanced now, when previously other policies ranging from voluntary guidelines to wage-price controls were attempted? Second, what is the likely impact of a TIP, if implemented? This section focuses on the first question; the next section treats the second.

A TIP and wage-price controls are two mechanisms designed to restrain wages. Though similar in intent, they differ in the relative importance given to the market mechanism as opposed to the political process in attempting to achieve the goal. Proponents of a TIP argue that it will minimize distortions in resource allocation because it interferes with the market to a lesser degree than do wage-price controls. An obvious point, but one that must be made, is the following: Where market imperfections exist, as they do in our society, it is not necessarily true that a more socially desirable allocation of resources will result from policies designed to let the market operate than from those explicitly interfering with the market process.[19]

While explicit arguments for a TIP are partially based on efficiency criteria, implicit in the position of the more politically sophisticated economists is the problem of the maintenance of social stability. Like Samuel Huntington, several policy-oriented economists have argued that too many demands are being made on the government, with a potential result being a loss of authority. According to Charles Schultze, the current chairman of the Council of Economic Advisers:

> The toughest challenge to the political consensus necessary to hold a free society together arises when society itself has to make explicit decisions about the fate of particular groups and communities. . . . As the volume of such decisions grows, the strain upon the political fabric grows at least proportionately.[20]

The social consensus may be threatened as those hurt by policies and those unsatisfied with the benefits they receive strenuously object. Also, people may become more aware of the basic contradictions that exist between major social groups. This may occur because naked political decisions about the distribution of income threaten a fundamental mystique of capitalism, that the fruits of the economic process are rewarded to those who are most productive through the voluntary decisions of individuals mediated by the impersonal workings of the market.

The market operates so as to mask the basic antagonisms, for people have difficulty understanding how the market achieves the results. A TIP, to a greater degree than wage-price controls, will continue to maintain this fundamental mystique of capitalism. By avoiding the necessity of a "social contract" between workers and capitalists, it will preserve, to a degree, the illusion of the existence of an apolitical technical solution to the question of distribution between workers and capitalists. An explicit questioning of the relative size of factor shares and governmental social and economic policy will be less likely to take place than under a social-contract form of incomes policy. A questioning of the relative size of factor shares, as well as a feeling of being unfairly treated by the current policy of voluntary wage-price guidelines, seems to lie behind the call of the leadership of the AFL-CIO for mandatory controls on all forms of income, including profits, interest, and so forth.

THE IMPACT OF A TIP ON BUSINESS AND LABOR

For a TIP to be implemented, a business consensus must exist that inflation must be combated and that restrictive monetary and fiscal policy alone are no longer feasible. Also, labor must be politically weak because TIPs, at least as currently formulated, place the major risk on workers. There is no guarantee that prices will respond in step with a slowdown in the rate of wage increases.

Several indicators point to a politically weak labor movement. Unions have a diminishing influence within the Democratic party, the party more likely to support labor initiatives. Within Congress, legislation important to the labor movement is continually being watered down, if not outright defeated. A most recent example is the labor law reform bill that was defeated by an unprecedentedly broad coalition of business groups.[21] Public opinion is becoming more unfavorable toward unions, especially in light of the public's perception that the actions of unions are one of the chief causes of inflation.

A politically weak labor movement is likely to be one characteristic of the context in which TIP proposals are discussed and possibly implemented. Assuming such a political situation, this section discusses the likely impact of a penalty-employer TIP (in which employers pay a penalty tax if they grant a wage increase in percentage terms over a specified threshold level) on factor shares and production and distribution at the firm level. The timing of a TIP, its nature, and the adjustments made in the incomes policy on the basis of events occurring outside its realm are treated.

The timing is important because a complete analysis of a TIP must include whether a change in a relationship occurred, as well as whether the status quo was maintained. A lack of change in the status quo is not evidence of the lack of impact of a policy if undesirable changes from

the point of view of the policymaker or the politically powerful would
have occurred without the policy.

The wage-price controls of the Nixon administration were designed to
exert downward pressure on wages to attempt to guarantee that they
responded in the "normal" fashion to slack in the labor market.[22] There
was concern in the business community over the potential for excessive
wage increases, especially in light of the effect of the Vietnamese War-
induced inflation on real wages. Pressure from the business community
was one of the important factors that led the Nixon administration to
adopt controls.[23] The Carter administration's voluntary guidelines are
timed to influence the large number of major contracts being bargained
over this year. Some of the major negotiations involve firms and unions
in the trucking, rubber, clothing, food-processing, electrical, and auto
industries.

With this history in mind, it seems that a TIP will be implemented
when business and government feel that wages are either rising at too
quick a pace, however defined, or have the potential for doing so. It is
impossible to conceive of any type of a TIP being implemented because
profits are rising at too fast a rate. Thus, a TIP will have the effect of
either freezing income shares or shifting the distribution of income toward
capital and away from labor. Laurence Seidman speculates on the possibility of a TIP's operating to shift the distribution of income toward
labor, assuming the degree of competition increases in the economy
causing the price markup over unit labor costs to decline.[24]

Such a shift appears unlikely for several reasons. First, with wages
being restrained, there is no guarantee that the price markup over unit
labor costs will remain constant. Firms with market power may fail to
reduce their price increases in line with the decline in wage increases.
Second, even if prices follow wages, they do not do so immediately. The
length of the lag is crucial and some feel it to be substantial.[25] Third, if
the share of capital were to decline, business confidence would deterio-
rate. Capitalists would go "on strike," refusing to invest, and the government would respond by developing policies aimed at coaxing them back
into investing. Such policies would shift the distribution of income back
toward capital. Without a politically strong labor movement, there is little
to limit the government from following policies solely geared to the needs
of private capital accumulation.[26]

However, several volatile sectors — for example, oil and food — seem
to be distorting the economywide relation between prices and unit labor
costs, making it difficult to predict the future behavior of income shares.
Such conditions, if they continue, or other "shocks" that may arise will
make implementation of, and predictions about, a TIP more difficult.

Questions of equity will become more fiercely debated. The crucial issues here are risk and burden. Who will bear the risk of volatile price movements? Who will bear the burden if they do occur? Under a TIP, workers bear the risk of uncontrollable price increases and are likely to bear the burden as well.

While it is possible to conceive of various schemes designed to protect real wages (real-wage insurance), it is impossible to conceive of the real wages of all workers actually being protected. This is so on both economic and political grounds. Real-wage-insurance proposals generally consist of tax rebates given to wage and salary workers if prices rise above a specified target and their wage increases remain below a specified target. The nature of the rebate, as well as the composition of those eligible to receive it, differs among the various proposals. Depending on the rate of inflation and the allowable rate of wage increase, for real wages of all workers to be protected, outlays from the federal budget may significantly worsen the budget deficit or lead to reductions in other elements of the budget. The reductions will be likely to take place in elements of the "social wage" of workers or those unable to work. In such instances, while real wages will be protected, actual living standards will not. A significantly larger budget deficit may worsen inflation, though the actual impact of the deficit on inflation has been exaggerated by political leaders aiming to provide justification for cuts in social spending, as well as to mollify political conservatives.

Carter's real-wage-insurance proposal and the response to it in Congress support the previous predictions concerning risk and burden. First, Carter's proposal for real-wage insurance is capped at 10 percent, with no protection being granted for any inflation above that level. Second, many workers are not covered, including those working in companies with less than fifty workers, many of whom are in low-wage jobs in the secondary labor market. Third, such a proposal, weak as it is, is having extreme difficulty in Congress. While the AFL-CIO has lessened its opposition to this specific proposal and is not against all forms of wage insurance, business seems to be against it. With a weak labor movement, it seems that business feels that any form of wage insurance is unnecessary, even one as weak as the Carter proposal, which in all likelihood will become weaker as time goes on. Also, as the rate of inflation continues to exceed the Carter administration's prediction, it becomes more likely that real-wage insurance, if passed, will worsen the budget deficit. This, together with the recent push for a balanced federal budget, is one more strike against it.

Real-wage insurance could be provided if other sources of tax revenue increase — for example, if corporate tax rates are increased if the wage target is met, but after-tax profits rise above some threshold for the entire corporate sector (or economy as a whole).[27] This is unlikely to occur in the assumed political context. A token increase in the tax rate is likely to occur only if it is needed to maintain the legitimacy of the program in the eyes of the populace.

In addition to speculating on more macrolevel questions, it is important to look at the effect of a TIP at the level of the firm. Focusing merely on the macrolevel issues can hide a differential impact of a TIP on employer-employee relations in different contexts — for example, in the secondary or primary labor market.

The effect of a TIP on firms in the secondary labor market seems relatively straightforward. In a slack labor market, a TIP will be unnecessary. With a relatively tight labor market, a TIP may still be unnecessary if wage increases below the penalty level are feasible for attracting an adequate number of desirable laborers. If problems of retaining workers evolve as workers move to higher wage establishments, a TIP will make the employer more resistant to granting high wage increases and more willing to search for other workers. Hiring and training costs are rather low and labor relatively homogeneous in this sector. Most unions based in the secondary sector are relatively weak, and the threshold level set by a TIP will likely be the ceiling on wage gains under collective bargaining.

It is in the primary labor market where the impact of a TIP is more complicated and more important to analyze. Collective bargaining in the primary labor market will be looked at first, followed by noncollective bargaining situations. While approximately 25 percent of the labor force is organized, the response of unions to a TIP and the effect of a TIP on them will impact on many nonunion workers. Union wages spill over to a degree into the nonunion sector. The publicity given to important negotiations (for example, the Teamsters' negotiations) will influence the attitudes and actions of other workers in regard to a TIP.

The two critical issues are the attitudes of workers toward a TIP and the relative bargaining strength of labor and management prior to and after the institutionalizing of a TIP. This focus on attitudes represents a belief that a maximizing model of collective bargaining is inadequate and should be replaced by a less rigid formulation incorporating notions of reserve power that, for whatever reason, labor, or management, or both have not used in the past.

The attitude of workers will be a function of elements inside and outside the firm. First, a quite important factor will be whether the administration can convince workers that the program is equitable, that everyone is making a sacrifice. If this campaign is successful, expectations of workers will fall and the level of conflict between labor and management will decline, with the success of a TIP likely resulting. Volatile price increases in necessities will be a strong factor working against the success of such an ideological campaign. Second, the attitude of the union leadership and the standing of the leadership will be important. To the degree that the leadership is willing to cooperate and that workers accept the leadership as legitimate, the likelihood of a TIP succeeding with a minimum of labor strife is increased. Third, whereas a TIP mainly tries to affect the distribution of income, recent changes, if any, in the nature of work will influence workers' response and reaction. Capitalists are unsatisfied with the rate of growth of productivity. This is coupled with attempts to limit the ability of health and safety agencies to force improvements in the work place, for they are said to be inflationary and to limit productivity. Management will attempt to improve productivity. The quality of life in the work place will differ depending on which changes are instituted, be they "speedup," elimination of "restrictive" work rules, or introduction of new machinery. Any tensions arising out of this process will feed back on workers' willingness to cooperate with a TIP.

The previous points show that the attitudes of workers toward a TIP may change their exploitation of their bargaining strength by influencing the nature of their demands and the vigor with which they pursue them relative to employers. This is likely to influence wages gained and the length and frequency of strikes. Relative bargaining strength, holding attitudes constant, must also be examined. A penalty TIP is designed to increase the resistance of employers who have acceded too easily to union demands in the past. By implication, it is argued that their market power has allowed them to pass on increased labor costs to consumers through price increases. The tax penalty will increase the costs of "laziness" at the bargaining table.

The effectiveness of this policy will vary depending on the relative bargaining strength of the two parties before its implementation. While on balance it is likely to strengthen employers and result in lower wage increases and increased tension at the work place, a perverse case of its weakening an employer should be mentioned. While most long strikes are won by management, there can be cases where a union has the strength to win one. In such a case, a relatively weak employer, with the help of the threat of a penalty, will hold out longer but will eventually settle on terms similar to the union's demands prior to the strike. Given that the tax penalty is assumed to affect the behavior of management, the final settlement is likely to be above the threshold level, with the company paying a penalty. In this example, the company will be weakened by both the costs of a lengthy strike and a penalty TIP.

The previous situation is likely to be relatively rare. While a TIP will strengthen the employer, the degree to which it will result in lower wage increases will depend on union goals and strategy and the ability of the employer to pass on the tax penalty to the consumers. Assuming that unions hold some reserve power and that workers are interested in their wages relative to those of other workers, as well as the growth rate of their own wages, it is possible that a TIP, rather than resulting in lower wage increases, will yield similar wage increases with greater labor strife and longer and more frequent strikes. This strife will be minimized by the degree to which the tax penalty can actually be passed on. Such passing on is more likely where the lower the price elasticity of demand, oligopolistic industries bargain as a unit with a union, or where there is a known pattern that will exist even though a union bargains individually with each member of the oligopoly. On the other hand, cases will arise when even under these assumptions for workers, lower wage increases occur with increased strife.

Increased attention will be given to productivity issues inside the firm. First, those firms penalized by a TIP and facing that situation because of a strong union rather than an ability to pass on a TIP penalty will need increases in productivity to maintain profitability. Second, those unions hurt by a TIP will desire to improve conditions of work in reaction to their inability to gain higher wages. This increased bargaining over non-wage issues also took place during the Nixon administration's controls period.[28]

This will be increasingly serious now, as there is a productivity crisis and employers will try to gain "givebacks" from unions. Unions may become more militant over work-place issues, and the potential exists for increased numbers of wildcat strikes over working-condition questions. While productivity bargaining can still occur with a TIP, an employer will desire more productivity gains than previously for an equivalent wage increase. This is especially true if a penalty tax must be paid and is likely to be true otherwise if a TIP succeeds in limiting wage increases elsewhere.

The impact of a TIP on nonunion firms will be influenced by events in the union sector to the degree that union wages normally spill over into that sector. The employer will need to balance wage patterns with the cost of paying a penalty tax if necessary. The initial reasons for the pattern, as well as for the ability of the union to gain wages above the threshold, will determine the extent to which a pattern is broken. If high wages were granted to the union because of a need to attract workers, then the same forces will likely cause the nonunion firm to maintain the pattern, assuming the firm competes for similar labor. If high wages were granted to the union more on the basis of union power, then the pattern may be broken, depending on the extent of the tax penalty, the ability to pass it on, the fear of unionization, and worker morale. It is likely that some patterns between union and nonunion firms will be broken.

Patterns between unions may also be affected. In cases where a particular union has settled for above a threshold wage increase, other unions will likely need to exert more effort to force employers to respond to their wishes. The degree of strife or discontent that will develop can be gauged by studies of previous instances where similar patterns have been broken.

Within firms, wage relations within the internal labor market and between union and nonunion employees may have to be reevaluated. This will be a problem to the degree that the economically more powerful employees are able to maintain their pattern of wage increases while those less powerful receive less as the employer tries to avoid a penalty tax. Morale problems are likely to develop, especially if the expected pattern of wage increase as a worker moves up the hierarchy within the internal labor market is significantly affected.

In all these cases, it is impossible to specify the exact probability of any of the conditions developing. The basic point has been to show the differential impact of a TIP on different workers, as well as the potential for increased strife between labor and management. In short, those with strong bargaining power are more likely to continue to do well. Those with limited bargaining power are more likely to bear the brunt of the struggle against inflation. The condition of the latter group will improve to the degree that lower rates of unemployment actually result from the implementation of a TIP.

CONCLUSIONS

Restrictive monetary and fiscal policy, tax-based incomes policy, and wage-price controls are three mechanicsms designed to fight inflation. One of the reasons business interests prefer the use of restrictive demand management to the other policy options is that, although amounting to an attack on labor's strength, it is not recognized as such by most people. The resulting wage restraint is perceived as occurring because of the

forces of "supply and demand," rather than because of conscious government intervention in the conflict over the distribution of income.

Yet at the current time, an anti-inflationary policy based merely on
restrictive monetary policy with some cuts in public expenditure would
only have a chance for success if unemployment were to increase to
extremely high levels. While monetarists and search theorists would
proclaim the value of unemployment to the unemployed (value of leisure
time, voluntary searching for other jobs, and so forth), social conflict
might develop instead.

Given the inability of Keynesian "fine-tuning" to operate as its proponents hoped and the likely failure of monetarist policies because of
inflationary biases in the economy, an incomes policy of one form or
another seems probable. Currently, voluntary wage and price guidelines
are being tried. While employers "wrap themselves in the flag" and
patriotically enforce the wage guidelines, prices continue their upward
movement. If prices continue to behave in such a manner in the near
future, it is only a matter of time before guideline-busting (or "guideline-
redefining") wage settlements occur or tense strikes result in the face of
employer resistance.

These guidelines are likely to fail to stop the inflationary spiral. In this
context, TIP proponents have become more vocal, claiming that the use
of the tax system is all that is needed to solve the conflict between
workers and capitalists over the distribution of income. I am skeptical
that mere technocratic tinkering can solve what is essentially a political
problem. Also, the particular nature of any incomes policy that is created
will depend on the relative political power of different groups in the
society. At the present time, labor and its allies are extremely weak,
while corporate interests are on the upswing. Those economists who will
be listened to on the issue of the need for an incomes policy and the type
of incomes policy to be created will be those whose ideas depart little
from the preconceptions and interests of those being advised. That is
why a TIP, if implemented now, is likely to operate so as to be biased
against workers relative to capitalists.

Given that this is a policy-oriented conference, I can be criticized for
not presenting an alternative policy to remedy American capitalism.
Rather than concluding with a package of suggested policies, logically
consistent but politically infeasible at the current time, I will end, as I
began, with a quote from Keynes. Keynes, in discussing international
capitalism, said, "It is not intelligent, it is not beautiful, it is not just, it
is not virtuous — and it doesn't deliver the goods." [29] Given such a
condition, more extensive changes are needed than mere tinkering with

the tax system to truly remedy the social and economic problems in our society.

NOTES

1. Richard Kahn, "Some Aspects of the Development of Keynes's Thought," *Journal of Economic Literature* 16 (June 1978):557.

2. For a more extensive discussion of the worker-capitalist relation in the process of production, see Richard Edwards, *Contested Terrain: The Transformation of the Workplace in the Twentieth Century* (New York: Basic Books, 1979).

3. For an example of the rhetoric of scarcity, see President Carter's statement accompanying his proposed budget for the current fiscal year. He said: "In formulating this budget I have been made acutely aware once more of overwhelming demands upon the budget and of the finite nature of our resources." *New York Times,* January 24, 1978, p. 24.

4. Inflation may increase uncertainty, making long-range planning more difficult. It may increase speculation, a generally unproductive activity with potentially destabilizing effects. Social conflict may worsen, for virtually everyone, feeling cheated by inflation, will strive to make up their losses by increasing their demands.

5. Michael J. Crozier, Samuel P. Huntington, and Joji Watanuki, *The Crisis of Democracy: Report on the Governability of Democracy to the Trilateral Commission* (New York: New York University Press, 1975), p. 113.

6. Craufurd D. Goodwin, ed., *Exhortation and Controls: The Search for a Wage-Price Policy, 1945–71* (Washington, D.C.: Brookings, 1975), pp. 385, 387.

7. *Economic Report of the President* (Washington, D.C.: U.S. Gov't. Printing Office, 1979), p. 128.

8. Edward F. Denison, "The Puzzling Drop in Productivity," *Brookings Bulletin* (Fall 1978):12.

9. Some suggestive evidence concerns the coverage given by recent journalistic accounts of labor-management relations to the demands of management for "givebacks" from labor in the work process designed to improve productivity.

10. In a maximizing framework, increases in monopoly power or changes in the strategies of those who have this power are needed for monopoly power to cause inflation. However, the extent and location of concentrated economic power influences the degree to which inflationary impulses are transmitted throughout the society.

11. There are many different explanations in the literature for the development of internal labor markets. They range from those emphasizing job-specific training to those emphasizing the use by employers of internal labor markets to stifle the development of class consciousness among their workers. For an example of the explanation based on training, see Peter B. Doeringer and Michael J. Piore, *Internal Labor Markets and Manpower Analysis* (Lexington, Mass.: D.C. Heath, 1971), chapter 2. For an explanation based on class-consciousness considerations, see Katherine Stone, "The Origins of Job Structures in the Steel Industry," *Review of Radical Political Economics* 6 (Summer 1974):61–97.

12. C.R. Livernash, "The Internal Wage Structure," in *New Concepts in Wage Determination,* edited by G.W. Taylor and F.C. Pierson (New York: McGraw-Hill, 1957), p. 140.

13. Public sector workers are being ignored in this paper, for recent wage settlements in the public sector have been relatively low and the "urban fiscal crisis" and "taxpayer revolt" have created an extremely unfavorable bargaining atmosphere for these workers.

14. Economists disagree on the empirical importance of wage interdependence and historical wage relationships. Eatwell, Llewellyn, and Tarling, in a study of twenty industries in fifteen countries, including the United States, from 1958 to 1967, find that the average interindustry dispersion of labor productivity increases was quite large. Also wage increases in each country were highly correlated with those that occurred in the three industries in which labor productivity was rising the fastest. John Eatwell, John Llewellyn and Roger Tarling, "Money Wage Inflation in Industrial Countries," *Review of Economic Studies* 41 (October 1974):515–23. On the other hand, Flanagan, in a study of American wage setting from 1959 to 1975, argues against the importance of wage interdependence. Robert J. Flanagan, "Wage Interdependence in Unionized Labor Markets," *Brookings Papers on Economic Activity,* 1976:3, pp. 635–73.

15. In many instances, lower-level production employees are laid off on the basis of seniority with some rights of recall based on accumulated seniority. Thus, they maintain a stable relationship of sorts with the firm.

16. For a more extensive discussion of this point, see Edwards, *Contested Terrain,* pp. 157–59.

17. Julius S. Brown, "How Many Workers Enjoy Discretion on the Job?" *Industrial Relations* 14 (May 1975):196–202.

18. For an elaboration on changing attitudes toward work, see Richard Sennett, "The Bosses' New Clothes," *New York Review of Books,* February 22, 1979, pp. 42–46. At the same time as I was writing this section, the *Wall Street Journal* had a series of articles dealing with the issues of worker absenteeism and productivity growth in which similar points were made concerning negative attitudes toward work. *Wall Street Journal,* March 13, 1979, pp. 1, 16; March 14, 1979, pp. 1, 33. For an article skeptical of these sorts of journalistic accounts, see Robert J. Flanagan, George Strauss, and Lloyd Ulman, "Worker Discontent and Workplace Behavior," *Industrial Relations* 13 (May 1974):101–23. Their conclusion concerning the ability of conventional economic variables, such as unemployment and the demographic composition of the work force, to explain productivity change is contradicted by studies, such as Denison's, of more recent productivity trends.

19. The theory of the second best, the basis for this assertion, is presented in R. G. Lipsey and K. Lancaster, "The General Theory of Second Best," *Review of Economic Studies* 24:11–32.

20. Charles L. Schultze, *The Public Use of Private Interest* (Washington, D.C.: Brookings, 1977), p. 75.

21. A very interesting discussion of the development of the broad coalition of business groups can be found in Thomas Ferguson and Joel Rogers, "Labor Law Reform and Its Enemies," *Nation,* January 6–13, pp. 1, 17–20.

22. Arnold R. Weber and Daniel J.B. Mitchell, *The Pay Board's Progress: Wage Controls in Phase II* (Washington, D.C.: Brookings, 1978), p. 139.

23. Ibid., p. 263.

24. Laurence Seidman, "Tax-Based Incomes Policies," *Brookings Papers on Economic Activity,* 1978:2, p. 336.

25. For an interesting discussion of these two issues, see the paper by Thomas Mayer in this volume.

26. There are certain circumstances in which this weapon of business can lose most of its effectiveness. For a discussion of these conditions, unlikely to occur in the American

political economy in the relatively near future, see Fred Block, "Cooperation and Conflict in the Capitalist World Economy," *Marxist Perspectives* 2 (Spring 1979):88.

27. Lawrence Klein and Vijaya Duggal make such a proposal. Seidman discusses it in Seidman, "Tax-Based Incomes Policies," p. 340.

28. Arnold R. Weber and Daniel J.B. Mitchell, "Further Reflections on Wage Controls: Comment," *Industrial and Labor Relations Review* 31 (January 1978):153.

29. John Maynard Keynes, "National Self-Sufficiency," *Yale Review* 22 (Summer 1933):760.

9 INNOVATIVE INCOMES POLICIES:
A Skeptic's View
Thomas Mayer

The substantial inflation we have experienced for more than ten years now has been remarkably stubborn. This may suggest that it is not just the result of a temporary lapse in macropolicy or of OPEC's misbehavior, but that it is the payoff of following employment-oriented policies rather than price level–oriented policies. Once the public realizes that the government will try to keep recessions short, it responds to falling demand, not by reducing prices, but by reducing output.[1] Since the public knows better than to trust the government's statements about what it will do and learns only by experience, a mere announcement that the government will now no longer tolerate inflation would not suffice, and it would take a long and severe recession to bring the inflation rate down substantially by monetary and fiscal policies. Hence, it is not surprising that incomes policies have been advocated. But traditional incomes policies have compiled a sorry record both in the United States and in foreign countries, so that there is much to be said for trying to develop new kinds. This is

The author is indebted for helpful comments to Martin Bronfenbrenner, Robert Hetzel, Charles Lieberman, Frederick Mishkin, Boris Pesek, and Steven Sheffrin.

197

so regardless of whether one believes that the causes of inflation are to be found in "demand-pull" or in "cost-push." Even if an inflation is due entirely to demand-pull, it could take a great deal of unemployment to eliminate it by demand management if firms and labor expect that aggregate demand will soon become excessive again.

I will, therefore, discuss only the effectiveness and costs of incomes policies and not the quite different issue of what caused our present inflation. Since specific incomes policies have different costs and chances of success, I will discuss three specific ones: the TIP tax-based incomes policy plan of imposing a special tax on corporations that grant excessive wage increases, the Lerner plan of requiring firms to purchase permits from other firms if they want to raise wages by more than the norm, and Arthur Okun's wage-insurance plan.

THE TIP PLAN

The TIP plan as proposed by Henry Wallich, Sidney Weintraub, and Laurence Seidman would impose a higher corporate income tax rate on those corporations that grant wage increases above a certain norm.[2] The additional revenue thus obtained would be offset by cutting some other tax, perhaps the standard corporate income tax rate, so that total tax collections would be approximately constant.

This TIP plan has three important advantages over outright wage controls. First, it allows the market mechanism to operate since a firm willing to pay the extra tax *can* raise wages by more than the norm. However, this advantage is only a matter of degree. TIP, like outright controls, would create distortions because it would create an additional wedge between the marginal productivity of labor and the wage rate. For example, an industry with an excess demand for labor may be unwilling to pay the penalty of exceeding the wage norm and hence may attract less labor away from other industries than it would in the absence of TIP. Similarly, assume that the marginal productivity of labor is rising equally in two firms. One of them is a firm with large profits and the other a firm with very low profits. Under a TIP system the first firm might be unwilling to raise wages above the norm because to do so would cost it a large amount of after-tax profits, while the second firm would be more willing to raise wages. Labor might then move from the first firm to the second firm. Thus, TIP, like outright wage controls, would cause distortions, and while these distortions would be less than those of outright controls, it is far from clear just how much less they would be.

A second way in which TIP is superior to outright wage controls is one that its proponents have not raised but that seems important: Outright wage controls tend to collapse after some time. A powerful union in a strategic position — for example, the coal miners in Britain — can break the controls system by striking until they receive a higher settlement, and that is the end of wage control. Under TIP, this situation is less likely because the employers could settle with the union. Admittedly, the difference between TIP and outright controls is a matter of degree because it is *possible* that firms would refuse to settle a strike until the government promises to exempt them from the TIP penalty. While it is, of course, something one can just conjecture about, it seems to me that TIP would be more robust in this way than straightforward wage controls, in part because corporations having to pay higher taxes are less likely to generate as much public sympathy as workers demanding higher wages.

Another advantage of TIP is that since it strikes directly at profits, it has a bigger chance of being enacted than does outright control of wages in the absence of price controls. And price control does much more damage than wage control because product markets respond more to prices than do labor markets in which quantity adjustments seem more important.

But the fact that TIP is superior to outright wage controls is not sufficient condition for supporting it. One has to consider the costs and benefits of TIP compared to those of a free labor market. The benefit of TIP is, of course, that it would lower the rate of wage increases.[3] But this is a benefit only if it also reduces the rate of price increases, and it is not clear that it would do so over a horizon of *several years*. Obviously, the reduction in the rate of wage increases would work to reduce the inflation rate, but there is the danger of an offsetting effect: Firms might pass the penalty forward in higher prices.

WOULD A TIP PENALTY BE PASSED FORWARD?

Some economists have mentioned the possibility that a TIP penalty tax might be passed forward in higher prices.[4] How likely is this? Consider a firm in a typical labor market — that is, a nonunionized one. Assume that this firm uses marginal cost pricing and that it faces an upward-sloping curve of labor so that to produce more, it has to raise wages.

The higher wage rate — and any TIP penalty it incurs — is then part of its marginal cost. Thus, in this situation, by raising marginal costs, TIP would raise prices.

Arthur Okun [12], after stating this point, rejects it. His argument is that unorganized firms pay higher wages, not primarily to obtain sufficient labor, but to maintain the morale of their work force. But this argument is questionable. First, where is the empirical evidence that this is indeed the case? Second, and more fundamentally, one should ask why firms care about the morale of the work force. The obvious answer is that high morale raises production. But if so, then a TIP penalty and all other costs of raising wages are still part of marginal costs. If a firm has to raise wages by, say, 10 percent to raise output, then this wage increase is part of its marginal cost, regardless of whether it is needed to raise the quantity or the quality of the work force. Only if the firm is concerned with morale and wage equity for some other reason than the effect on its output does any TIP penalty not enter its marginal costs and hence its price.

The story is very different if the firm faces a strong union and has a choice between either granting a certain wage increase and paying any TIP penalty this involves or not producing at all. In this case, once the firm decides to produce at all, it has to pay the TIP penalty, so that this penalty then is part of its fixed costs, rather than its marginal costs.

So far I have assumed that firms set prices on the basis of marginal costs and marginal revenues. It is not clear how applicable this marginal cost model is. To what extent is the widely observed markup pricing just a rule of thumb approximation that in the longer run yields similar results to marginal cost pricing? So instead of assuming marginal cost pricing, assume that firms typically set prices by adding to their direct costs a fixed markup that is arbitrary from the point of view of marginal cost pricing. The question then becomes whether firms would treat a TIP penalty as part of their direct costs or whether they would perhaps adjust their markups for it. Unfortunately, the information needed to answer this question does not seem to be available. To be sure, at present, accountants measure labor costs without any allowance for taxes other than payroll taxes, but this might change under TIP since TIP, by raising the indirect cost of labor, would give firms an incentive to change their way of measuring labor costs.

Wallich and Weintraub [20] have argued that a TIP penalty could not be passed on because it would cost different firms different amounts depending on their profitability. But in industries with strong price leadership, the dominant firm might simply set price high enough to cover the expected TIP penalty for the substantial majority of firms. This *might* result in more than 100 percent of TIP being passed on.

Laurence Seidman [17] has also suggested that even if a TIP penalty is passed on, the inflation rate would rise only temporarily and would decline subsequently.[5] If the penalty is passed on, it raises the price level only once and for all at that particular time, while, on the other hand, the moderation of wage pressures that result from TIP helps to hold down the inflation rate year after year; hence, eventually the price level is lower with TIP than without it. But if the initial rise in prices enters subsequent wage bargains (and monetary policy is accommodative), it may take a long time before the anti-inflationary effect of TIP outweighs its inflationary effect. Would Congress be willing to keep TIP this long?

Another factor that contributes to the uncertain effect of TIP on prices is that the revenue gained from the TIP penalty would be offset by a cut in some other tax. If the adoption of TIP results in a cut in payroll taxes, then the net tax passthrough into higher prices would probably be reduced since a payroll tax is more likely than a TIP tax to be passed on in higher prices. But if the TIP penalty is offset by lowering the standard rate of the corporate income tax, then the answer is less clear. It depends on the extent to which the corporate income tax is currently passed on in higher prices. If the corporate income tax does not in large part enter prices, imposing a TIP penalty and lowering the corporate income tax correspondingly could well raise the inflation rate temporarily. On the other hand, if the corporate income *is* passed on into higher prices, then TIP, coupled with a lowering of the corporate tax rate, could reduce the inflation rate. But in another way, a situation in which the corporate income tax is passed forward is not favorable for TIP because it suggests that a TIP penalty would be passed forward too. Hence, if TIP is instituted and the revenue gain offset by cutting some tax that is not passed forward, then the net effect of the tax change itself could be to raise prices, and this would offset at least some of the effect of curbing wage increases.[6]

The upshot of all of this is that we cannot be certain what a TIP penalty would do to prices over a period of several years; in general, we know little about the effect of taxes on the supply side. My guess — but it is no more than a guess — is that TIP, whatever its other faults, would tend to lower the inflation rate at least somewhat. But should we economists go before Congress and advocate an anti-inflation policy that *might* for several years raise, rather than lower, the inflation rate? As a practical matter, the only way we might possibly convince Congress to impose TIP would be if we declare that we are certain — or almost certain — that TIP would lower, rather than raise, prices; and I for one would feel most uncomfortable doing so.

THE COSTS OF TIP

Any benefits that TIP could provide in curbing inflation would come at considerable cost. Having already discussed the misallocation of resources that TIP would generate, I will now take up five additional costs. All but the first of these apply to virtually any incomes policy. They are the potential reduction in labor's share; the politicizing of the income distribution; the danger that monetary and fiscal policies would become too expansionary; the creation of compliance costs, enforcement costs, and loopholes; and the problems created by incomplete coverage. Obviously, the importance of these problems, particularly the compliance and loopholes problems, depends in large part upon how long TIP would be in effect. A very short-term TIP would not have such large costs.

First, there is the danger that TIP could lower labor's share of national income, though its proponents reject this possibility. Wallich and Weintraub argue that "the average markup of prices over unit labor costs has been remarkably constant. . . . Of all time series in economics that of k, the average markup is most nearly constant, in the short run and the long run. Annual fluctuations rarely exceed one or two index points. We can rely on k to remain firm."[7] But is the markup really so constant? In the short run this does not seem to be the case. Robert Gordon has found that

> price change responds to wage change with a substantial lag. The short-run impact of a wage deceleration would be to limit labor's share of the income distribution. The wage deceleration of the early 1960's in response to slack labor markets, together with wage guidelines, helps to explain why the share of profits in gross national product was so high in 1964 and 1965. And the British experience with voluntary incomes policy in the past few years has indicated that prices follow wages with a lag sufficiently long to cause a squeeze on labor's share that lasts for a year or more.[8]

Similarly, Albert Reese concluded that

> the view that price inflation merely mirrors wage inflation has been somewhat shaken by the events of recent years. From 1973 to 1974 the consumer price index rose by 11.0 percent, while average hourly earnings in private non-agricultural industry rose only 8.2 percent, producing a decline of 2.5 percent in real hourly earnings. Although the events of 1974 were highly unusual, the labor movement certainly cannot be blamed for wanting insurance against their repetition.[9]

In addition, even if the share of labor in national income is constant on the level of individual firm, profits would *in some cases* rise substantially if wages are held down, and this would generate opposition to TIP.[10]

More fundamentally, any historical evidence that the average markup is constant comes from data generated over a period when we did not control wages and let prices change freely. As we know from the work of Robert Lucas, evidence that a particular parameter has a particular value under one policy regime does not necessarily tell us that it will be the same under a different policy regime [10]. Specifically, why has the average markup been so stable in the past? One possibility is that in the past whenever prices rose, wage responded fairly soon so that the old markup was quickly reestablished. If we now limit the rise in wages, this old relationship will no longer hold and markups will rise. Another possibility is that in the past when demand increased, firms did not raise prices until wages rose too, since this would make it easier for them to coordinate prices. But if firms now believe that wages will not rise, will they forego the price increase or will they raise prices in any case despite the greater difficulty of coordinating them? To illustrate this point, assume that wages are strictly controlled and that aggregate demand is raised sufficiently so that firms can sell all their potential output and still have many unsatisfied customers. Would they really keep prices down and markups constant in the longer run?

The obvious answer to this question suggests that one cannot rely on markups remaining constant regardless of what happens to aggregate demand. Rather, to keep them constant, aggregate demand would have to be held down sufficiently to reduce the temptation to raise prices and markups. It is to the credit of Henry Wallich, Sidney Weintraub, and Laurence Seidman that they have recognized that TIP is complementary to, and not a substitute for, appropriate monetary and fiscal policies. This means that it would not be feasible to hold down by a TIP tax the inflationary consequences of trying to reduce the unemployment rate to, say, 4 percent. If this were tried, markups would rise substantially, and the political response would be to impose price controls. It is, therefore, far from clear that TIP can be used over the longer run to lower the natural rate of unemployment substantially, as Seidman has suggested [16], though it might help a bit. How much it can help depends on how markups respond to continually strong markets, and this is hard to say.

The second cost of TIP is that it would further politicize the income distribution. TIP may give employees the idea that the government is on the side of the corporations and that corporations will use their power over the government to impose various devices to hold down wages and raise markups.[11] This may help spread the idea that a better way to raise one's income than relying on the rewards generated by the market is to gain power and influence over the government. This in turn *may* result in a serious threat to liberal democracy. One can well argue that a major reason why people are willing to play the game by democratic rules and not try to win elections by various dirty tricks, of which the devices used by the Nixon administration are just a mild harbinger, is that it does not really matter all that much who runs the government. But once a substantial proportion of the public believes that losing control over the government will reduce its income substantially, it may not be willing to yield power gracefully. I am not saying that giving the government substantial power over the distribution of income would *necessarily* destroy democracy and freedom, but it might happen, and in view of the great loss this would entail, it is not a danger to be dismissed lightly.

Another, less dramatic danger from politicizing the income distribution is that by making the government a more valuable prize, it would increase the amount various groups spend to gain control over it, and these expenditures are largely a waste from the national viewpoint. Moreover, since crude direct methods of redistributing income lack political appeal, governments often redistribute incomes in hidden ways that, being indirect, have a large resource cost. A prime example here is agricultural price supports.

To be sure, the income distribution is already to some extent politicized, and control over the government does generate economic benefits even without TIP; however, TIP would make this problem worse.

A third problem with TIP is that its imposition could easily lead to more expansionary monetary and fiscal policies. Again, it is hard to evaluate the likelihood of this danger, but it could readily result in TIP's, in this indirect way, causing a major rise in the inflation role. It seems that something like this happened during the Korean War when one of the arguments used in favor of a highly expansionary monetary policy was that we could rely on our system of price controls to hold down inflation. This might well turn out to be the main disadvantage of TIP.

A fourth cost of TIP consists of adding to our tax system another tax with substantial loopholes and high enforcement and compliance costs. Since these problems have been discussed in much detail by two Treasury experts [4], I will only mention them briefly. One set of these problems relates to the initiation of TIP. How should corporations locked into long-term wage contracts be treated? Would they have to pay TIP on the basis of agreements made before it was enacted? This seems unfair, particularly if the corporation is not given the right to reopen the contract. On the other hand, to exclude wage increases already set in long-term contracts would be unfair to those corporations and unions that signed shorter-term contracts.[12] Besides, there is much to be said against abrogating contracts.

Apart from these start-up problems, there are many potential loopholes. One way to avoid the TIP penalty is to settle for a lower wage increase but to reduce either the hours worked or work intensity. For example, employees could be given additional, badly policed sick leave or not have their pay docked for tardiness. This would not only create a loophole, but could also lower productivity significantly. Moreover, workers could be paid in the form of more pleasant working conditions, instead of in higher hourly pay that would be a misallocation of resources. In addition, firms could agree to liberalize pension plans and offer other fringe benefits that involve no current outlays.

Another problem is created by the complexity of the corporate structure. Wage agreements may be made at the plant level, but the tax-paying unit may be a multiplant corporation or even a conglomerate. In general, when making an agreement with one union, management would sometimes not know whether this would trigger a TIP penalty because it would not know for what it will settle with other unions. And then there is the problem of how to treat overtime. Should firms that now face a stronger demand for their products than they did in the previous year be penalized by TIP because the law forces them to pay for overtime work at time-and-a-half rates? But if there is an adjustment for overtime wages, what is to prevent employers from giving employees some regular time off and allowing them to make it up by overtime work the next week? Another problem is that firms could lower their average wage rates by contracting out work that is highly paid and could also use spurious promotions without pay increases to pretend that they are keeping the pay for each grade of labor within the norm. Finally, there are nasty technical problems relating to corporate mergers and spinoffs and to the establishment of new firms. To be sure, all these problems could be solved in some rough-and-ready fashion, but they would create inequities and distortions. These enforcement problems would, of course, be less severe if TIP were applied only to, say, the 100 largest firms, but this suggestion, made by some TIP adherents, raises another problem to which I now turn.

If one disregards the administrative difficulties just discussed, there is much to be said for applying TIP to the whole economy. One reason for this is that it would obviously provide a more effective curb on wage increases. Second, unless it applies to the whole economy, it would distort the allocation of resources between the covered and uncovered sectors. Obviously, if wages rise faster in the uncovered sectors, labor will tend to flow to these sectors. Third, if certain firms are exempted, awkward problems of wage comparisons are created; if only large firms are covered, unions may have to settle for lower wages for identical work at large firms than at small firms. More generally traditional wage patterns would be threatened [19]. This equity problem might seem unimportant since many people feel that the large unions that negotiate with large companies are in part responsible for inflation. But leaving aside the question of whether large unions are indeed responsible for inflation, there is the nasty fact that many large unions deal with small companies, rather than with industrial giants;[13] hence, holding down only the wages paid by large corporations would create an equity problem. It is easy for economists to respond that the alternatives to TIP are further inflation or substantial unemployment, and since both of these create great inequities, why worry about the inequities of a TIP program? But Congress may not buy this argument. It is one thing for Congress to let market processes inflict inequities, but it is a more serious matter for Congress to do so itself. This attitude may strike economists as naive, but it is not. The government can do great harm. Unless we impose some restraint against its acting inequitably, the public has every right to feel insecure; hence, there is something to be said for not using the government to impose a small inequity even if this prevents it from curing larger market-imposed inequity.[14]

Thus, if a tax penalty on excess wage increases is to be imposed, both resource allocation and equity considerations suggest that it should be on an economywide basis. But this would greatly increase enforcement and compliance costs since small and unincorporated firms often keep only rudimentary accounts [4]. By contrast, if only firms with 100 or more employees — who surely have good records — would be included, then only 1 percent of all firms would be covered; however, they account for more than 60 percent of total employment [4].

But even if one is willing to pay the high enforcement and compliance costs and apply TIP to all corporations, it would still be very much a partial tax. In 1977, corporations accounted for only 61 percent of national income, and even if one assumes that the federal government can control the wages of both federal and state and local employees, this would bring the percentage of national income covered to only 75 percent. And not all corporations would feel the impact of TIP because many have no net income.[15] In 1973 such corporations without net income accounted for 37 percent of all corporations and for 11 percent of total gross corporate receipts.[16]

Where does this leave us? Obviously, one can compile an impressive list of costs and disadvantages for most policy measures, and one must choose the lesser evil. Does TIP qualify on this basis? I think not, because in addition to the weaknesses just discussed, there exists another plan, really a variant of the standard TIP proposal, that is far superior. This is Abba Lerner's ingenious wage-permit plan to which I now turn.

THE WAGE-PERMIT PLAN

Abba Lerner has proposed that firms wanting to raise wages be required to obtain permits [9]. Each firm would be given annually a certain number of permits so that wages could, on the average, rise by a given percentage, perhaps equal to the increase in labor productivity. A firm wanting to raise wages beyond this would have to purchase wage increase permits from another firm that intends to raise its wages by a lesser amount. This system would have several major advantages over TIP. First, there is no danger that the higher labor costs of firms buying these permits would be translated into a higher inflation rate because what one firm loses by buying the permits another firm gains by selling them. For the whole economy, both average and marginal costs would be unaffected.[17] Second, the wage-permit plan would not distort resource allocation as much as TIP would, though it would still distort it to some extent; for example, it would encourage the substitution of capital for labor. Under TIP a company has an incentive to raise wages by no more than the norm, but it has no incentive to keep them much below the norm. But with a wage-permit plan, the ability to sell the wage permits provides an incentive to limit wage increases just as much for companies that are below the wage norm as for companies that are above it. Moreover, under TIP, but *not* under the permit plan, the penalty is applied in an inefficient way because its magnitude depends not only on the size of the wage increase, but also on a purely extraneous factor, the profitability of the company.

However, the wage-permit plan is still subject to other problems that afflict TIP.[18] It *could* lower labor's share of national income, it would further politicize the income distribution, and it could provide an excuse for following excessively expansionary monetary and fiscal policies. Moreover, there would be serious problems of enforcement and substantial compliance costs, and these *may* be just as bad or perhaps even worse than for TIP.

All the same, the wage-permit plan's superiority over TIP is substantial. I believe that its adoption in more or less the form advocated by

Lerner would be a "good thing." While it could not curb inflation in the absence of tight fiscal and monetary policies, it would help to reduce the unemployment cost of bringing the inflation rate down. To be sure, there would be much evasion and misallocation of resources, but as Tobin said, "It takes a heap of Harberger triangles to fill an Okun gap."[19]

IDEAL V. ACTUAL POLICIES

But all the same, I would be quite uneasy if I heard that Congress is seriously considering the adoption of a wage-permit plan. Since the free market has many faults and imperfections, *in principle* government policies should be able to improve its functioning substantially. But actually, the visible hand of government is even clumsier than the invisible hand of private self-interest. Again and again, legislation is proposed that promises to do much good and yet in practice does more harm than good. For example, while in principle a good case can be made for protecting infant industries, most economists would probably not like the trade policy that would emerge from legislation that purports to protect infant industries; there would be many senescent "infants." Similarly, agricultural price-support legislation looked a great deal better on the drawing boards than it does in actual operation. Hence, before advocating new legislation, we should ask ourselves how the legislation that is likely to emerge from Congress and from the tender ministrations of the enforcement agency is likely to differ from what we originally proposed.

One way any wage-permit plan or TIP plan could well be changed in Congress is by its proponents having to buy labor's support by offering various concessions. These could consist of imposing some price controls or even a commitment to aim at a, say, 5 percent unemployment rate.[20] The latter is particularly likely if the wage-permit plan is sold as a surefire way of stopping inflation without unemployment. And such high-pressure sales tactics may be needed to get it adopted. Moreover, liberal support may have to be bought by exempting low-paid workers, and *low paid* may be defined very broadly.[21] Beyond this, industries providing certain "necessities," such as housing, could clamor for exemptions so that they can produce sufficiently for our "needs." And export industries, as well as those that are import competing, would have a good case for exemptions in their own eyes and perhaps in the eyes of Congress. Moreover, small firms could argue that it would be "unfair" to allow big business to bid up the price of wage permits. Hence, there is a danger that a wage-permit plan would eventually turn into a system of *relative* wage taxes and wage subsidies.

Apart from this, what else could go wrong? Unfortunately, this question is hard to answer because we economists have paid virtually no attention to the problem of what determines the gap between the programs we propose and the way these programs actually function. It would be a good idea if everyone presenting a proposal for a new policy would discuss not only the advantages it would have if it were to work as planned once it is adopted, but also the various ways in which it could be corrupted in practice.

WAGE INSURANCE

A wage-insurance plan, which is an outgrowth of a plan suggested by Arthur Okun [12], has been proposed by the administration. This plan would, with a number of exemptions, insure those employees who are willing to limit their wage demands against the inflation rate's exceeding 7 percent. This, for all its ingenuity, is an exceedingly dangerous proposal.

To see why, consider first a more extreme version of the Okun plan that insures *all* incomes fully against an inflation rate greater than 7 percent. Assume further a permissive monetary policy that finances any resulting deficit at a given interest rate; assume also that the Pigou effect is unimportant. Then, perhaps as a result of an external shock, let prices rise by, say, 8 percent. The government, in compensation, obligingly raises everyone's income by 1 percent. The inflation rate then just takes off for the wild blue yonder. Put differently, there is much opposition to indexing the tax system because this would remove an automatic stabilizer. But the wage-insurance plan would be much worse than indexing in this respect: It not only eliminates the tendency for inflation to generate a surplus, but it would also mean that a higher inflation rate generates a greater deficit.[22]

To be sure, the Okun plan is not the extreme plan just discussed since it would have an income limit above which no compensation would be paid. But in a wage-insurance plan actually adopted by Congress, this income limitation *may* be omitted. As the treatment of capital gains in recent tax legislation shows, Congress is not indifferent to the welfare of the upper-middle class. In general, there is a danger that the idea may catch on that the government, being responsible for inflation, should compensate people for the losses inflation imposes on them. The Great Depression brought us unemployment insurance; perhaps the current inflation will bring us inflation insurance and in this way set off a much greater inflation. All in all, the Okun plan, while it is ingenious and *might* work, is much too risky.[23] Clever ideas often make bad policies.

CONCLUSIONS

Hence, while I like the wage-permit plan and would like to see it adopted *in the form suggested by Abba Lerner,* I am unsure that this is politically feasible. If it proves not to be, what then? One possibility is to aim at high employment and more or less to ignore the inflation rate. This policy has many advocates who (rightly) point out that an additional 1 percent unemployment is much worse than an additional 1 percent inflation. But this formulation misstates the issue for several reasons.

First, the unemployment cost of reducing inflation is a once-and-for-all cost, while a higher inflation rate continues year after year. To be sure, eventually expectations and contracts are all adjusted to this higher inflation rate, and after that it does little damage. But this could take a long time. Second, in the long run, one cannot buy much of a reduction in unemployment by allowing a higher inflation rate.

Third, the choice is not just one between permitting the inflation rate to rise from, say, 7 percent to 8 percent or having the unemployment rate rise from 6 percent to 7 percent. A 1 percent rise in the inflation rate may well be the most probable outcome of a policy that tries to hold the unemployment rate down. But, in deciding between two courses of action, one should not look just at their most likely effects, but at a wide array of possible effects accompanied by their respective probabilities. If this is done, then the inflation problem looks much more serious because there is a significant probability that the inflation rate may accelerate. It is not only double-digit inflation that we have to worry about; we also have to worry about what the first of these digits will be. Even the possibility of hyperinflation cannot be entirely dismissed, highly improbable though it is. I am more worried about the small possibility of a great acceleration of the inflation rate than about the much larger probability of a small raise.

Insofar as the really serious problem is not our current inflation rate but the (perhaps smaller) danger that it will accelerate substantially, one can make a reasonable case for trying to stabilize the inflation rate at its present level rather than trying to bring it down. This would not require creating large-scale unemployment except insofar as sellers continue to raise the rate of increase of their prices and wages because they do not believe that the government will stick to its policy. Unfortunately, a promise to draw the line at, say, 9 percent inflation may seem like the first of a series of steps in surrendering to accelerating inflation. "He who fights and runs away, lives to *run* another day."

A policy of just stabilizing the inflation rate rather than bringing it down could also be justified by arguing that a substantial proportion of the contracts that are currently in force were made in the expectation of something like a 7 percent inflation rate. Issuers of bonds with a 10 percent coupon rate would certainly have something to complain about if suddenly the inflation rate fell to zero. This whole issue of whether to bring the inflation rate down or to stabilize it at its current level deserves much more attention than it has received. For example, it would be useful to have estimates of when contracts (including retirement schemes) currently in force were made and how much longer they have to run.

But whether one wants to bring the inflation rate down or merely stabilize it at its present level, there is much to be said for no longer treating inflation as merely an unfortunate by-product of our necessary and desirable full employment policy. We *may* be better off stabilizing the price level (or the inflation rate) and letting employment take care of itself.[24] Since a decline in aggregate demand would then be accompanied by a decline in prices (or in the inflation rate), such a policy would indirectly also be an employment policy. Moreover, we could still take action on an ad hoc basis if unemployment on a very large scale occurs. By breaking inflationary expectations, a repeal of the Employment Act and of the relevant sections of the Humphrey-Hawkins Act would probably do much more to curb inflation than TIP would.

NOTES

1. See [3].

2. This could take the form of a special surtax for those raising wages excessively or a special lower tax bracket for those that do not exceed the norm. I will discuss only the former penalty case, but many of the issues raised also apply to a "reward TIP."

3. Albert Reese [15] has questioned the extent to which TIP would reduce wage increases, but in reply see Mitchell [11]. For a detailed discussion of why TIP would lower wage settlements, see Wallich and Weintraub [20] and Kotowitz and Portes [7]. However,

in the case of a monopolist who is also a monopsonist, this need not be the case — see [8].

4. See, for instance, [15]; Modigliani in [2].

5. In addition, Seidman argued that if the tax rate is set close to 100 percent, it cannot be shifted because this would require much too great an increase in prices [17]. But a tax rate close to 100 percent would involve many inefficiencies. More generally, the fact that firms would have to raise prices substantially to pass a high TIP tax rate forward completely does not argue in favor of TIP because it suggests that even if only a part of the tax is passed forward it would raise prices substantially.

6. Moreover, TIP would create *some* inefficiencies, and a lowering of productivity tends to result in a higher inflation rate.

7. Henry Wallich and Sidney Weintraub, "A Tax-Based Incomes Policy," *Journal of Economic Issues* 5:3.

8. Robert J. Gordon, "Comment," *Brookings Papers on Economic Activity,* 1978:23, p. 353.

9. Albert Reese, "New Policies to Fight Inflation: Sources of Skepticism," *Brookings Papers on Economic Activity,* 1978:2, p. 459.

10. See [2].

11. However, the fact that the TIP penalty tax is imposed on corporate income and not directly on wages may help here. See [5].

12. Moreover, unless TIP is made retroactive, corporations could quickly agree to wage increases while Congress is considering TIP.

13. The dozen largest unions in the private sector include the Teamsters, carpenters, laborers, retail clerks, meat cutters, and hotel workers.

14. To a considerable extent, one can look at laissez-faire as an agreement that nobody will use the government as an economic weapon against anyone else.

15. Compare [14].

16. There are, of course, fewer corporations that have no net income over a span of, say, three or five years. Hence, TIP might be applied to any firm that paid excessive wage increases in any three or five previous years. See [21]. But this assumes that TIP will stay in effect for several years.

17. The gain of the selling firm would lower its marginal, as well as average, costs since the greater its output, and hence the more people it employs, the more permits it would have available to sell.

18. The MAP plan described in the Lerner-Colander paper in this book avoids some of these difficulties, but it has its own administrative problems.

19. James Tobin, "How Dead is Keynes?" *Economic Inquiry* 15:468.

20. Gardner Ackley has suggested some price control as a likely trade-off for the adoption of TIP [1].

21. In 1973 under the Nixon wage controls, the low income exemption from wage controls covered almost half of all production and nonsupervisory employees in the private nonagricultural sector [15].

22. Admittedly, as William Nordhaus points out in his paper in this book, a procyclical policy may sometimes be desirable since we may want to accommodate an exogenous inflationary shock. But in the example just given, wage insurance would more than just accommodate the initial inflationary shock; it would allow the inflation rate to rise by much more than that.

23. In practice, it would also be quite complex and subject to many loopholes. See [1].

24. Would not abandonment of our high employment policy lead to a substantial increase in unemployment? Not necessarily; it is by no means clear that our employment policy is actually reducing the unemployment rate to a significant extent any more.

REFERENCES

[1] Ackley, Gardner. "Okun's New Tax-Based Incomes-Policy Proposal." *Economic Outlook* 5 (Winter 1978):8–9.

[2] ———, et al. "Symposium." *Brookings Papers on Economic Activity,* 1978:2, pp. 507–23.

[3] Cagan, Phillip. "The Reduction of Inflation by Slack Demand." In *Contemporary Economic Problems.* Edited by William Fellner. Washington, D.C.: American Enterprise Institute, 1978, pp. 13–45.

[4] Dildine, Larry, and Sunley, Emil. "Administrative Problems of Tax Based Incomes Policies." *Brookings Papers on Economic Activity,* 1978:2, pp. 363–90.

[5] Fogarty, Michael. "Fiscal Measures and Wage Settlements." *British Journal of Industrial Relations* 11 (March 1973):29–61.

[6] Gordon, Robert J. "Comment." *Brookings Papers on Economic Activity,* 1978:2, pp. 349–53.

[7] Kotowitz, Yehuda, and Portes, Richard. "The 'Tax on Wage Increases.'" *Journal of Public Economics* 3 (1974):113–32.

[8] Latham, R.W., and Peel, D.A. "The 'Tax on Wage Increases' When the Firm Is a Monopsonist." *Journal of Public Economics* 8 (October 1977):247–53.

[9] Lerner, Abba. "A Wage-Increase Permit Plan to Stop Inflation." *Brookings Papers on Economic Activity,* 1978:2, pp. 491–505.

[10] Lucas, Robert. "Understanding Business Cycles." *Carnegie-Rochester Conference Series on Public Policy* 5 (1977):31–68.

[11] Mitchell, Daniel. "Comment." *Brookings Papers on Economic Activity,* 1978:2, pp. 478–82.

[12] Okun, Arthur. "Discussion." *Brookings Papers on Economic Activity,* 1978:2, pp. 353–57.

[13] ———. "The Great Stagflation Swamp." *Challenge* (November–December 1977):613.

[14] Poole, William. "Discussion." *Brookings Papers on Economic Activity,* 1978:2, p. 399.

[15] Reese, Albert. "New Policies to Fight Inflation: Sources of Skepticism." *Brookings Papers on Economic Activity,* 1978:2, pp. 453–77.

[16] Seidman, Laurence. "Tax-Based Incomes Policies." *Brookings Papers on Economics Activity,* 1978:2, pp. 301–49.

214   THOMAS MAYER

[17] ———. "Would Tax Shifting Undermine the Tax Based Incomes Policy?"
      Journal of Economic Issues 3 (September 1978):647–76.
[18] Tobin, James. "How Dead is Keynes?" *Economic Inquiry* (1977):459–68.
[19] Ulman, Lloyd. "Comment." *Brookings Papers on Economic Activity,*
      1978:2, pp. 483–88.
[20] Wallich, Henry, and Weintraub, Sidney. "A Tax-Based Incomes Policy."
      Journal of Economic Issues 5 (1971):1–19.
[21] Weintraub, Sidney. *Capitalism's Inflation and Unemployment Crisis.*
      Reading, Mass.: Addison-Wesley, 1978.

V COMPLEMENTS TO DECENTRALIZED ANTI-INFLATION SCHEMES

10 LABOR MARKET POLICIES AND INFLATION

Isabel V. Sawhill

It is now rather widely accepted that macroeconomic policy cannot by itself simultaneously produce both full employment and price stability. In fact, recent events in most of the industrialized part of the world suggest that it cannot even come close. This state of affairs contrasts sharply with the decade of the 1960s when fine-tuning was in vogue and when the economic report of the president could confidently predict that the business cycle might soon be eliminated. It was a time during which the nation's leading economists, taking their script from Keynes, successfully made the case for discretionary fiscal policy to both the president and the American public. Not only was their faith infectious, but their good works also showed up in all of the economic indicators, and as a result, their influence grew. Even in those halcyon days, however, structural problems did not go unrecognized, and some experimentation with wage-price guidelines and manpower programs occurred. Nevertheless, these policies were clearly an addendum to the macro text.

With the events of the 1970s behind us, much of this has changed. The disease of stagflation has become more virulent. During this decade, the unemployment rate has averaged slightly over 6 percent, while the inflation rate has hovered around 7 percent. If earlier experiments with incomes policies or manpower programs had any effect, it has not shown up in the aggregate statistics. In addition, there is now far less agreement about how to define full employment and a great deal more modesty among economists about their ability to explain the underlying causes of inflation and unemployment. Lacking a new overarching paradigm with wide acceptability within the discipline, research has become more compartmentalized, and policymakers have had to content themselves with "muddling through."

It is in this environment that the search for new ways of improving the trade-off between inflation and unemployment is taking place. As Arthur Okun has put it, the debate is joined between the hawks, the doves, and the eagles. The hawks take a hard line on economic policy, suggesting that deflationary policies, well advertised and maintained over a sufficiently long period, will burst the balloon of inflationary expectations and enable us once again to have a relatively noninflationary level of full employment. They do not appear to be concerned about the costs of pursuing a low-growth, high-unemployment economy in the interim, even though most estimates suggest that an extra percentage point of unemployment (maintained for a year) will buy, at most, half a percentage point reduction in inflation [15].

The doves, perhaps still inebriated from the success of the 1960s, or perhaps just deeply concerned about the social and political implications of what the hawks are proposing, would maintain a very high-employment economy in the hopes that the inflationary costs would be small and in any case worth the benefits to be gained. They are optimistic that the short-run Phillips curve that prevails during expansions is relatively flat, just as the hawks are optimistic that the one that prevails during recessions is relatively steep. In fact, any asymmetry in the trade-off that exists over the cycle probably runs in the other direction.

Finally, there are the eagles — and I count myself one — who believe that the costs of pursuing either of these two paths would be intolerable and that it is therefore imperative to find some other alternative.

Two such alternatives are commonly believed to hold considerable promise. The first is some kind of incomes policy, including those schemes that rely on taxes, either as a carrot or a stick, to induce more socially responsible wage-price behavior. Here, the argument that I find compelling is that an exogenously induced reduction in wages and prices will permit a rather large increase in employment and output at any given rate of inflation, thereby leaving everyone much better off than before. Since most of the other papers in this volume examine these approaches, I will have little more to say about them.

A second way to improve the trade-off between inflation and unemployment (or to reduce the unemployment rate consistent with nonaccelerating inflation) is to place greater emphasis on selective labor market (or manpower) policies. In the remainder of this paper, I attempt to review and evaluate the evidence on the efficacy of this latter approach. As an eagle, I have my biases. I want to believe that both of these two approaches — incomes policies *and* selective labor market policies — can work. But the case for relying on either or both is far from airtight. So, in addition to reviewing the theory and the existing evidence on selective labor market policies, I include some thoughts on what we still need to learn if we are to move with confidence to a greater reliance on this particular approach. Toward the end of the paper, I also attempt to compare, at least in a broad way, selective labor market and tax-based incomes policies and explore the relationship of one to the other.

THE PROMISE OF SELECTIVE LABOR MARKET POLICIES

In a textbook model of the economy, labor is treated much like any other commodity. Any shift in demand or supply is expected to lead to an adjustment in wages with the result that unemployment, beyond some frictional minimum, should not exist. Observations of the real world do not conform very well to this model. Not only does the *level* of unemployment typically exceed what could reasonably be explained by frictional or cyclical factors alone, but also the *structure* of unemployment appears to be quite impervious to change.

In the face of these facts, one suspects that wages perform their equilibrating role very crudely, that they mostly adjust upward in response to excess demand in a particular market and hardly ever downward in response to excess supply, that any adjustments that do take place occur only very slowly, and that all kinds of institutional constraints influence the outcomes. In the latter category, we might mention the existence of unions; cultural discrimination by race, sex, or social class; personnel practices geared to long-term employer-employee relationships; the high costs of hiring and training new workers; minimum wages; a lack of complete information about the labor market on the part of both employers and job seekers; family or community ties that reduce mobility; and high reservation wages set by income transfers and other sources of nonearned income. These and other institutional complexities are quite pervasive and capable of explaining a good deal of "structural unemployment." Thus, we are left with a situation in which wages may not always perform their market-clearing function, in which there is no single auction market for all types of labor but rather a multitude of partially segmented markets and consequently a wide dispersion of unemployment rates around the national average.

Selective labor market policies are designed to deal with this kind of market failure. Given the uneven incidence of unemployment, a nondiscriminating dose of macroeconomic policy will be inflationary unless the economy is operating so far below its potential that virtually every labor market has excess capacity. As one moves closer to full employment, an increasing proportion of these markets become tight, with the result that wages and prices are bid up long before the very high rates of unemployment in other markets have fallen very far. Thus, the economy tends to exhaust its supply of, say, prime-age white males long before it has made much of a dent in the unemployment rate of, say, minority teenagers.

Labor market policies can respond to this situation in three ways. First, special job creation programs can be aimed at loose labor markets. The objective is to translate as much of an increase in labor demand as possible into rising employment, rather than into rising wages. The fiscal stimulus is focused on those groups and areas with high rates of unemployment on the assumption that wages are less responsive to increases in demand in these markets. Currently, there are a number of programs that operate, more or less, on this set of principles. Public service employment under the Comprehensive Employment Training Act (CETA) offers federally subsidized jobs in local government and nonprofit agencies to the low-income, long-term unemployed. The targeted-jobs tax credit, enacted in 1978, effectively increases the demand for low-income youth and some other disadvantaged groups by subsidizing their wages. Finally, the allocation of funds under a number of different programs (CETA, public works, revenue sharing) depends on local area unemployment rates.

A second role for selective labor market policies is to influence the supply side of the labor market through education and training programs. There are a number of distinct contributions that these supply-side policies can make to the inflation problem. One is to ease the skill bottlenecks that push up wages in tight labor markets over the short run. Another is to improve the long-term rate of increase in productivity so that any exogenously produced increase in money wages will affect labor costs and prices as little as possible. Still another is to raise the productivity of the most disadvantaged groups to a level commensurate with the wage floor set by social or legal minimums or by income transfer programs and thus to reduce the amount of structural unemployment attributable to these factors.

The third way in which labor market policies can improve the trade-off between inflation and unemployment is by reducing frictional or "search" unemployment. A considerable proportion of measured unemployment represents the voluntary movement of workers in and out of the labor force and between jobs. Although some search may contribute to a better match between worker and job, much of this search is inefficient and should not require an individual to become unemployed in order to find a new position. Thus, better labor market information and placement assistance, such as that provided by the federal-state employment service, are generally believed to be one way of improving the inflation-unemployment trade-off.

If successful, all the above programs should improve the functioning (efficiency) of the labor market, moving it closer to the textbook model in which everyone is paid what they are worth and there is no excess unemployment in any market. Such programs may simultaneously be designed to produce a fairer distribution of income and employment opportunities (equity). Whether or not such programs can actually achieve these two objectives is an open question. No attempt will be made here to assess their ability to achieve equity objectives; instead the focus is very much on their ability to improve the efficiency of labor markets and the inflation-unemployment trade-off. However, it should be noted that programs that operate in the real world tend to represent compromises between various objectives, and any evaluation of them must take their hybrid character into consideration. In the end, the political system may need to choose from among various objectives the one deemed to be most important. My own view is that equity will not be well served in an economy with underutilized resources and that underutilization will be the norm until we find new ways to deal with inflation. This view is a modern variant of Paul Samuelson's "neoclassical synthesis" [19]. The old neoclassical synthesis held that a market economy would produce the best of all possible worlds once macroeconomic policy had eliminated involuntary unemployment. The new neoclassical synthesis is less sanguine and more interventionist, but it is still hopeful that labor market or incomes policies to deal with structural unemployment and inflation can save the market system from chronic stagflation and possible crisis or collapse.

THE ABILITY OF SELECTIVE LABOR MARKET POLICIES
TO IMPROVE THE INFLATION-UNEMPLOYMENT TRADE-
OFF

The arguments sketched in the preceding section about the "promise" of labor market policies on the inflation-unemployment front represent to a large extent the currently prevailing wisdom among supporters of these programs. This wisdom is backed up by very little in the way of (1) a theoretically detailed modeling of the process by which the expected effects are to take place, (2) empirical testing of the resulting models using standard analytical techniques, or (3) an evaluation of the actual effects of current programs on inflation and unemployment.

In the remainder of this section, I attempt to give the flavor of recent work in each of these areas. No claim is made that this review is exhaustive. Rather, the purpose is to highlight the kinds of issues that are being, or need to be, addressed.

Theoretical and Empirical Issues

The case for an active labor market policy is based on the assumption that "structural" and "frictional" unemployment exist. But can these two concepts be rigorously defined? And once defined, can they be shown to exist? I know of no one who claims to have a completely satisfactory answer to these questions. It may turn out that the concepts themselves are in need of revision.

If there were an equivalence between the distribution of job vacancies (by duration, location, skill level, wage being offered, and so forth), on the one hand, and the distribution of unemployment, on the other, then one might claim that only frictional or search unemployment existed and could be explained in terms of a scarcity of knowledge (about the above distributions) and the consequent need for time to acquire it. Presumably, a giant computer that contained detailed information on these distributions could eliminate frictional unemployment. Economies of scale and the public-goods nature of such information could justify making this a government monopoly. One of the problems with the current employment service is that it is *not* a monopoly and in many cases is producing an inferior product relative to its competitors, which include private placement agencies, help-wanted ads, and more informal networks. Even if a complete listing of jobs were feasible, one suspects that the job market is a little like the marriage market — neither party to the transaction wants to make a decision based on statistical information alone. More-over, it is not clear why job search cannot take place just as efficiently on the job or before entering the labor force as while unemployed. Finally, there is no reason to assume that more information would reduce the measured unemployment rate since it might increase job turnover or labor force entry at the same time that it reduced the duration of search.

For all the above reasons, there may have been too much emphasis both on search unemployment and on the potential of better labor market information to reduce it. Although one early study of the efficacy of manpower programs estimated that a $2.4 billion expansion of resources available to the employment service might reduce the noninflationary level of unemployment by half a percentage point, this estimate did not go unchallenged [8, 10]. The more recent evaluation literature has not even attempted to quantify potential benefits. In fact, no one knows whether the incidence and duration of unemployment is much affected by the existence of a public labor market exchange. It seems reasonable to assume that more information improves the efficiency of the search process — either by shortening its duration or by improving the quality of the matches — and that reducing the costs of this information should lead to greater utilization. But we cannot say by how much.

Compared to frictional unemployment, structural unemployment is, if anything, still more elusive. It is alleged to occur when the characteristics of workers do not match up with the characteristics of jobs. Overall, there may be a rough balance between demand and supply, but in indi-vidual submarkets — defined by location, skill level, demographic, or other characteristics — different degrees of disequilibria exist. Thus, there may well be excess unemployment in some markets combined with excess vacancies in others. If wage adjustments are asymmetrical — increasing in response to excess vacancies but exhibiting downward rig-idity in the face of excess unemployment — then the economy will have an inflationary bias as a result [11,20].

Assuming such disequilibria exist, the more fundamental question is: Why do wages not perform their market-clearing function? Much of the recent debate about the efficacy of labor market policies has centered on this issue [18]. Two polar cases can be described: one in which relative wages are completely flexible in response to any shift in demand or supply and one in which they are completely inflexible for institutional reasons.

In the flexible wage model, the existence of high unemployment in a particular labor market is viewed as the equilibrium level for that market, reflecting high turnover rates rather than any excess supply. Redirecting

demand toward such markets, through the use of public service employment or wage subsidies, for example, will only serve to raise relative
wages for the affected groups. This upward wage adjustment in turn
leads to an eventual substitution of nonsubsidized for subsidized workers
in the economy as a whole, with no net increase in employment for the
target groups and no *permanent* improvement in the inflation-unemployment trade-off. The impact of training programs can be analyzed in a
somewhat analogous fashion. These programs increase the supply of
skilled workers that can be expected to put downward pressure on the
relative wages of this group and induce, over the longer run, a new set
of occupational choices [12].

In the rigid wage model, various institutional factors, such as minimum
wages, are held to be responsible for the relatively high unemployment
observed in some labor markets. In this case, the supply of low-produc-
tivity workers is relatively elastic over the relevant range; that is, they
would be willing to work at wages below the minimum if there were any
effective demand for their services. A subsidized job program can create
this demand with little or no upward pressure on wages, assuming that
the jobs offered pay the minimum wage or less. As a result, such programs can increase employment and output with little inflationary cost.[1]

In sum, the efficacy of direct job creation programs hinges on the
factors thought to explain the relatively high unemployment rates in some
markets and the implications of the explanation for the wage adjustment
process assumed to take place in response to a labor market intervention.
Thus, a job creation program targeted on low-income youth will have a
less inflationary effect if their unemployment is caused by the minimum
wage than if it is caused by a high rate of voluntary turnover. Put more
generally, the major issue is the extent to which structural unemployment
exists where the latter is defined as a condition of excess supply that will
not be eliminated by market forces in a reasonable period of time. Clearly,
over the long run wages may adjust, but in a dynamic economy new
disequilibria will appear as rapidly as old ones disappear, and we then
need to ask: How long is the short run, and will the political system
tolerate pockets of high unemployment over this period? If not, is there
any hope that structural interventions can be effectively tailored to a
constantly changing set of disequilibria, in particular labor markets
brought about by shifts in demand, technological or demographic
changes, foreign competition, and so forth?

Another continuing puzzle is why it is that unemployment rate differentials by age, race, sex, location, and skill level are so persistent over
time. Their persistence suggests that structural unemployment is not just

a matter of temporary disequilibria in particular labor markets. Rather, there may be some structural barriers — such as those created by discrimination, minimum wages, and income transfer programs — that lead to persistently high levels of unemployment for certain groups. In principle, such barriers should be tackled directly rather than by means of labor market policies, since the latter are often a second-best solution. But in practice, labor market policies may be the only acceptable or politically feasible response.

One possible source of persistently high unemployment rates for some groups is the availability of nonearned income from other family members, illegal activity, or income transfers. These sources of income can set a floor under reservation wages that is above the market-clearing level. The resulting gap between acceptable wages and what the market is willing to pay may prolong job search and create a high level of voluntary unemployment.

Most of the increases in the nonaccelerating inflation rate of unemployment (or NAIRU) in recent years have been attributed to shifts in the composition of the labor force by age and sex. Adjustments for these compositional shifts are presumably a crude way of adjusting for the growth of nonearned income or some other factor associated with high levels of structural or frictional unemployment. A much more defensible procedure would be to estimate the effects of nonearned income on the duration of unemployment and the increase in the unemployment rate that can be attributed to longer durations of unemployment induced by increases in nonearned income. Whether minimum wages, nonearned income, inadequate information, labor force mobility, or other factors account for the higher unemployment rates observed for certain groups, the effects of these factors need to be measured *directly,* their trends estimated, and policy solutions tailored to the findings.

While we are far from understanding the basic causes of the persistently high unemployment rates experienced by some groups and the implications for policy, some empirical work has been done on how to identify particular markets where selective policies can be used to increase employment in relatively noninflationary ways. In the case of direct job creation programs, one would like to identify groups whose wages are not very responsive to increased demand — groups that are on flat segments of their Phillips curve. In the case of training programs, one would like to identify occupations in which rising wages fail to induce the appropriate skill investments in a reasonable period of time — that is, sectors with steeply sloped Phillips curves. In the past, unemployment rates have typically been used as a proxy for discriminating between these various markets, but the recent literature stresses the need to focus on the relevant wage responses in each market, as well as on elasticities of substitution between markets. It is hoped that the estimation of these parameters can add some precision to the concepts of long-term structural imbalance and segmented labor markets [9].

Some recent evidence on these matters suggests that the rate of wage inflation *is* relatively unresponsive to the unemployment rates of groups who traditionally experience high unemployment — youth, women, and the unskilled [2,4,14]. Some other evidence suggests that over a *longer* time period, labor markets adapt quite well to shifts in demand and supply [12]. Overall, however, the research base is quite thin with the result that we understand very little about how labor markets work and thus how to intervene most successfully. Some progress has been made in disaggregating the unemployment rate, both demographically and with respect to its component flows (hires, quits, and so forth) [6], but little work has focused on the determinants of labor market transitions, why they vary between groups, and the way in which they influence the process of wage inflation.

Program Evaluation

Given the scale of current programs, the number of factors that impinge upon economywide rates of inflation and unemployment, and the theoretical uncertainties already alluded to, it may be unrealistic to expect to be able to identify the impact of labor market policies on macroeconomic objects [1]. However, given the importance of the issues, it is somewhat surprising that there has been so little systematic data collection from, and monitoring of, existing programs.

Evaluations of training programs generally deal with their impact on postprogram earnings. Thus far, the lack of good longitudinal data with a built-in control group has hampered efforts in this area. Even assuming a program-induced increase in earnings or occupational skill level, the ultimate effects on inflation and unemployment cannot be readily quantified, although at least one researcher has made a heroic effort [Johnson in 21]. It is also clear that only a tiny fraction of the manpower budget has been directed toward upgrading workers to provide those skills in greatest demand so as to ease inflationary bottlenecks in specific markets. Most training programs are of very short duration and are focused on entry level jobs.

Evaluations of public service employment under CETA have been largely directed toward ascertaining the net employment effects of such programs [13]. There is no definitive evidence on whether these programs have *shifted* the composition of overall demand toward workers on relatively flat Phillips curves, although recent changes in the targeting of the program and limits on the wages that can be paid are expected to have this effect. But until recently, the program has not been highly targeted and could not have had much effect on the trade-off between inflation and unemployment.

Turning to direct job creation programs in the private sector, there are some evaluations of the New Jobs Tax Credit (NJTC), which was in effect during 1977 and 1978.[2]

Evaluations of the NJTC indicate (1) that many firms were ignorant of its existence, (2) that many of those who knew about it did not qualify (for example, because their employment levels failed to expand sufficiently), and (3) that about one-quarter of those who knew about the credit and had established that they were eligible to receive it reported a conscious effort to increase employment as a result of the credit. Three separate studies confirm that the program has had a positive impact on employment levels, and at least one also shows a significant reduction in prices as a result of the credit [4,5,7].

In 1979, the NJTC was replaced by a new tax credit targeted on disadvantaged youth, eighteen to twenty-four years old, and some other hard-to-employ groups. Evaluations of this credit are still being planned and are plagued by the usual methodological and data problems. The focus, however, is on measuring increases in the employment of eligible groups. Such increases may be at the expense of noneligible groups, or they may represent net increases in employment. In either case, it will be difficult to ascertain the effect on wages, productivity, and inflation. Theoretically, tax credits or wage subsidies can reduce marginal costs, expand employment and output, and lower prices. Depending on the extent to which any one-shot price reduction influences future wage and price increases, such programs could have longer-run effects on the rate of inflation [3].

Even a brief discussion of these evaluations points up the difficulties in assessing the ability of labor market policies to reduce unemployment in relatively noninflationary ways. Future work will have to proceed on two fronts: Better evaluations will be needed to measure direct program impacts, and better theoretical and empirical models will be needed to analyze or simulate the indirect effects on the economy.

LABOR MARKET AND INCOMES POLICIES

If they are to successfully manage the economy over the coming decade, policymakers will need every tool in the economic kit, including some that have not yet been invented. Still, some evaluation of the relative merits of different strategies and of where they fit into a broader policy framework is needed.

One way to approach this task might be to ask how much of current inflation is the result of (1) the continued adjustment of current wages and prices to past wage and price increases; (2) specific cost-increasing measures associated with external events, the government's own actions, or the independent market power of large unions and corporations; (3) excess demand in particular labor or product markets; and (4) more generalized excess demand. If one believes, as I do, that these factors are listed more or less in the order of their relative importance as explanations of *current* inflation, then clearly an incomes policy is essential to unwind the momentum of that inflation. Simultaneously, we need to insure that the other three factors do not sow the seeds of *future* inflation in the same way that the events of the late 1960s and early 1970s produced much of our current problem.

Viewed in this context, incomes policies have some short-run curative properties not shared by labor market policies, and the latter might be more appropriately classified as long-run preventive measures. It must be recognized that labor market policies have no power to prevent that portion of inflation caused by exogenous shocks to existing cost structures. In this sense, it would clearly be inappropriate to put all, or even most, of one's eggs into the labor market basket. By the same token, if we want to escape relatively permanent dependence on some form of wage-price controls, the development of a more effective set of selective labor market interventions applied on a larger scale than in the past may be a necessary addition to the policy arsenal.

Even at their current level of about $12 billion a year, these programs are not cheap. While tax-based incomes policies carry some significant budgetary costs, most incomes policies appear to be a bargain when compared to employment and training programs. On the other hand, the *real* economic costs of labor market policies are undoubtedly lower, at least if one accepts the conventional wisdom that says that incomes policies introduce distortions and inefficiencies into the system while employment and training programs improve the functioning of the labor market and the productive potential of the economy.

As a final observation, it is worth noting that a great deal of attention has been devoted to the inadequacies of the unemployment data and the need to recalculate the unemployment rate consistent with nonaccelerating inflation. It is argued that as a result of changes in the composition of the labor force and the growth of income transfer programs, the unemployment rate does not have the same meaning today as in the past and that any given rate of unemployment represents less labor market slack than previously. Congressional hearings, conferences, and even an entire commission's efforts have been devoted to these issues. Curiously, there has not been a similar degree of interest in the inflation statistics. Yet, one could make a very similar set of arguments with respect to the changing significance of these data. In particular, the failure to measure the value of cleaner environments, safer work places, higher quality products, and other possible additions to real output lends an upward bias to the measured rate of inflation. Given the widespread indexing of wages and other payments to the CPI, if this bias exists, it will not only lead to the setting of unrealistic goals but will also contribute directly to the wage-price spiral. Thus, unless existing price indices are subjected to the same scrutiny as the unemployment statistics, there is the danger that full employment will be redefined to the point where there are just enough unemployed people to keep the statistical "inflation" in the inflation rate under control.

NOTES

1. It is sometimes further argued that even if the relative wages of the subsidized workers do rise, the process is self-limiting because both employers and employees are sensitive to the need to maintain prevailing wage differential. Even more importantly, equilibrium unemployment rates are not independent of wage levels; turnover is significantly lower in higher-wage jobs. Consequently, the upward adjustment in the relative wages of low-paid workers has offsetting effects and need not prevent their unemployment rate from falling [2].

2. The NJTC provided firms with credits equal to 50 percent of the increase in the FUTA wage base over 102 percent of the previous year's base, subject to various limitations, such as a "cap" of $100,000 in credits for any one firm. The FUTA base for 1977 consisted of wages paid of up to $4,200 per employee. Thus, a firm that expanded its employment could receive 50 percent of a new worker's first $4,200 of earnings as a tax credit.

REFERENCES

[1] Ashenfelter, Orley. "Reducing Unemployment without Inflation." Statement before the Committee on the Budget, U.S. House of Representatives, February 6, 1979.

[2] Baily, Martin Neil, and Tobin, James. "Inflation-Unemployment Consequences of Job Creation Policies." In *Creating Jobs: Public Employment Programs and Wage Subsidies* (Washington, D.C.: Brookings Institution, 1978).

[3] Bishop, John, ed. *The Potential of Wage Subsidies.* Final report to the Employment and Training Administration. Washington, D.C.: U.S. Department of Labor, 1979.

[4] Bishop, John, and Haveman, Robert. "Targeted Employment Subsidies: Issues of Structure and Design." Paper given at the Conference on Creating Job Opportunities in the Private Sector, October 19–20, 1978, sponsored by the National Commission for Manpower Policy.

[5] ———. "Selective Employment Subsidies: Can Okun's Law Be Repealed?" Paper presented at the 91st Annual Meeting of the American Economic Association, Chicago, August 29, 1978.

[6] Ehrenberg, Ronald G. "The Demographic Structure of Unemployment Rates and Labor Market Transition Probabilities." Washington, D.C.: National Commission for Manpower Policy, 1979.

[7] Eisner, Robert, "Employment Taxes and Subsidies." In *Work Time and Employment.* National Commission for Employment Policy, Special Report No. 28, forthcoming.

[8] Hall, Robert E. "Prospects for Shifting the Phillips Curve through Manpower Policy." *Brookings Papers on Economic Activity,* 1971:3, pp. 659–702.

[9] Hamermesh, Daniel S., and Grant, James. "Econometric Studies of Labor — Labor Substitution and Their Implications for Policy," Michigan State University, Econometrics Workshop Paper No. 7709, June 1978.

[10] Holt, Charles C.; MacRae, C. Duncan; Schweitzer, Stuart O.; and Smith, Ralph E. "Manpower Proposals for Phase III." *Brookings Papers on Economic Activity,* 1971:3, pp. 703–23.

[11] Holt, Charles C., "Improving the Labor Market Tradeoff between Inflation and Unemployment." *American Economic Review* (May 1969): 135–46.

[12] Johnson, George, and Blakemore, Arthur. "The Potential Impact of Employment Policy on the Unemployment Rate Consistent with Nonaccelerating Inflation." Paper presented at the 91st Annual Meeting of the American Economic Association, August 28, 1978.

[13] National Commission for Manpower Policy. Interim Report to the Congress, *Job Creation through Public Service Employment,* Report No. 6. Washington, D.C.: U.S. Gov't. Printing Office, 1978.

[14] Nichols, Donald. Statement before the Joint Economic Committee, U.S. Congress, February 9, 1979.
[15] Okun, Arthur M. "Efficient Disinflationary Policies." Paper presented at the 90th Annual Meeting of the American Economic Association, December 28, 1977.
[16] ———. "The Great Stagflation Swamp." *Brookings Bulletin* 14, no. 3 (Fall 1977): 1–7.
[17] ———, and Perry, George L., eds. "Innovative Policies to Slow Inflation." *Brookings Papers on Economic Activity,* 1978:2, special issue.
[18] Palmer, John L., ed. *Creating Jobs: Public Employment Programs and Wage Subsidies.* Washington, D.C.: Brookings, 1978.
[19] Samuelson, Paul A. *Economics,* 9th ed. New York: McGraw-Hill, 1973.
[20] Tobin, James. "Inflation and Unemployment." *American Economic Review* (March 1972).
[21] U.S. Congress. Joint Economic Committee, Hearings on the Effects of Structural Employment and Training Programs on Inflation and Unemployment, February 9 and 21, 1979.
[22] U.S. Department of Labor, Office of the Assistant Secretary for Policy, Evaluation and Research. *Conference Report on Evaluating the 1977 Economic Stimulus Package.* Washington, D.C.: U.S. Gov't. Printing Office, 1978.

11 SOME NEGLECTED MICROECONOMICS OF INFLATION CONTROL

Martin Bronfenbrenner

We owe to Professors Lerner, Wallich, and Weintraub, and more explicitly to their proposals for microeconomic incomes policies (MAP, TIP, and so on), a revival of interest in a much broader range of intermediate microeconomic policies — which the skeptics call gimmicks — for control of inflation and mitigation of inflationary expectations. I call their proposals "intermediate" because they fall short of outright long-term wage and price controls; the administration of TIPs is therefore hoped to be less threatening to civil liberties. At the same time, TIPs are intended to be less recessionary — less stagflationary, if you please — than the conventional delayed-action medicine of monetary disinflation, that is, decelerated monetary growth.

I propose to move a few steps further along microeconomic lines, concentrating on purely short-term proposals unless otherwise indicated. My proposals will ignore TIP almost entirely and will be divided among ten fields. I cannot hope to go into administrative details, but since (unlike most proponents of incomes policies) I envision most microeconomic interventions as primarily crisis remedies, I claim to be justified in reliance on rough-and-ready, that is, arbitrary, administrative discretion plus standard procedures for the "textbook cases." These procedures would, I fear, be stifling and dictatorial over the long term, but no short-term administrative alternatives seem to be available.

Here are the ten areas in which I believe I may have something to offer: taxation, public expenditures, public-service pricing, trade regulation, tariff and nontariff protection, labor relations, immigration, agriculture, land policy, and finance and banking.

SLICING THE SALAMI

Before embarking on a number of necessarily brief proposals under these ten heads, I propose to talk economic theory and explain my own peculiar reconciliation of the microeconomic and macroeconomic approaches in inflation control.

I consider myself basically a "macro man," closer to monetarism than to fiscalism and closer to Chicago than to either Cambridge. The macro or aggregative approach to inflation, of which I accept 90 percent wholeheartedly, sees inflation as primarily a monetary phenomenon resulting from the growth rate of the money supply outpacing the growth rate of real output.[1] In this view, microeconomic pressures of the cost-push variety serve to "shift the cargo" of inflationary pressure — concentrating it in sector A, where costs are being pushed, and reducing it in the more competitive sector B. The converse is true of controls and incomes policies, either voluntary or compulsory. They reduce inflationary pressure in the highly visible sector A and sweep it under the rug to sector B. At times, they can sometimes conceal or repress inflationary pressure until a later period (après l'élection, le déluge). At best, microeconomic controls can provide a welcome breathing spell for macroeconomic measures to come on stream, but they have more commonly been used in practice as excuses to postpone such measures — with their accompanying risks of recession — to the indefinite future.

The imperfections of competition — monopolies, cartels, trade unions, farm lobbies, collective bargaining, administered prices[2] — leave room for independent cost-push inflation only if the degree of monopoly available to the price and wage setters or administrators is *rising*. Otherwise, each monopoly, cartel, or union is supposed to be already in the neighborhood of its optimum position. Its cost-pushes are matters of ancient history only. It has no motive to push costs or prices up further, unless, of course, its power is on the rise, a case the conventional macroeconomist discounts as unimportant.

But I find myself in what I consider more than marginal disagreement with this separation of inflation from imperfect competition. What the conventional account omits, I think, is monopolists', cartels', and unions' reserves of potential or unexercised economic power at any particular point in time. In a world of incomplete and unreliable information and guesstimates about consumer demand and outlier demand — with trust-busters, socialist nationalizers, consumer activists, and regulatory bureaucrats around every corner — I think I see the representative imperfect competitor or economic pressure group proceeding with some caution, approaching its best estimate of its optimum position a little at a time, rather than aiming at this position in one fell swoop. The Hungarian dictator Matyas Rakosi called such a process "slicing the salami" in his theory of public choice in an encroaching Stalinist dictatorship. I propose to use the same expression here as well.

Given an inflationary history over the past few years, with optimum prices increasing over time, it seems safe to assume for our representative imperfect competitor a substantial gap between his actual and optimal price or wage, with the actual price or wage the lower of the two and in process of catching up.

Not only are actual prices and wages charged by imperfect competitors systematically below their optima during inflationary periods, the optima are themselves also rising for two reasons independent of the observed overall inflation rate and the observed macroeconomic control policy. The first reason is the "passthrough" or "escalation" phenomenon, assuming (without proof) reactions to the recent price movements of related prices and wages in a series of mutual adjustments to be convergent, but only slowly so. The second reason for exogenous movements of national optimum wages and prices may be increasing confidence in eventual monetary and fiscal validation or accommodation by the public authorities to bargained, administered, or otherwise "artificial" price and wage increases precisely as though they had been acts of God.

These shifting and possibly increasing gaps between actual and optimal prices and wages each imperfect competitor proposes vaguely to close in the relatively near future, even if macroeconomic policy turns disinflationary.[3] This hypothesis suggests why, over a short or medium term, prices and wages may continue to rise in spiral patterns of stagnation with no simple-minded "quantity theory" or other monetary reason for their doing so. In our and Rakosi's terms, these are intervals of salami slicing pure and simple.

It is the adjustments of imperfect competitors' prices and wages to their optima, or to prices and wages in related sectors, that microeconomic "gimmickry" may perhaps restrain for a period long enough for disinflationary macroeconomic policies to attain credibility and end accommodation-inspired rises of optimum prices and wages. In our un-

professional lingo, microeconomic policy can put a stop or brake to
salami slicing by imperfect competitors.

INDEXATION AND COUNTERINDEXATION

A second theoretical preface relates to indexation. I am one of many
economists to have favored at least a partial indexation to protect taxpayers, bondholders, and fixed-income people in general from certain
unfavorable effects of however much inflation can be traced to governmental monetary and fiscal policies or to the full amount of inflation
(whichever is less).[4] While many of the proposals below are intended to
act as "indexators" in much the same way as formal indexation, others
are not. These others may rather exaggerate certain unfavorable effects
of inflation on particular individuals and groups and may even be called
anti-indexation proposals. Our problem is whether such inconsistencies
can be explained and rationalized.

I rationalize the inconsistencies only crudely in terms of broad economic pressure groups rather than individuals. The argument is that
organized business, organized labor, organized agriculture, and the government can gain inflation subsidies or avoid inflation taxes at the expense
of the unorganized remainder of the population to whom the inflation tax
is essentially shifted.[5]

Some anti-inflationary proposals may accordingly be presented as
equivalents to indexation for groups outdistanced by inflation, although
the process of indexation is itself seldom an anti-inflationary one. Other
proposals, however, are for counterindexation penalties against members
of one or another group who have gained by past cost-pushes, or by
voluntary or compulsory macroeconomic accommodation or validation
of these past cost-pushes, or by both.

But all this is unfortunately overaggregated. One person's particular
organization may be weak or his or her affiliation to a strong organization
may be tenuous. Consider one who raises poultry or livestock, who may
be a net loser from inflationary agricultural supports on feed-grain prices.
Another example is the "subemployed" nonunion worker. At the opposite extreme is the strong individual member of the weak unorganized
group. A case in point is a wealthy widow, basically in a fixed-income
position but owning not only her own home but also substantial additional
holdings of real estate and other inflation hedges. From such ambiguous
cases result inequities and unfairnesses in my proposals that I recognize,
but that I hope can be overlooked for the short term. The greater number

of my suggestions are accordingly short-term ones only. Between crises, they should at most be relegated to the backburner, cold storage, or placed on some standby basis, but they should not be forgotten. The occasional exceptions to this "short-run-only" generalization will be indicated as we discuss them.

TEN SHORT-TERM ANTI-INFLATION ALTERNATIVES

Taxation Proposals

Thus, despite the formidable obstacles to its equitable long-term administration,[6] I find myself on balance in favor of a TIP experiment over a short term, although not on the permanent basis sometimes suggested. As a more permanent reform, I also favor the indexation of the tax brackets in progressive taxes, meaning primarily the federal income tax.

Along with TIP, and perhaps more important than TIP, a thoroughgoing anti-inflationary tax program should include revival of the World War II excess profits tax on corporations and enactment of an incremental income tax on individuals.

To indicate a problem that excess profits taxation might ease, let me construct an oversimplified case. A firm has output and sales of x, a wage bill of w, explicit land and capital charges of k, and gross profits y so defined that $x = w + k + y$. With a constant labor force and wage rates rising in line with average productivity, output and sales become αx, with $\alpha > 1$, and the payroll becomes αw. Capital costs remain k — fixed, perhaps, by long-term contracts — while gross profits become βy. The difficulty is that not only is $\beta > 1$ but $> \alpha$ gross and probably also net of taxes.[7] This excites labor hostility and discontent if the gap $\beta-\alpha$ is large.

The case for an incremental income tax on individuals parallels the case for an excess profits tax on corporations. Indeed one might call it an excess profits tax on noncorporate business. Like the excess profits tax, it discriminates against those who happen to have inflation-unrelated windfalls, such as major promotions, in periods of inflation. Such discriminatory features can be mitigated by high exemptions plus exclusions of young people and others taking their first full-time jobs.

Commodity taxes, whether of the excise, sales, or value-added (VAT) variety, present special problems for inflation control. Insofar as price index numbers are based on prices gross of tax, increases in these taxes raise measured price levels. These increases may have further undesirable inflationary consequences in the presence of escalation-type arrangements. Neutrality as between direct and indirect taxes could be achieved with a wider scope for the commodity taxes if prices were reported net of all such taxes. Such reporting could be done quite easily on the basis of the conventional (but not universally accepted) assumption of complete forward shifting to consumers.[8]

Changes in state and local property-taxation systems could go far to eliminate the attractiveness of real estate, including both raw land and obsolete buildings, as a hedge against inflation. They might therefore indirectly act to mobilize middle-class disinflationary sentiment. This topic, however, we discuss separately in the subsection on land proposals.

Public Expenditure Proposals

Let me dispute at the start the common belief that public expenditures, especially deficit-financed public expenditures, are themselves uniquely inflationary, more so than private expenditures of equal size. There are, however, two grains of truth in this popular superstition: (1) Public expenditures have been historically less "productive" or "efficient" — less GNP-generating on the supply side — than private ones, and (2) central governments are uniquely tempted to finance expenditures by direct or indirect money creation by treasuries or central banks, when they find adequate taxation unfeasible politically or when they cannot sell their ordinary debt securities on the security markets — which, in some developing countries, may not even exist!

The most important form of administrative control over public expenditures may be *impoundment,* the refusal to spend appropriated funds. This may in extreme cases approximate a macroeconomic policy tool. It was adjudged illegal when attempted by President Nixon, but only because it was attempted without congressional authorization. In crude form, it could be based on an agreed overall expenditure ceiling. Then, in case total appropriations exceeded this ceiling, the administration could be empowered to "impound" part or all of the difference, that is, refuse to release certain appropriated funds.[9]

More than incidentally, the impoundment device could be used to delay or suspend the enforcement of environmental, safety, health, and similar public controls with high cost inflationary impact, without the trauma of reconsidering the underlying control legislation.

Sanctions against firms that may be adjudged, presumably by an anti-inflation authority, to be engaging in price gouging or in collusion with wage gouging could be imposed. They could be excluded from bidding for public contracts. The use of their products or services by successful contractors could also be enjoined. Perhaps more generally, governments could exercise their dormant monopsony powers in an anti-inflationary direction by refusing to let public contracts at inflationary prices, that is, by impounding the appropriations for particular projects until the submission of reasonable bids.

Public Service Pricing Proposals

We have listed governments, particularly central governments, among the economic pressure groups gaining by inflationary finance at the expense of the general public.[10] The gains of any particular public body could be reduced sacrificially by self-denying programs of inflation control that freeze public service prices for central government enterprises and government corporations and force heavy losses on, for example, post offices, public housing, public schools and hospitals, and national railroads in consequence of inflationary financing. This would also bring disinflationary pressure on private firms competing with the public ones. On the other hand, similar freezing of civil service wages and salaries is dangerous. It often has the side effect of encouraging corrupt practices of all sorts, which are difficult to eliminate after the inflation has run its course.

Trade Regulation Proposals

Many economists, including my teacher Henry Simons, have proposed from time to time a uniform and severe federal incorporation law tax to replace the "competitive depreciation" features of the various state regulations. My long-term support for this particular reform is derivative from Simons in particular, but its application to the inflation problem is not. I should like to see the continuation of an apparently valuable privilege, namely, carrying on business in the corporate form, made legally dependent upon the firm's acceptance of inflation-control orders relating both to output prices and to output mixes.[11] At the same time, I should expect such orders, including rollbacks along with price fixing, to be limited in number — limited, that is, to a relatively few basic products such as steel, fuels, transportation, and utilities, plus a few cases of egregious misconduct, such as that exemplified by the clothing trades in World War II.

As an inferior substitute for a federal incorporation law with anti-inflationary teeth in it, one might at least hope for amendment of the basic antitrust statutes so as to include explictly both price and output behavior during inflationary periods as evidence about "reasonableness" and "performance" in corporate actions. Such evidence is introduced frequently in lawsuits involving divestiture, dissolution, and lesser penalties under both federal and state antitrust laws.

Tariff and Nontariff Protection Proposals

As a sanction against cost-push behavior in protected industries, the inflation control agency should be given discretionary authority to suspend partially or completely any tariff or quota protection — the so-called antidumping duties included — on products whose leading domestic producers are adjudged to be violating price and wage orders, disregarding voluntary guidelines or guideposts, or violating "hold-the-line" agreements previously made.

Labor Policy Proposals

In a natural and compassionate reaction against employer monopsony and its supposed consequences on imperfectly competitive labor markets, legislative floors have been put under wages and working conditions and support provided for unemployed workers. In addition, trade unions, once adjudged illegal combinations at common law, were first legalized and then fortified with special privileges and immunities under laws governing torts and restraint of trade.

Not surprisingly, in a democracy dominated numerically by urban employees rather than family farmers, the reaction against workers' "unequal bargaining power" went too far. Concessions to labor (or unconcern with whatever any national or local labor organization might win for itself) have become at least temporarily the order of the day. These concessions have had minimal regard for the consequences in productivity, costs, prices, inflation rates, and private sector employment.[12] Their net effect is the so-called English Disease, which is apparently spreading with the speed of the medieval Black Death. The cure of this disease is in my opinion necessary to the control of stagflation. It is probably impossible either on a short-term basis or without risking a serious confrontation between the ostensible government and the organized labor movement.[13]

My private and drastic long-term suggestion has been for legislation to divide unions into A and B categories. The union choosing A status should retain its privileges under New Deal legislation (including such precursors as the "anti-injunction" Norris–La Guardia Act), but must accept compulsory arbitration of its labor disputes (with anti-inflation agency representation on arbitral boards in crisis situations), must forgo closed-union practices, and must accept responsibility for damages caused by unofficial or wildcat strikes by its members. Class B unions may reject arbitration, but employers are to be free to refuse collective bargaining with such unions, to oppose them by "unfair labor practices," and to transport and maintain strikebreakers (even from abroad) in any strike or lockout involving them.

During short-term inflationary flareups at least, we should consider temporary rollbacks of minimum wages or at least moratoria on scheduled minimum-wage increases. We should likewise consider, subject to minimum-wage restrictions, suspension of existing restrictions on the temporary immigration of contract laborers (as under the former *bracero* program for Mexican immigrants in southwestern agriculture). The subsection below on immigration discusses the point in greater detail.

The suspension or preferably the outright repeal of "prevailing wage" limitations on federal government employment and contracts (the Walsh-Healey and Bacon-Davis acts) has been proposed so often as no longer to merit the title of "neglected" microeconomic inflation control. All we need to do here is to second the motion that similar provisions in much state and local legislation deserve similar treatment.

The final entry under this head is purely statistical. Unemployment statistics should be published, wherever possible, net as well as gross of job vacancies. Job vacancies, furthermore, should include openings in less desirable fields such as domestic service and agricultural labor. The anti-inflationary point here is entirely indirect — to redress the balance between the (overstressed) "employment" problem and the (understressed) "inflation" problem in the public eye and the public consciousness.

Immigration Proposals

There seems little doubt that movements of temporary immigrant labor from low-wage countries and regions of southern and eastern Europe, the so-called *Gastarbeiter,* have played an important role in the superior anti-inflationary performance of both Germany (Federal Republic) and Switzerland since approximately 1950. Given the proximity of Latin America to the United States and the desire of so many Latin Americans to immigrate there, even illegally, there seems no reason for the United States to abstain from the same *Gastarbeiter* devices used by the West Germans and the Swiss, not to mention the Americans themselves in the *bracero* arrangements with Mexico.

The use of foreign labor under contract as temporary immigrants, including their use as strikebreakers, needs some justification. It should be remembered, however, that the existing prohibition of immigration to contract laborers dates from the 1870s. This was more than half a century before the enactment of the first federal minimum-wage law; it was during a period of widespread money illusion and international economic ignorance as well. There is now less danger of *Gastarbeiter* receiving less than the minimum wage, even in agriculture, and less danger of immigrant failure to consider American living costs. In the European cases also, agencies from both source and host countries monitor *Gastarbeiter* conditions with a view to minimizing both "exploitation" of the immigrants and displacement of indigenous labor.

The American volunteer Army program could also be salvaged by overseas recruitment of potential immigrants. That is to say, aliens recruited abroad for the U.S. armed services could be offered the status of nonquota immigrant after one term of service or the status of permanent residence or even U.S. citizenship after two tours of duty.

Agriculture Proposals

Two wrongs don't make a right is one of those normative maxims that is positively untrue in pressure group relations. After tariff protection and the antitrust "rule of reason" had been conceded to organized business at consumer expense and after the "Labor New Deal" had been similarly conceded to organized labor, organized agriculture's turn came on an ostensibly temporary postwar-reconstruction basis. The principal economic concession to the farm lobby has been a set of no-recourse loans at varying percentages of "parity" prices for six major crops, reinforced at times by production restrictions. Subsequent trends have been to raise the percentages of parity and to recompute parity itself upward by including rapid inflation elements in farm costs and in "prices paid by farmers." (The inclusion of taxes among the prices paid by farmers is particularly unfortunate for the fiscal approach to inflation control, as per the subsection above on taxation proposals.)

Most market economists, I believe, would like to see the demise of the entire support-price system but fear that such a demise may have to await the parallel weakening of the prior concessions to organized business and labor. In the meantime — an unduly long meantime, in all probability — we should be content with three reforms: exclusion of taxes from the parity base, moratoria on support-price increases during inflationary periods, and subjection of federal appropriations for no-recourse agricultural loans to the general limitations of impoundment.

Land Proposals

Under this somewhat misleading heading, I am including suggestions about gold, as well as about land, since both are important inflation-hedge assets.

Land — raw, underdeveloped, or underutilized land — enters into inflation in both economic and psychological ways, the latter being more important. While the inflation of land prices is a consequence rather than a cause of general inflation, the speculative holding of land out of use (or in inferior uses) reduces production and supply and therefore raises prices much as any ordinary cost-push factor does.[14]

The psychological argument is indirect. Their holdings of inflation-hedge assets, of which real estate is the most important, give holders of these assets a vested interest in inflation and, more important, a vested interest against disinflation. By definition, an inflation hedge is an asset whose price both rises and falls with greater amplitude than the general price level and is related positively to the inflation rate. Their holders' wealth positions therefore rise with inflation or "acceleflation" and fall with deflation or disinflation. Their improving wealth positions — asset effects — offset at least partially any unfavorable income or consumption effects of inflation. (The negative inflation tax, or inflation subsidy, or their stock of assets offsets at least partially any inflation tax on their flows of income.) Conversely, deflation not only deprives these holders of anticipated gains but may impose positive and real capital losses if the total demand for these assets is dominated by inflation-hedge considerations.

Without accepting a full single-tax position, I also believe that the shifting of property taxation from improvements to land is a useful long-term reform quite apart from implications for inflation control. It would free land for superior uses, as well as encourage investment in both housing and industrial plants.

But let us return to the inflation-control problem. An additional and often more drastic penalty to discourage real estate speculation in inflationary periods (buildings, in this case, along with land) has been suggested frequently and applied rarely in connection with urban and rural land reform in developing and reconstructing countries. It empowers either central or local governments to limit compensation in cases of eminent domain — which may itself be extended to include public housing — to some fixed percentage, presumably greater than 100, of assessed valuation for property tax purposes.

We pass on to gold. This is a quantitatively much less important inflation-hedge asset than real estate. It is, however, an asset over which the U.S. government and the International Monetary Fund together exercise substantial control because of their existing holdings. My suggestion is that these holdings be "dumped" over a relatively short period with a guarantee *against* repurchase at any fixed price, precisely to disrupt the world gold market and decrease inflation complacency in the influential upper reaches of the country's income and wealth distributions. If it were also to induce further dishoarding of privately held gold stocks in the Far East, in South Africa, in the Soviet Union, among French peasants, or anywhere else, so much the better.

Finance and Banking Proposals

We have argued or at least asserted that long-term inflation control requires substantial reduction of the monetary growth rate and its subsequent maintenance at a rate approximating the growth rate of the real economy.[15] This statement, conventional enough in itself, evades such important macroeconomic issues as the definition of money, "Rules vs. Authorities in Monetary Policy,"[16] and the time path over which monetary growth rates might optimally be reduced. We shall continue to evade these issues in what follows, precisely because they are essentially macroeconomic.

This section concentrates instead upon the political economy of sugarcoating monetary tightness to render it palatable to a populist public and opposing politicians' initial reaction to short-term disinflationary success, which has been to relapse into monetary growth reacceleration. My assumption here is that such reaction is due less to the strains of monetary tightness itself — meaning primarily the initially high nominal interest rates it entails — than to its coupling with the continued low nominal rates available to the average small saver.[17]

To sweeten the bitter pill of tight money, I propose three varieties of sugarcoating, or rather sweet-and-sour sauce:

(1) Give the ordinary individual saver the benefit of higher nominal interest rates and incidentally increase the funds available for short-term investment without simultaneously heightening inflationary pressure. For this purpose, we should remove at least temporarily all ceilings on either checking or savings accounts at commercial banks or other financial intermediaries. In addition to encouraging saving and discouraging disintermediation, this proposal would have the secondary statistical effect of increasing to nearly unity the correlations between published series on various definitions of money (M_1, M_2, . . . , M_n), so that it would make minimal difference which one was used.

This proposal is not without its costs and risks. It may increase the nominal capital losses sustained by holders of outstanding securities, both bonds and equities, in consequence of the rise in interest rates. Savings and loan associations, with assets tied up in long-term mortgages at current or recent interest rates, would face heavy withdrawals and disintermediation by their depositors. If this occurred on a large scale, savings and loan associations might be forced into the undesirable expedient of requiring long notices before deposits can be withdrawn.

(2) Temporarily revive the Federal Reserve System's Regulation W, a World War II restraint upon consumer credit. This regulation was a first approach to credit rationing. It was aimed at minimizing the demand for loans and the rise of market interest rates and also at channeling credit into "productive" uses. The admittedly cumbersome regulations required minimum down payments on loans for purchase of consumer goods, more rapid principal repayments, and therefore larger weekly or monthly payments by consumers than had been customary. It may have had the unwelcome side effect of channeling scarce consumer durables to the well-to-do, who could most readily pay cash or secure credit for other ostensible purposes, while denying them to the poor. But it did not affect a more patently inflationary form of "unproductive" credit — the accumulation and hoarding of speculative inventories of raw materials and outputs at all stages of production.[18]

(3) Legalize and widely use — but not retroactively use — variable-rate mortgages. With a variable-rate mortgage, the home buyer or other mortgagee who signs his or her mortgage at a period of unusually high nominal interest rates avoids being "locked in" to this high rate for the life of the mortgage.[19] A typical variable-rate mortgage specifies the rate

applicable each year as, say, the federal government bill rate plus x, the federal funds rate plus y, or perhaps the prime borrowing rate plus z — with (x, y, z) all positive — of the previous year, either as an average over the year or as of the year's end.

Nobel Prize economist Friedrich von Hayek has suggested several times a multiple currency system as an anti-inflation device. While I see great merit in his proposal as an inflation preventive, I fear that it might be worse than useless in inflation control.

Hayek proposes that "legal tender" for the monetary satisfaction of obligations to pay specified amounts in private contracts be whatever the contracting parties agree to make it. It may be a domestic (government) currency, a foreign (government) currency, the private currency issued by a particular bank regardless of country, a specified standard commodity such as gold, or an artificial (symmetallic) bundle of such commodities.[20]

Suppose that, under the Hayek proposal, the policies of the U.S. government gave rise to widespread fears of accelerated American inflation. Contracts could then be made and enforced in terms of German marks, Swiss francs, Japanese yen, gold bullion, or composite commodities.[21] The declining acceptability of the U.S. dollar, both as a store value and a standard of deferred payments, would immediately affect the demand for it. People's willingness to hold it would decrease, and the velocity of its circulation would rise. This would in turn affect prices immediately, with shorter and less variable lags than economists have found between money and prices under the existing regime. The hope is that these immediate reactions would alert the government to what it was doing and that the unfavorable responses would strengthen the forces for repeal or modification of its "inflationary" policies.

So far so good, but the chronic inflation status quo is significantly different. With a ten-year history of acceleflation, let us say, the extension of the legal tender privilege to foreign currencies and to commodities would have an immediate inflationary effect. It would set off or accelerate the flight from the dollar into these foreign currencies and commodities, which would in turn increase velocity and increase the inflation rate. This increase would naturally offset any anti-inflation measures that might currently be in progress and increase the time span required for restoration of monetary stability.

The Hayek proposal, in conclusion, is a fair weather insurance policy against future inflationary adventures. In the midst of an existing inflation, it does more harm than good. Its inaguration should be postponed until inflation has been checked decisively.

THE CONTROL AUTHORITY

For the libertarian — including myself — the most threatening feature of the foregoing compendium is the power allotted at several points to an inflation-control or price-control authority of some unspecified kind. In some instances, these powers include the imposition of direct controls at points the authority deems strategic, although not "across the board." In other instances, these powers relate to the selective enforcement of controls that are on their face indirect. Can anything be said to excuse such concessions to the bureaucracy?

What I have in mind as an inflation-control authority is a small, high-level agency patterned on the Council of Economic Advisers or the Board of Governors of the Federal Reserve System rather than a gargantuan sprawl, such as the Department of Health, Education and Welfare or the World War II Office of Price Administration. I should also like to see it staffed for short terms with rapid turnover by persons on loan from other governmental agencies, from the private sector, from the universities, and from consumer organizations, including Nader's Raiders.

Might not such arrangements lead to chaos? To hasty, arbitrary, incoherent, and inconsistent judgments by overworked and harassed economists, statisticians, and lawyers who may never have met a payroll? Yes, it might. Would it exclude rancor, ineptness, incompetence, unfairness, even corruption? No, it would not, though turnover would certainly reduce the attractions of corruption to both the corrupter and the corruptee. The system would, however, hold power madness to a minimum and forestall vested interests in inflation control as a way of life. The key defense against the bureaucrat, in any case, is temporal limitation of his authority. If microeconomic inflation controls, fair or unfair in individual cases, are allowed to work and are accompanied by suitable macroeconomic policies, even chronic inflation can be cured, I believe, more quickly, though perhaps not more painlessly, than most onlookers suspect.

Foreign occupation forces essentially independent of domestic opinion have cured inflations in short order when they wanted to. American forces have illustrated this in Germany and Japan, with "deflation-disinflation models — for export only." A German or Swiss occupation of America could illustrate it again. The issue is whether Americans can themselves do it at home without the benefit of gnomes of Zurich or of Frankfurt on the Main, and quickly enough to escape the dead hand of controls for controls' sake.

NOTES

1. This summary statement abstracts from changes in taste, technology, and social institutions that affect the velocity of circulation of money. It also abstains from inquiring *why* monetary authorities, whoever they may be, permit the excessive growth rate of the money supply. In economic jargon, our statement avoids "blaming anyone" and evades any inquiry as to the extent to which the money supply is "exogenously" (independently, arbitrarily) regulated by these authorities.

2. Let us ignore *buyers'* economic power (monopsony, oligopsony), with its interest in beating down prices, as largely irrelevant to inflation control. A study of *deflation* control might, and sometimes did, concentrate on this aspect of "the higgling of the market place."

3. An *autocratically imposed* disinflationary or deflationary macroeconomic policy may invalidate this sentence, at considerable cost in temporary recession and unemployment. Witness the "currency reform" recession in occupied Germany and the "Dodge Line" recession in occupied Japan.

4. What is to be indexed under indexation proposals? At a minimum — progressive tax brackets, interest and principal payments of public securities, and obligations under social security schemes. (Additional indexations and escalations are, of course, contracted privately.)

5. Governmental bodies gain in two principal ways: by lowering the real value of their nominal public debt and its service charges, and by the movement of taxpayers into higher tax brackets of progressive taxes, thereby increasing public revenues as percentages of taxpayer income. In addition, the central government gains initial command over whatever "fictitious values" may be created by the financial system specifically to finance its deficit.

6. Compare Arthur M. Okun and George L. Perry, eds., *Curing Chronic Inflation* (Washington, D.C.: Brookings, 1978), particularly the contributions of Larry L. Dildine and Emil M. Sunley, and of Albert Rees. See also Joseph A. Pechman in *Challenge,* November-December 1978. To glimpse the magnitude and multiplicity of these administrative difficulties, consider the applications of TIP to a new firm, to the several components of a firm that has split up, to a firm that has changed its output mix, or to a firm that has changed its technology in a substantial way.

7. The algebraic proof is elementary. We have $\alpha x = \alpha w + k + \beta y$ and also $x - w = k + y$. Combining these expressions, we get:

$$\alpha(k + y) = k + \beta y.$$

The solution of the equation for β is:

$$\beta = \alpha + (\alpha - 1)\frac{k}{y} \, ,$$

which exceeds α since $\alpha > 1$.

8. Some statistical difficulties are involved when taxes are levied in whole or in part at the wholesale level, as in the case of manufacturers' excises and VAT.

9. Legislative authorization for impoundment would presumably be hedged in with limitations in aid of particular regions, expenditure categories, and so forth.

10. See note 5, above.

11. What "output mix" regulation may overcome is the propensity of many firms, producing goods from automobiles to toothpaste, to shift their outputs away from standard types to higher-margin deluxe ones or to devise cosmetic "improvements," name changes, and model changes as covers for price increases.

12. Dr. Barry Bosworth of the American price control agency was even muzzled (summer 1978) after the plausible suggestion that with employee compensation comprising 75 to 80 percent of the U.S. national income, wage inflation might be the key to cost and price inflation — particularly, I might add, if employment were simultaneously to be maintained. (The muzzling was apparently on political, rather than economic, grounds, with special attention to the November 1978 elections.)

13. The British electorate was not ready for such a confrontation in 1974, when the government of Prime Minister Edward Heath was repudiated in the middle of a major coal strike, despite his party's slogan "Who Governs?"

14. My "salami-slicing" rehabilitation of cost-push inflation theories does not apply to land. As inflation progresses, however, the demand for land as an inflation hedge increases and with it whatever imperfectly competitive economic power that may be exercised by the owners of strategically located plots. To some extent, then, we are dealing with an instance of systematically increasing economic power by the landlord group, increasing economic power being a necessary condition for cost-push as seen by conventional macroeconomics. (But I reject as entirely unrealistic the single-taxers' construct of an aggregative "land monopoly.")

15. The finance and banking topics in this section impinge upon the jurisdiction of the Federal Reserve System, and I am presently affiliated with one of the Federal Reserve banks (San Francisco). Let me therefore stress my own responsibility for these proposals. They were written before I joined the bank as visiting scholar, and they do not purport to represent the views of the Federal Reserve System or of any of its component authorities, agencies, and so forth.

16. To quote the title of Henry Simons's classic article (*Journal of Political Economy*, February 1936).

17. If a nominal, money, or market interest rate is (to a first approximation) the corresponding real rate plus (or minus) whatever rate of inflation (or deflation) is anticipated generally in the money market, the rise in nominal interest rates due to tight money should be reversed as inflation psychology evaporates. The historical evidence for this "snapback" theory of nominal interest is impressive. In addition, the major complication, the so-called Gibson paradox, relates nominal rates directly to the price level itself along with its rate of change.

18. Member banks of the Federal Reserve System were instructed to avoid the granting of credit for inventory speculation but apparently hesitated to offend steady customers and depositors. (I owe this paragraph on consumer credit regulation to conversations with a former colleague at the University of Wisconsin in Madison, Dean James S. Earley.)

19. By the same token, this person's neighbor or competitor who has taken out a mortgage at an unusually low-rate period is subject to periodic increases when interest rates are rising.

20. The provision for private currencies appears to me to be a weak spot in the Hayek proposal. It does not, for example, seem to pay enough attention to the problems arising during the "free" (or "wildcat") banking period of U.S. monetary history in the generation immediately before the Civil War.

21. Actual payment could, of course, continue to be made in U.S. dollars, but the *number* of these dollars would presumably depend upon exchange rates and commodity prices at the time of payment, rather than at the time of the original contract.